**For *Blindside: Why Japan is Still
on Track to overtake the U.S. by the Year 2000***

"Fingleton is merciless as regards the conventional economic view of Japan, and persuasive as to what is right. *Blindside* is an important and interesting book, and it will have a large, well-rewarded, and sometimes angry audience."

—J.K. Galbraith, author of *The Affluent Society*

"A brilliant book."

—Pat Choate

"Fingleton has written a brilliant book full of fresh insights that explode carefully nurtured myths about Japan, as well as much conventional wisdom."

—Clyde Prestowitz, author of *Trading Places*

"Crisp, well-written, well-executed."

—"Adam Smith," *New York Times Book Review*

"This provocative and informed analysis is an antidote to the recent flurry of critiques that see Japan's current economic trroubles as the same old omens of decline."

—*Publishers Weekly*

"This gracefully written bool⎯⎯⎯⎯⎯⎯⎯⎯⎯⎯⎯⎯ icated treatment yet of how the ⎯⎯⎯⎯⎯⎯⎯⎯⎯⎯⎯⎯ ⎯nglo-American capitalism."

—Chalmers Johnso⎯⎯⎯⎯⎯⎯⎯⎯⎯⎯⎯ *Miracle*

"Provides an important corrective to some of the euphoria about America's competitiveness comeback in high–tech."

—Leslie Helm, *Los Angeles Times*

"President Bill Clinton has recommended it."

—European Business News

"Controversial."

—Barbara Rudolph, *Time*

"At elite private seminars and on the Internet, [people] are excitedly picking over Fingleton's thesis."

—Robert Guest, *Daily Telegraph*, London

"Widely acclaimed."

—*Sunday Tribune*, Dublin

"One of the ten best business books of the year." —*Business Week*

For *In Praise of*
Hard Industries: Why Manufacturing, Not
the Information Economy, Is the Key to Future Prosperity

"One of the ten best business books of 1999." —Amazon.com

"Eamonn Fingleton is a bravely original-minded writer, whose challenges to the prevailing wisdom of the time are based on detailed reporting and always worth considering. His skeptical look at the software/Internet boom is important while the boom is going on and will seem even more intriguing once it is over."

—James Fallows, author of *Breaking the News*

"In his new book about why manufacturing, not the information economy, is the key to future prosperity, Eamonn Fingleton exposes so many hypes and punctures so many myths that the few hypes and myths that he furthers can be forgiven against the benefit of this powerful critique of the conventional party line."

—Ralph Nader, Washington, D.C.

"It is close to impossible to get Americans today to understand that an economy based on manufacturing and an economy based on finance are not equivalent. Manufacturing provides jobs for the largest number of citizens; finance is the non value-adding but crisis-provoking segment of modern society. Japan is the world's leading manufacturing country; the United States is the stronghold of finance capitalism. This is the best book on why that distinction matters. It is indispensable reading for Americans who wonder what the world will be like after Wall Street's bull market ends."

—Chalmers Johnson, author of *MITI and the Japanese Miracle*

"Eamonn Fingleton's remarkable tour de force demolishes dangerous myths—mainly that large economies like America's can flourish indefinitely while down-sizing and exporting its vital manufacturing industries, and that U.S. business is leading a 'post-industrial' world towards a bright, non-industrial, all-digital future. This powerful book must make policy-makers and managers think again, and should make them act decisively to meet a grave challenge."

—Robert Heller, author of *The Fate of IB*

BOOKS BY
EAMONN FINGLETON

Blindside:
Why Japan Is Still on Track to
Overtake the U.S. by the Year 2000

In Praise of Hard Industries:
Why Manufacturing,
Not the Information Economy,
is the Key to Future Prosperity

The Penguin Money Book
(with Tom Tickell)

HOW ECONOMIC DOGMA
IS DESTROYING
AMERICAN PROSPERITY

UNSUSTAINABLE

EAMONN FINGLETON

Thunder's Mouth Press • Nation Books
New York

UNSUSTAINABLE:
How Economic Dogma is Destroying American Prosperity

Copyright © 1993, 2003 Buttonwood Press

Previously published as *In Praise of Hard Industries*
in 1989 by Houghton Mifflin

Published by
Thunder's Mouth Press/Nation Books
245 West 17th Street, 11th Floor
New York, NY 10011

Nation Books is a co-publishing venture of the Nation Institute
and Avalon Publishing Group Incorporated.

Library of Congress Cataloging-in-Publication Data

Fingleton, Eamonn.
    Unsustainable : how economic dogma is destroying U.S. prosperity / Eamonn Fingleton.
        p. cm.
    Rev. ed. of: In praise of hard industries. 1999.
    Includes bibliographical references and index.
    ISBN 1-56025-514-5
        1. Manufacturing industries—United States—Forecasting. 2. Manufacturing industries—OECD countries—Forecasting. 3. Industries—United States—Forecasting. 4. Industries—OECD countries—Forecasting. I. Title: Economic dogma is destroying U.S. prosperity. II. Fingleton, Eamonn. In praise of hard industries. III. Title.

HD9725.F56 2003
338.4'767—dc22

2003061623

9 8 7 6 5 4 3 2 1

Book design by Kathleen Lake, Neuwirth & Associates, Inc.

Printed in the United States of America
Distributed by Publishers Group West

●

For Yasuko

●

CONTENTS

AMERICA AT THE BRINK INTRODUCTION

This book's analysis of the future of the American economy is a sombre one—so sombre indeed that when it was first aired in an earlier version in 1999, the reaction of many readers was not so much shock as outrage. In updating the argument for this edition, I would have liked to have struck a more optimistic note. But in some ways the facts are even more troubling now than they were in 1999.

The case I presented in 1999 was that America's then ecstatic infatuation with the so-called New Economy (the economy of computer software, the Internet, entertainment, finance, and other "sophisticated" services) was misguided. America, I argued, was squandering vast resources on untried and, in many cases, patently unworthy New Economy businesses. Meanwhile, it was utterly mistaken in turning its back on its manufacturing base. I was concerned in particular about the wholesale erosion of

America's advanced manufacturing industries, which had been the font of American prosperity and power in the previous century.

Startling though my critique of the New Economy may have seemed in 1999, events in the interim have done much to vindicate it. Certainly, following the flaming out of so many erstwhile high-flying software and Internet stocks in 2000 and 2001, fewer people today imagine that the New Economy walks on water. But the more important part of my argument—that, in neglecting its advanced manufacturing industries, the United States is courting long-term economic enfeeblement—has yet to prevail in the court of public opinion.

The most dispiriting aspect of the events of the last four years has been the way the American establishment has chosen to ignore the deeper meaning of the stock market debacle. American opinion makers have missed something that will be obvious to future historians—that the absurd overvaluation of New Economy stocks in the late 1990s was no isolated mishap. Rather it was part of a much larger pattern of American economic self-delusion. Another important manifestation of that self-delusion is the equanimity with which the United States has viewed the decline of its manufacturing industries in recent decades. Like the New Age talk that propelled the dot-com debacle, the American establishment's indifference to the plight of American manufacturing industries is based on no rigorous analysis. The key commonality between the two cases is an *a priori* belief that whatever the market dictates is, in all circumstances, unquestionably right.

Caught in the crash, the United States was like a man who, after years of vaguely suspecting that all was not well with his health, suddenly underwent a frightening heart attack. Yet, instead of acting decisively to have his illness properly diagnosed and treated, he chose to deny the devastating significance of his symptoms.

This attitude of denial—even more stubborn than I could have anticipated in 1999—makes me particularly concerned about the long-term outlook for the American economy. If a 70 percent drop in the NASDAQ market does not shake people's economic illusions, it is hard to know what will.

Let's be clear: I have nothing against the New Economy. Not only is it here to stay but, on balance, it is a great force for good. Certainly, companies like Amazon.com, eBay, and Yahoo! have ingenious and innovative business models that serve real needs. Indeed, I fully expect that in due course at least some of the New Economy stocks will surpass their pre-crash levels. But the New Economy is no panacea; and to the extent that its benefits continue to be overestimated by policymakers and opinion leaders, it distracts attention from America's fundamental problem, the disastrous decline of America's once–world-beating advanced manufacturing industries.

One thing is certain: few members of the American economic establishment have emerged from the bubble with much credit. As other observers have already sufficiently documented (see in particular John Cassidy's *Dot.con)*, the bubble unmasked countless Wall Street stock promoters as, at best, quacks. (This would hardly have come as a surprise to anyone who had read the 1999 version of *Unsustainable*. Although my strictures about Wall Street's ethics may look unexceptional today, when they were first made in 1999, Wall Street's apologists tried to dismiss them as "overblown.") Meanwhile, those in the press who so uncritically fell for Wall Street's euphoric talk in the late 1990s revealed themselves as dupes. Yet, these same people—the quacks and the dupes—continue for the most part to guide America's economic course today. And even after the crash they have expended hardly a moment on self-reflection concerning the debacle they helped create in the late 1990s.

Yet, painful though it may be for the quacks and the dupes, it is important that they recall—and try to learn from—the inanities of the bubble era. Here are a couple of prime slices of bubble-era lunacy:

- Dubbing itself "the gateway to world cool," Boo.com was one of the most hyped new companies of the late 1990s—and one of the most absurd. Its 400 employees drew big salaries, travelled in style, and had fresh fruit delivered daily. It lost $185 million in an attempt to position itself as a global online retailer. Still hopelessly unprofitable a year after the stock market crash began, it was shut down in May 2001. Among "smart money" investors who lost heavily were J.P. Morgan and Goldman Sachs.

- Rufus Griscom, co-founder of a minor-league Internet site called Nerve.com, was quoted saying, "It's incredibly powerful to feel that you are one of seventeen people who really understand the world." The comment appeared in *New York* magazine on March 6, 2000. A week later the NASDAQ crash began. To be fair it should be added that Nerve.com survived the crash—but then as it is a sex site, the secret of its business model is one that probably more than seventeen people are privy to.

- Webvan filed to issue an initial public offering in August 1999, just two months after it had begun selling groceries over the Internet. As disclosed in its prospectus, it was expected to lose more than $500 billion in its first three years. Even so, the offering was a huge success and investors valued the business on the first day's trading at $8 billion. Webvan's chief financial officer was quoted in *Business Week* describing the company's strategy as the "first back-end re-engineering of an entire industry." Less than two years later, Webvan ignominiously closed after spending $1.2 billion on a nationwide distribution network. As recorded by John Cassidy, the Webvan business model had a basic flaw—most people prefer to drive to their local grocery store and pick out their own tomatoes.

MANUFACTURING: AN AMERICAN BLINDSPOT

So much for the absurdities of the late 1990s bubble. But, as I have mentioned, the case for manufacturing is the core of my argument. The decline of American manufacturing has continued apace in the four years since the first edition was published.

I will leave the full explication of the argument until later. But, at this stage, the important point to note is that most Americans literally do not know what modern manufacturing is. Misled by the American media, they have come to think of manufacturing as merely assembly work—in other words, labor-intensive work that if the American economy were in robust good health, America could happily delegate to low-wage nations like Mexico and China. Those who think of manufacturing as mere final assembly fail to ask some important questions. Who, for instance, makes the high-tech components required in such assembly? And who makes the advanced materials used in such components? Even more to the point, who makes the machines—typically highly sophisticated and minutely precise machines—that make such components and such materials? It cannot be emphasized too strongly that assembly is not serious manufacturing. It is merely the last stage in a long series of manufacturing processes. And it is in the earlier processes that serious manufacturing is done. Such manufacturing— advanced manufacturing—is the very antithesis of the low-wage assembly work of the American media stereotype. For a start, it is typically both far more capital-intensive and—surprising as it may seem—far more knowhow-intensive than most areas of the New Economy. As such it scores over the New Economy in several crucial ways: it creates a wider range of jobs than the New Economy and, measured by the level of worker skills and capabilities required, higher wages. Manufacturers, moreover, typically export more than ten times as large a share of their total output as service companies.

This last point is particularly topical. For, virtually unnoticed by the American media, America's trade position has deteriorated to the point where disaster is now staring policymakers in the face. After decades of competing in an utterly unfair world trading system—outrageously more unfair than most of the American media have understood—many American manufacturing industries have dwindled almost to nothing. And the result is that imports have been flooding in, even in years when the American economy has stagnated. As of 2002, the American current account deficit had reached a record $503 billion, a rise of 28 percent on 2001. Even more shockingly, it represented nearly ten times the deficit of a decade earlier and was an increase of 138 percent on the $221 billion recorded in 1998, the last full year before the original version of this book went to press.

One reason all this is not better understood is that it has been hidden by the trend towards outsourcing. Many advanced American manufacturing industries—the sort that have traditionally leveraged their productivity with large amounts of sophisticated production know-how and advanced equipment—still exist in name but they have become deeply hollowed out by better financed European and East Asian rivals.

By far the biggest winner from the trend has been Japan. Despite an image as an economic basket case, Japan has now passed the United States in total manufacturing output—and has done so with a workforce less than half of America's. Even more startlingly, Japan's output of advanced manufactured products—high-tech components, key materials, and sophisticated production equipment—is now estimated to exceed that of the United States by a factor of at least five. Moreover, although Japan's manufacturing success continues to be attributed to low wages, wages in Japan are now actually higher than in the United States.

How can these facts be reconciled with the press's suggestions that the Japanese economy suffered a disastrous "lost decade" in the 1990s? They can't, of course. Not for the first time, the press has gotten the Japan story completely wrong. And—again not for the first time—the problem has been in the press's choice of sources. Just as the press was persuaded by dubious sources to overestimate America's strengths in the 1990s, equally dubious sources led it to underestimate Japan's. It is, of course, true that Japan suffered major financial problems in the early 1990s in the wake of the implosion of Japanese real estate and stock prices. But as I was almost alone among Tokyo-based observers in the late 1980s in predicting Japan's financial crash (see the notes at the end for further elaboration), I can claim to understand that crash better than those who did not predict it. We will have more to say about the Japanese financial crash later. For now, let's note that the problems in Japan's financial sector have done little if anything to hold back the basic engine of Japanese prosperity, Japan's superstrong manufacturing sector.

THE TRADE CRISIS IN PERSPECTIVE

Given that the United States has now incurred large and generally rising current account deficits for two decades, even America's most
serenely detached ivory-tower economists are becoming alarmed. This
emerged clearly from a poll I conducted in 2000. In a project undertaken
for the Boston-based magazine *The American Prospect*, I contacted the
ten American-born economists who had most recently received the
Nobel Prize to ask whether the current account deficits were too high.
As most of these economists were strong believers in free markets, they
might have been expected to see no problem. After all, given their commitment to doctrinaire laissez-faire theory, they could readily have
explained away the deficits as simply an expression of the market's
unfathomable and supposedly infallible wisdom. In reality, only one of
the Laureates was prepared to offer such an unqualified endorsement.
The others either voiced misgivings about the trend or embarrassedly
refused to comment.

In truth, there is much to be alarmed about. The 2002 deficit represented fully 4.7 percent of America's gross domestic product. This ranked
as America's largest percentage trade gap since records began in the
1880s. It stood in particularly stark contrast to America's days of greatest
relative economic success in the first seven decades of the twentieth century. That was a period when thanks mainly to the extraordinary exporting prowess of America's then huge manufacturing industries, America
showed a trade surplus in all but eleven years—and did so despite the fact
that American wages were then five to ten times higher than those of
nations like Japan and Germany.

Even America's notorious trade crisis of the early 1970s seems
insignificant by recent standards. The current account deficit represented
just 0.1 percent of GDP in 1971 and 0.5 percent in 1972. Yet, it was the
prospect of the 1972 deficit—considered such a disgrace for the United
States at the time—that forced President Nixon to break the dollar's traditional and semi-sacred link with gold.

Not only is that 4.7 percent 2002 deficit unprecedented in American economic history but it is shocking by all previous world standards. As I have shown in an article at my website (www.unsustainable.org), other major nations have incurred percentage deficits comparable to recent U.S. levels only at times of extreme economic distress, such as during the two World Wars or in the immediate aftermath of those wars. The nations whose records I studied were Canada, France, Germany, Italy, Japan, and the United Kingdom. Full disclosure: as current account numbers do not exist for several of these nations in earlier periods, the analysis by default relied on records for visible trade. This, however, is not a significant qualification as the visible trade numbers are believed to approximate closely the current account experience—and invisible trade was negligible at relevant times.

America's pattern of worsening trade balances correlates closely with declining manufacturing employment. As the Washington-based economist Pat Choate has pointed out, the United States lost more than four million labor-intensive manufacturing jobs in the ten years to June 2003. Of these, more than half disappeared in just the last thirty months of the period.

The result is that manufacturing's share of total employment had fallen to 10.7 percent by 2003—versus 18.2 percent in 1989 and 33.1 percent in 1950.

Manufacturing's falling share in total employment in turn correlates closely with a pattern of stagnant middle class income growth. The most obvious indication of how badly the American middle class has done in recent years is that these days most families need two incomes—that of a mother as well as a father—to maintain the sort of lifestyle that fathers alone could deliver a generation ago. As recorded by Alan Tonelson in *Race to the Bottom*, Bureau of Labor Statistics data show that over the last forty years, two-earner families have moved from being the exception to being the norm in American life. In 1960, fewer than 27 percent of all married women living with their husbands worked. By 2000, the figure had risen to 62 percent. Forty years ago, moreover, only 19 percent of such women with children under six years of age worked. By 2000, this share was 63 percent.

SELLING THE FAMILY SILVER

If the immediate problems associated with the decline of manufacturing are troubling, the consequences for America's long-term future are positively frightening. Because its manufacturing base has shrunk so drastically, the American nation is like a household whose income can no longer keep up with its spending. To pay the bills, it must either run up credit or sell the family silver. Neither option is attractive. Loans must be repaid in the end and in the meantime interest mounts up. As for selling the family silver, one can do that only once. Thus, one can live beyond one's means for a while but eventually there is a reckoning. And the longer the reckoning is avoided, the more painful it is likely to be when it finally comes.

The same logic applies to nations. It is a fundamental fact of economic life that every dollar a nation incurs in current account deficits must be funded by a dollar of foreign finance. In the case of the U.S. trade deficits, much of the foreign funding comes in the guise of foreigners buying U.S. Treasury bonds. Some comes from foreign banks lending to American counterparts. And much of the rest comes from foreigners buying American real estate and equities.

In an increasingly troubling trend that has its roots in the trade imbalances, foreigners are even buying some of America's largest corporations outright. In effect, the United States is selling the family silver. Within the space of a single generation it is presiding over the disposal of much of its industrial and commercial base. This base, need it be added, required the enterprise of many earlier generations of Americans to build.

Such erstwhile pillars of American industry as Amoco and Chrysler have been bought by foreigners. In 2002, Lucent, heir to the fabled technological riches of Bell Labs, sold its optical fiber business to Furukawa of Japan. Meanwhile, IBM announced the sale of its disk drive business, a crucial high-tech operation that has played an historic role in the development of the global computer industry. Again the buyer was Japanese, in this case, Hitachi.

Large parts of Wall Street have also come under foreign control. Names like Scudder Investments, Bankers Trust, First Boston, Alliance

Capital, Republic Bank, Kemper Corporation, Alex Brown, and Dillon Read may still sound American but these former pillars of the American financial establishment are now controlled from places like Zurich, Frankfurt, Paris, and London.

LexisNexis, long America's best known news database, is foreign–owned and its only major rival, Factiva, is 50 percent foreign–owned. Even the American book publishing industry is now largely foreign owned. On one estimate, German companies alone now account for more than half the industry. American publishers that are now German-owned include Random House, St. Martin's Press, Doubleday, Crown, and Farrar, Straus & Giroux. Even President Bill Clinton's memoirs are to be published by a foreign owned publisher—the Knopf imprint of Random House (Random House was taken over by the German Bertelsmann group in 1998).

Already, the United States has sold so much of its asset base that its economic standing on the world stage has been significantly undermined. While this may not be obvious to the American public, it is shockingly clear in national asset/liability figures compiled by the International Monetary Fund. These show that between 1989 and 2000, America's net foreign liabilities ballooned from $47 billion to $2,187 billion. By comparison, the experience of Japan, the supposed basket case of the world economy, was entirely the opposite. In contrast with the United States, Japan has long enjoyed a positive net financial balance with the rest of the world and its net foreign assets at $1.16 billion as of 2000 represented a near quadrupling since 1989.

Perhaps the most alarming news of all is that America's problem of foreign indebtedness is now feeding on itself. In the words of the prominent British fund manager and financial commentator Marshall Auerback, America has entered a banana republic-style "debt trap." The nub of the problem is in the vast and ever rising flow of dividends and interest payments that the United States must now remit abroad to foreign owners of American assets. This problem has been significantly exacerbated by the expenses of the 2003 Iraq war, which will be borne in almost their entirety by the United States (this is in sharp contrast with the Gulf war of 1991, which was largely financed by America's allies). In a paper published in June 2003 by Chalmers Johnson's Japan Policy Research Institute, Auerback sketched out this truly alarming prognosis:

> If the U.S. did not have to borrow to pay interest on its debt, the ratio of the trade deficit to GDP would likely remain manageable. Unfortunately, the U.S. is a country with a trade deficit and must also borrow [abroad] to pay the interest on its debt. Because the interest rate on that debt exceeds the U.S.'s growth rate, the compounding of capitalized interest payments alone will tend to raise the nation's relative indebtedness. . . . I expect that the chronic U.S. current account deficit and mounting external debt will ultimately raise long term U.S. interest rates. And this, in turn will speed up the compounding of the interest due on the U.S. external debt and will make the debt trap dynamics even more vicious. At that point, what author Charles Kindleberger calls a "credit revulsion" might ensue, producing a catastrophic outcome for the U.S. economy.

Auerback is not alone in fearing the worst. Even the U.S. government's own Trade Deficit Review Commission has strongly hinted that America's current account imbalances are spiralling out of control. In an unusually outspoken report in November 2000, it suggested that, even assuming the trade deficit did not deteriorate further, the current account deficit could reach 7.5 percent of GDP by 2010. Implicit in the commission's devastating analysis, whose publication was discreetly timed to coincide with the interregnum period after the Presidential election, was that the increase would be driven by rising debt service costs as America's foreign debt was likely to reach nearly 60 percent of annual GDP in 2010, versus a mere 16 percent in 2000.

By all accounts, the outlook has worsened since 2000. As of the summer of 2003, Washington-based Pat Choate was predicting that, absent drastic policy changes, America's current account deficit could reach 8 percent of GDP before the end of the decade.

Just how alarming this figure would be is clear from a glance at financial history. An analysis of the official records of the Group of Seven nations shows that the only occasion when a major nation has incurred a deficit of comparable size was in 1924. On that occasion, the nation in question was Italy and its deficit represented 7.7 percent of GDP. This is hardly a record the United States would want to surpass. After all, Italy's economic problems in 1924 were so intractable that they paved the way for Mussolini to seize dictatorial powers in January 1925.

In truth, on unchanged policies, the United States is headed for disaster—though probably the ultimate outcome will be closer to the fate of the Ottoman empire than to that of Mussolini's Italy. Certainly, like the Ottoman empire in its last decades, America is becoming more and more beholden to a few major capital-exporting nations. The most important of these are Japan and China. As both these nations closely regulate their financial institutions, this means that unaccountable bureaucrats in Tokyo and Beijing will increasingly function as the ultimate bankers to a financially distressed United States. The consequences for American power—and indeed for Western leadership of the world community—are hard to exaggerate.

THE POLICY CHALLENGE: FACING A CATCH-22

Clearly, drastic policy changes are long overdue. Ranged ominously in opposition to effective change, however, are several hugely powerful interest groups. The most notable is the Washington foreign trade lobby. Almost by definition, it can be counted on to oppose any effort to reduce the trade imbalances. Representing powerful corporations based in Japan, Germany, France, the Netherlands, and elsewhere, the foreign trade lobby employs some of the most skilled propagandists in Washington and has a long record of extraordinary success in quashing earlier American efforts to achieve fair trade.

Another formidable interest group opposed to a sensible trade policy is corporate America. Although in former times, many American corporations were prominent in the fight to open foreign markets, now they have crossed over to align themselves with their foreign competitors in the foreign trade lobby. The reason is that they have found they can profit hugely by outsourcing—in plain English, importing—from certain low-wage nations, and particularly from nations that have deliberately rigged their markets to capture American jobs. The principal case in point is China, which keeps its manufacturing costs ultra-low by (a) suppressing workers' wages at gunpoint and (b) manipulating currency markets to keep the Chinese currency hugely undervalued. In truth, corporate America is now deeply complicit in the rise to world power of a frighteningly authoritarian regime in Beijing. All this represents the ultimate vindication of Lenin's famous remark that, in competing for short term profit, the capitalists will sell the rope with which the communists will hang them.

In fighting interest group politics on this issue, the American nation should be able to count at least on the solid support of the American press. In reality, however, the American press has long been in the foreign trade lobby's corner. Increasingly since the mid-1980s, key reporters—particularly elite reporters in Washington who disproportionately shape the press's economic thinking—have embraced the view that America's trade deficits "don't matter." Even the editors of the *New York Times* seem to have bought into this ultimate inanity. Certainly, they no longer seem to think trade is worth the serious coverage it received in the 1970s and 1980s. By the early years of the new century, the *Times's* coverage of the monthly trade imbalances had dwindled to almost nothing—even as those imbalances reached levels that just a few years earlier would have been considered unthinkable.

The absurdity of the "trade-deficits-don't-matter" thesis is discussed at length in a recent paper I published in 2003 in the economic journal, *Challenge*. The paper, co-authored with Senator Ernest F. Hollings, pointed out that the thesis had its origins in editorial articles written in the mid-1980s by the Japanese management consultant Kenichi Ohmae. Ohmae and other de facto spokesmen for the foreign trade lobby have skilfully exploited the press's commitment to an extreme version of laissez-faire. Believing that markets can do no wrong, press commentators have been readily persuaded that even efforts to shield American manufacturers from dumping by foreign rivals are an interference in the market's "all-seeing wisdom."

What in practice should the United States do? To many economists, the obvious policy remedy is a drastic devaluation of the dollar. With a lower dollar, the price of America's exports in foreign markets would fall. Thus American exporters would gain share in these markets and U.S. exports would surge. Perhaps more important American producers would increase their market share at home, as the devaluation forced up the prices of competing imported goods.

Thus, at a stroke, the current account deficits would be sharply reduced. At least that is the textbook theory. Unfortunately, the real world doesn't work quite like this. While in the long run the effect of devaluation would undoubtedly be to alleviate the deficits, in the short run, it would exacerbate them. This is because, as Pat Choate points out, America no longer makes—and worse, no longer is capable of making—many goods essential to the American economy's daily functioning. Thus, in the short run the textbook prediction that devaluation would lead to American manufacturers taking a larger share of the home market is simply invalid. Instead, the United States would have to continue willy-nilly to import and in the wake of devaluation, the dollar-denominated cost of its imports would increase. Choate's conclusion is that even a 50 percent devaluation would not significantly cut the current account deficit.

Another obvious policy tool is tariffs. As Pat Buchanan has documented, tariffs enjoy an honoured place in the history of American economic policy. As many Americans will remember, even such a staunch Republican as President Richard Nixon used temporary tariffs, in combination with devaluation, to fight the American trade crisis of 1970-71. What fewer Americans will remember—though it is well worth recalling—is that this formula proved successful in restoring America's trade to broad balance.

Nonetheless, tariffs have gotten terrible press in recent decades. Indeed in the eyes of the perennially misguided American establishment, they are the economic equivalent of anthrax—a weapon whose deployment is simply inexcusable in any circumstances. Thus, when President

George Bush resorted to tariffs in 2002 as part of a desperately-needed rescue plan for the American steel industry, he was widely excoriated.

As Marshall Auerback points out, United States suffers a special problem because its economy accounts for such a large proportion of world consumption. He comments: "When it [the United States] tries to improve its trade balance through devaluation or through restrictive demand management, its sheer size affects the economies of its trading partners adversely and to an appreciable degree. Understandably, they object and resist." In Auerback's view, foreigners' resistance will force America to raise interest rates—and this will greatly exacerbate the problem of debt-trap economics.

In essence the United States is caught in an historic Catch-22: on the one hand, farsighted and austere policies are needed to rectify the deficits, but on the other, the American political system seems incapable of seeing beyond the next election. So is all lost? Perhaps not. Some critics of America's naïve brand of "one-way free trade" sense the political pendulum may at last be swinging their way. This is the view in particular of Alfred E. Eckes, Jr., an Ohio-based historian who in the early 1980s served President Reagan as chairman of the U.S. International Trade Commission. He believes that the recent trend for key American service industries to emulate manufacturing industries by outsourcing work overseas could prove to be the last straw for hard-pressed American voters. This trend, whose rapid rise was predicted in the 1999 version of this book, began creating increasing joblessness in American suburbia in the first years of the new century. And this, Eckes reasons, might finally foster the rise of a grassroots coalition with enough clout to make a real impact on the presidential election of November 2004. "We may be watching a sea change in public attitudes, as people gradually awaken to the fact that free trade is not a free lunch," said Eckes. "Now that engineers, accountants, Wall Street analysts, and even physicians are facing growing competition from low-paid professionals in India, the Philippines, and potentially China (as English-language skills improve), the articulate professional classes may come to appreciate what blue-collar America discovered in the 1980s."

DILEMMA FOR THE SPHINX

So much for the mood in Peoria. But in view of the massed opposition of the lobbyists and the press, a disgruntled electorate alone will probably not be enough to affect farsighted changes—at least not in time to avert an Ottoman empire-style denouement. Something more is needed—specifically, strong institutional leadership from within the American economic establishment. But where might it come from? One institution in particular comes to mind: the Federal Reserve. After all, the Fed is supposed to look out impartially for the best interests of the American nation. It is expected to be immune to lobbyists and its constitution is carefully designed to keep short-term political pressures at bay (a key part of the Fed's make-up is that its governors are nominated for a term of fully fourteen years). Thus, if any institution enjoys the independence to offer farsighted leadership it is the Fed, and in particular its famously Sphinx-like chairman Alan Greenspan.

Moreover, no American institution comes even close to the Fed in its potential power to influence media coverage of trade. But potential is the operative word. Where trade is concerned, Greenspan and his officials have hitherto been almost entirely silent.

Yet, arguably more than any other individual, Greenspan will be held responsible by future generations for the developing disaster. More perhaps than Bill Clinton, more even than George W. Bush (both of whom, let's be clear, will have plenty to answer for when the history of this crisis is written). In postponing action on an exceptionally thorny issue, Clinton and Bush at least can say they were deterred by the usual short-term political considerations. Greenspan has no such excuse.

Greenspan's current four-year term is due to expire in the summer of 2004. But in the spring of 2003, at the age of seventy-seven, he was appointed by President Bush to a further term of up to four years. Thus on present calculations Greenspan is likely to continue in his job until 2006, or even until 2008. This means he is set to become the longest serving Fed chairman ever, beating the previous nineteen-year record set in the mid-twentieth century by William McChesney Martin.

In truth, Greenspan should have retired long ago. Not only was he already too old when he was last reappointed in 2000, but, even overlooking for a moment his handling of the trade problem, he richly deserves to be put out to grass for other, more widely recognized failures. In particular, he has failed to stand up for fiscal commonsense in the face of George W. Bush's wildly irresponsible budget policy. He was also clearly derelict in his duty in his handling of the late 1990s stock market boom. After expressing early reservations in the mid-1990s, he later embraced the New Economy with the fervor of a true believer. In January 1999, he pronounced the wild technology stock speculation "good" for the capitalist system. As John Cassidy has noted, Greenspan could hardly have done more to promote the boom if he had allowed himself to be photographed buying stock in Amazon.com. Even as late as January 2000, as he was belatedly preparing to raise interest rates, he was praising the "awesome changes" supposedly being wrought by technology.

Of course, Greenspan's innumerable admirers suggest that any criticism of his handling of the bubble is mere Monday morning quarterbacking. Not surprisingly, this view is prevalent among press commentators who themselves were deeply complicit in pumping up the bubble. In self-defense, they point out that economic history is full of cases of intelligent people being caught up in financial manias. Take the South Sea Bubble, the notorious mania that gripped London in the early eighteenth century. Its many notable victims included even the great physicist Sir Isaac Newton. First, he made a fortune by getting in early and selling well. Then, just before the top, he jumped in again and suffered terrible losses in the subsequent crash.

But if bubbles prove infectious, this does not mean everyone catches the bug. Far from it. In the case of the late 1990s excesses, plenty of sceptics proved immune to the mass hysteria. In the business world, only the most notable cases in point were the virtuoso investors Warren Buffett and Julian Robertson. Others included the textile industrialist Roger Milliken and the press baron Rupert Murdoch. Skeptics in Washington included the economic commentator Pat Choate as well as Senators Ernest F. Hollings and Charles Schumer. Even in the press there were notable sceptics. Examples included James Fallows of *The Atlantic Monthly*, Allan Sloan of *Newsweek*, Alan Abelson of *Barron's*, and Jim Grant of *Grant's Interest Rate Observer*. In Britain, they included the author Robert Heller, as well as top editors of the *Financial Times*.

In truth, given his unrivalled access to confidential information about the world financial system's workings, Greenspan has less excuse than almost anyone for his bubble-era illusions.

As for the future, Greenspan faces a choice. The graceful thing to do would be to admit publicly what must now be becoming obvious to him: that he has consistently underestimated the seriousness of the trade trend. Following such an admission, he should resign to make way for a younger, more energetic person to tackle the already nearly intractable trade crisis. By that very act of nobly falling on his sword, Greenspan would powerfully dramatize the nature of the crisis and thus help galvanize the nation for the inescapably tough measures ahead.

If, by contrast, he hangs on, he may succeed for a few more years in sweeping the crisis under the carpet. But in the absence of drastic policy changes, the truth will come out sooner or later, probably in the form of an uncontrollable crash in the dollar's value.

By making a graceful exit now, Greenspan can hope to be remembered for his intellectual courage in admitting his mistakes. Certainly, he will salvage much of the enormous respect with which he has long been viewed by the American public. On the other hand, if he hangs on, the result in the end will be certain obloquy. He will be fated to be remembered as the man who lost America.

POSTINDUSTRIALISM
VERSUS
MANUFACTURING

PART 1

CHAPTER 1

THREE STRIKES AGAINST THE NEW ECONOMY

Time was you could hardly pick up a newspaper without reading glowing accounts of the golden prospects supposedly in store for the United States in the so-called postindustrial era. If media comment was any guide, almost everyone believed that new information-based businesses and other postindustrial activities had superseded manufacturing as the font of prosperity.

Just as in the early nineteenth century the United Kingdom exploited the bountiful possibilities of the manufacturing age to become the world's leading economy, a farsighted United States was now poised to lead the world in a leap to a still more sophisticated level of economic endeavor in the postindustrial age.

During the great dot-com stock market boom of the late 1990s, this euphoric view of the United States' so-called New Economy was rarely subjected to reality checking. Only later—after the prices of countless erstwhile high-flying New Economy stocks had tumbled by 95 percent or more—did the euphoria about postindustrialism come under serious scrutiny. Even then, the postmortems were notably superficial and were largely limited to a rediscovered interest in profits. Capitalism without profits is an oxymoron, it was discovered. As of this writing years after the dot-com crash, it is surprising how many of the myths that drove the New Economy boom remain unexposed.

The truth is that many of the fallacies driving the trend towards postindustrialism still pervade mainstream economic thought and action.

As I show in *Unsustainable,* there are major holes in the case for postindustrialism. Not only do those who advocate postindustrialism—let's call them postindustrialists—overestimate the prospects for postindustrial services, but they greatly underestimate the prospects for manufacturing. A major part of their problem is that they do not understand how sophisticated modern manufacturing truly is.

Before looking at the reality of modern manufacturing, however, let's first be clear about postindustrialism. The term covers a bewildering variety of businesses whose only obvious shared characteristic is what they are *not:* they are not manufacturing. Broadly defined, therefore, virtually all service industries might be considered part of the postindustrial economy. For the purposes of this book, however, we will bend over backward to be fair to the postindustrialists and judge their case on those areas of the service economy whose prospects they regard as particularly promising. We will, therefore, be focusing mainly on the information industry, which as defined for statistical purposes recently by the United States government, consists of publishing, movies, broadcasting, telecommunications, and computer software. We will also include within our definition of postindustrial services such other advanced areas of the service economy as financial services, data-base management, the Internet, consulting, accounting, advertising, and the law.

One confusing point that ought to be cleared up right away is that some statisticians have recently started classifying computer software as a manufacturing industry. This is obviously a perverse use of words and one that is explicable only as an effort by embarrassed government officials to cover up the extent to which *real* manufacturing has declined in certain key Western nations. Throughout this book, therefore, we will treat software for what it obviously is—a postindustrial service.

Our task is to weigh the economic merits of postindustrial activities against those of what might be called hard industries. This term is intended to denote capital-intensive, technically sophisticated forms of manufacturing. Thus, it excludes most types of final assembly of consumer products, which is a generally labor-intensive and unsophisticated activity. This distinction needs to be emphasized because postindustrialists implicitly define manufacturing to mean merely labor-intensive work of the assembly type. In so doing, they set up a straw man—for there is no question that, in an increasingly integrated world economy, many kinds of consumer products can no longer be assembled economically in high-wage nations. Overlooked by the postindustrialists, however, assembly is only the final, and generally by far the least sophisticated, step in the making of modern consumer goods. Earlier steps such as the making of components and materials are typically highly sophisticated. And even before the making of such components and materials, there is a still more sophisticated level—the manufacture of the *production machines* that make the world's components and materials.

These higher levels of manufacturing used to be the backbone of American prosperity in the days of undisputed American leadership of the world economy in the 1950s. Unfortunately for the United States, they have now migrated elsewhere—and in particular to nations that have adopted carefully honed national strategies to boost their manufacturing prowess.

One nation that has been outstandingly successful in expanding its share of advanced manufacturing in recent decades is Japan. The history of the Japanese electronics industry in particular is an object lesson in how a nation can climb the ladder of manufacturing sophistication. Having started out in the 1950s as a lowly assembler of imported components, the Japanese electronics industry long ago phased out most of its assembly operations to make way for more sophisticated activities— albeit activities that are almost entirely overlooked by consumers and even by business reporters and economic commentators. Among the most notable of such activities is making high-tech electronic components. The Japanese electronics industry has also moved heavily into making the advanced materials and production machinery used throughout the world electronics industry.

Among other nations that have been similarly successful in advancing to ever more sophisticated levels of manufacturing are Germany, Switzerland, Denmark, and Singapore—and, as we will see, in common with Japan, these nations have generally outpaced the United States economically over the years.

That said, we should make clear that this book does not seek to disparage *all* postindustrial activities. Nor does it hold up all manufacturing activities as inherently superior. In fact, advanced nations clearly need a mix of both. Apart from anything else, many postindustrial services are necessary to support and enhance a nation's manufacturing base. The point, however, is that postindustrialism should not be embraced blindly just because it is fashionable. Nor should nations lightly allow their manufacturing prowess to drain away.

For, as we will see, postindustrialism entails many hidden drawbacks. Of these the most important are

- an unbalanced mix of jobs
- slow income growth
- poor export prospects

In essence, these drawbacks constitute—in baseball terms—three strikes against the New Economy.

STRIKE ONE AGAINST THE NEW ECONOMY: A BAD JOB MIX

The most obvious problem with the New Economy is that it creates an unbalanced mix of jobs. Whether we are talking about financial engineering, legal services, computer software, movie-making, healthcare, broadcasting, database management, consulting, scientific research, or telecommunications, most postindustrial jobs are for people of considerably higher than average intelligence—typically people whose IQs rank in the top 20 percent in I.Q. tests, if not in the top 5 percent or even 1 percent. In this regard, postindustrialism contrasts sharply with manufacturing, which, of course, generally creates a well-balanced range of jobs.

For workers who lack the rarefied talents needed to succeed in postindustrial services, therefore, the United States' shift to the New Economy is little short of a disaster. In fact, their job prospects are so discouraging that even the postindustrialists don't bother to sugarcoat the pill. As estimated by the postindustrial economic commentator Michael Rothschild, up to 20 percent of the American work force will be marginalized by the move to an information-based economy. That amounts to a shocking 25 million people—or nearly four times the total number of jobless workers in the United States as of 2001!

Yet, Rothschild and his cohorts see the sacrificing of so large a share of the work force as not only inevitable but even acceptable—because the collateral advantages of postindustrialism for the rest of the economy are supposedly so large. They imagine in particular that postindustrialism is a formula for generally fast growth in incomes. Would that it were so. It is time to consider the second strike against the New Economy.

STRIKE TWO AGAINST THE NEW ECONOMY: SLOW INCOME GROWTH

That the United States' drift into postindustrialism results in weak income growth is one of the most serious, albeit one of the least recognized, drawbacks of the New Economy.

Yet, the evidence is undeniable. More than two decades after the United States began its fateful experiment in full-scale postindustrialism, international economic comparisons have consistently shown that Americans have lagged in wage growth in the interim. The point stands out dramatically in statistics for hourly compensation costs compiled by the Geneva-based International Labor Organization. According to the latest statistics available as of 2003 at the ILO's website, hourly compensation (wages plus benefits) in no less than ten nations exceeded that of the United States. The nations were Germany, Norway, Switzerland, Denmark, Belgium, Austria, Sweden, Finland, the Netherlands, and Japan.

Of these, Germany, Switzerland, Austria, Sweden, and Japan are particularly noted for the large share of their workforce engaged in manufacturing. Indeed with just two exceptions—Norway and the Netherlands—all the nations identified by the ILO as exceeding the United States in total hourly compensation also devote a larger share of their labor force to industry than the United States.

As for the Netherlands and Norway, neither nation constitutes a model for a deindustrializing United States. They owe their high positions in the compensation league table not to any special merits of their service industries but rather to their lucky endowment of natural resources: both are major exporters of natural gas and Norway owns much oil as well.

In any case, the absolute levels of incomes we have been discussing so far are less important than the pace of income growth. And here the facts are even more clearly against the postindustrialists.

A particularly appropriate starting point for any analysis of income growth is 1980. This was the year when the merits of postindustrialism were first widely debated in the United States. The debate began after the social philosopher Amitai Etzioni published a gloomy analysis of the United States' deindustrialization. His concern about the United States' then-incipient drift out of manufacturing was widely challenged by many feel-good commentators, who proceeded to enunciate the now widely accepted doctrine that a shift to postindustrialism boosts the United States' income growth.

In any event, American incomes as measured in non-inflation-proofed dollars grew by 207 percent in the twenty-one years to 2001. Although this may seem respectable, it pales by comparison with the performance of virtually every advanced nation that resisted the postindustrial trend. In South Korea, for instance, growth in dollar-denominated incomes was more than fivefold in the period and in Japan nearly fourfold. Perhaps even more significantly, virtually the only developed nations that lagged the United States' performance were the United Kingdom and Canada, two nations that by no coincidence have been at least as enamored of postindustrialism as the United States in the last two decades.

In view of the evidence of the real world, how come the postindustrialists ever considered the information economy a superior formula for income growth in the first place? In essence, they have been blindsided by a subtle fallacy in economic reasoning. This fallacy is clearly apparent in the views of, for instance, John Naisbitt, who as the author of *Megatrends* was one of the earliest cheerleaders for postindustrialism. Noting correctly that the wages of United States' postindustrial workers are generally much higher than the American average, Naisbitt goes on to jump to the completely fallacious conclusion that a general shift by the United States into postindustrialism will result in a general boost to wages. The fallacy here is Naisbitt's implicit assumption that postindustrial wages are high by dint of the innately superior economic virtues of postindustrial services. In reality, of course, the high wages paid in typical postindustrial activities such as software merely reflect the fact that such businesses generally recruit exceptionally intelligent and capable workers—in essence, workers who could expect to earn superior wages in almost any field they chose to enter. And in particular, such workers could earn at least equally high wages in a manufacturing-based economy. Meanwhile, Naisbitt utterly overlooks the plight of the rest of the work force, and in particular millions of ordinary workers who are left out in the cold by the shift to the New Economy. And it is their plight, of course, that is behind the United States' persistent underperformance in international comparisons of income growth.

Many postindustrialists question the methodology of surveys that show the United States has been losing out in long-run income growth. They maintain that the internal purchasing power of the dollar within the United States is greater than what one dollar can buy abroad if converted into local currency at market exchange rates. They therefore embrace a system of comparison in which "purchasing power parity" exchange rates are used to assign a lower-than-market valuation to wages earned by workers in Japan, Germany, Switzerland, Singapore, and other key foreign countries.

At first sight, this methodology seems to make sense. After all, if an American family is posted to, say, Singapore, it will soon discover that replicating an American lifestyle there is much more expensive than in Peoria. To the postindustrialists, therefore, the fact that Singaporean wages are typically somewhat higher than those in the United States hardly proves that Singaporeans are better off than Americans. But the postindustrialists forget that by the same token, citizens of Singapore who try to replicate their home-country standard of living in Peoria also face sticker shock. They may, for instance, need to maintain two or three cars just to get through the day—whereas in Singapore the supermodern public transport system is so comfortable and safe that even many well-off citizens see little need to own a car. The Singaporeans will also face sticker shock when it comes to educating their children. How much will they have to pay for private education to make sure their children get as good a start in life as they would in just an ordinary Singaporean state school? And, for that matter, is there any private school in Peoria, however expensive, that is as safe from the drug culture as an ordinary Singaporean school?

The postindustrialists' purchasing power parity method tends to throw up particularly anomalous results in the case of the United States' principal economic competitor, Japan. On a purchasing power parity basis, the Japanese come out looking distinctly less affluent than Americans. And this impression seems to be confirmed by the high prices the Japanese must pay for some obvious things such as housing, beef, and entertainment. But are the Japanese really so poor? Hardly. In fact on many of the most important *objective* measures, the Japanese are clearly richer than Americans. Take the most important measure of them all, life expectancy. This is a highly objective measure and, if the past is any guide, it is closely correlated with living standards. Remember that in the early years after World War II, the world's highest life expectancies were found in Sweden and Norway, nations that by common consent at that time led the world in affluence. These days, however, the Japanese are the world's longest-lived people. In the space of just sixty years, their life expectancy has gone from about ten years shorter than that of Americans to four years longer. The key factor driving this trend has clearly been rising living standards. In the circumstances, therefore, it is obvious that there is something wrong with a purchasing power parity methodology that portrays the Japanese today as significantly less affluent than Americans.

Essentially, there are many hidden flaws in the purchasing power–parity method. Thus, although it may accurately capture how the price of a McDonald's hamburger varies around the world, it is far from reliable in assessing less easily measured items—items such as infant care and preventive medicine, where superior Japanese standards do much to explain Japan's world-beating longevity experience.

Much more could be said about the major blindspots in the purchasing power–parity method. But all we need to note here is that purchasing power parity is an ethnocentric yardstick that should have no place in a scientific debate. What matters is the undeniable fact that, measured at market exchange rates, employers in many foreign countries pay wages that are considerably higher than American levels. Thus, it is a myth that manufacturing-oriented economies are ipso facto low-wage economies. As for the postindustrialists' suggestion that manufacturing economies are destined to suffer slower income growth than postindustrial ones, this is clearly even more misguided.

The result in the end is not only poorer income prospects for individual American workers but a general decline in the United States' economic strength. And this latter effect is greatly compounded by the New Economy's tendency to weaken the nation's trade position. To that subject we now turn.

STRIKE THREE AGAINST THE NEW ECONOMY:
A DEARTH OF EXPORTS

The third big drawback of postindustrialism is that it weakens a nation's prowess in overseas trade. It is a problem that has hitherto received remarkably little attention from the postindustrialists. In fact, such lead-ing advocates of postindustrialism as Daniel Bell, John Naisbitt, and Kevin Kelly make virtually no reference to exports in their writings. But there is no getting away from the fact that the export problem is not only obvious but extremely serious.

For a start, virtually all postindustrial activities are handicapped in export markets by basic and often insurmountable cultural differences. Take the new American information businesses that have mushroomed with the rise of the Internet. Virtually all their revenues come from within the United States. This reflects the fact that in overseas markets, their sales are hindered by several cultural and regulatory factors of which the most obvious is language. English may be a universal language but most non-native speakers are hardly more likely to be comfortable read-ing English-language websites than, say, English-language magazines.

Differing national tastes also limit the export potential for Internet-based information businesses: an American database of baseball scores, for instance, has little appeal in Britain, let alone in Germany or France.

In any case, many kinds of information are inherently local in appeal and therefore generate minimal exports. Information on traffic conditions in Vermont, for instance, is likely to be of little value in Virginia, let alone in Vietnam. Similarly, a database on Nebraskan car insurance rates has lim-ited value in North Carolina, let alone in the Netherlands or Nepal. The problems in exporting information are in fact endless. It is not surprising, therefore, that, as noted by Internet consultant Alfred Glossbrenner, American information providers' export sales are "negligible."

As we will see in Chapter 2, similar cultural problems are also much in evidence in curtailing the American computer software industry's export prospects. These problems are perhaps most obvious in the case of personal computer programs, which must, of course, be comprehensively altered for other nations' writing systems and customs. The costs involved cut deeply into the United States' export revenues. In particular, the so-called user interface—the array of commands and menus by which the user operates the computer—must be tailored to the user's culture. This means much more than merely writing the commands and menus in the user's national language. In the case of many application programs such as accounting and factory-management systems, the user interface may require a total makeover to fit the customs and procedures of other nations. In some cases, the user interface may even have to be tailor-made to suit the needs of individual companies within a single country. Thus, for all the hype about the United States' world-beating lead in software, most American software businesses generate little if any revenue abroad and therefore do remarkably little for the United States' chronically troubled balance of payments.

Culture is also a barrier to exports in many other highly paid information-based professions. The United Kingdom's famously strong advertising agencies provide a good example. Among the biggest and most globalized in the world, they shape the worldwide advertising activities of such globally active corporations as Ford, IBM, Philip Morris, Procter & Gamble, and Toyota. Nonetheless, their contribution to Britain's balance of payments is quite puny. The reason is obvious: most of the jobs involved in serving their global clients are not British jobs. To create advertising for the American market, for instance, British advertising agencies rely heavily on thousands of American advertising professionals in New York and elsewhere in the United States. And, of course, *a fortiori* in non-English-speaking markets such as Japan or Germany, British advertising firms must rely almost entirely on locally recruited professionals to serve clients in those countries. Thus, most of their foreign revenues are eaten up by costs incurred abroad. At the end of the day, all the British economy receives is a trickle of dividends on the capital invested overseas.

The story is much the same in other information-based businesses. Take the American legal profession. It accounts for fully 2 percent of the United States' gross domestic product, yet it contributes virtually nothing to America's balance of payments. In truth, with the exception of some foreign corporations operating within the United States' borders, few foreigners have any need for American legal advice.

So much for cultural barriers to postindustrial exports. But these are far from the only impediments limiting the United States' overseas sales of postindustrial services. Another key impediment to trade in postindustrial services is regulation in foreign markets, which is generally a much bigger problem for exporters of services than for exporters of manufactured goods. Regulation is a particularly serious problem in financial services, an industry that ranks second only to computer software in the hopes pinned on it by the postindustrialists. If you believe the postindustrialists, nations like the United States and the United Kingdom can look forward to rich pickings as other nations open their financial markets to overseas competition in the years ahead. Unfortunately, this prospect is largely fantasy. For a start, it ignores the fact that regulators in many overseas financial markets are not as "global" in their outlook as those of the United States, let alone those of that ultimate postindustrial pioneer, the United Kingdom. As we will see in Chapter 3, regulators in many key nations believe it is crucial to maintain their grip on their nations' financial systems, even if they rarely acknowledge this publicly.

Another major problem for many would-be postindustrial exporters is inadequate protection of their intellectual property rights. Essentially piracy in foreign markets severely depletes the flow of foreign revenues to many important postindustrial businesses, most notably computer software, movies, and music. Perhaps the most worrying aspect of the problem is that illegal copying of copyrighted work is getting ever easier thanks to technological advances. One reason why pirating is so rife in the CD industry, for instance, is that the investment needed to set up a CD replication operation is, in real terms, only a fraction of the cost of a record-pressing plant in the era of gramophone records. Now, of course, the rise of the Internet has made it even easier to profit from other people's work.

It is important to remember that piracy is a double whammy for American postindustrial exporters. First, of course, it deprives them of sales volume. But the second effect, while less obvious, is perhaps even more serious: it puts them into head-to-head competition with cut-price versions of their own products—with devastating implications for their pricing strategy.

As if the United States' poor prospects for exports were not bad enough, there is another problem with the trade side of postindustrialism—rising imports. At first sight, the idea of the United States importing postindustrial services on a large scale seems hard to reconcile with our observation that cross-border trade in postindustrial services is heavily curtailed by cultural and other barriers. But actually, there is no contradiction here because the barriers to trade in postindustrial services are in many cases not totally insurmountable. Rather, they are expensive to surmount. Typically, the only real problem in exporting postindustrial services is that postindustrial products have to be adapted considerably for foreign markets. Although this adds to costs and thus is a major drawback for high-wage countries, it is hardly fatal for low-wage countries.

The full seriousness of the import threat is apparent only when you realize that postindustrial services are highly labor-intensive—typically more so even than the most labor-intensive manufacturing activities such as the final assembly of televisions and radios. By definition in a labor-intensive industry, the cost of labor is a decisive factor in competitiveness. Thus, as global competition intensifies, the First World's postindustrial businesses can be expected to outsource more and more of their services from low-wage nations in the Second and Third worlds.

Even such a sophisticated business as the American computer software industry is far from invulnerable to the threat of third world competition. Of course, at first sight this seems hard to credit. After all, computer software is the ultimate "knowledge industry." As such, it is generally regarded as requiring a great deal of sophisticated know-how, not to mention a special streak of creativity that only a few countries are supposed to have. How can third world countries possibly aspire to go toe to toe with the United States in such an industry? Actually very easily.

Let's address the creativity argument first. All conventional wisdom to the contrary, there is little evidence that simply by dint of their nationality, Americans are more creative than other people—and certainly there is no reason to hope, as the postindustrialists do, that a purported edge in creativity will render the United States more or less invulnerable to foreign competition in the postindustrial era. In fact the evidence the postindustrialists adduce for their belief in superior American creativity is remarkably flimsy. They make much, for instance, of the fact that Americans are disproportionately successful in winning Nobel Prizes for science and technology. But is this a reliable measure of creativity. Actually no. Why? Because Nobel Prizes are awarded mainly for break-throughs in only one narrow field, *fundamental* science. And the success of a nation's scientists in fundamental science is a function far less of their inherent creativity than of how much government money is available for such science. As the United States government is by far the world's biggest spender on fundamental science, American scientists not surprisingly win more than their share of the prizes. We will have more to say about the creativity question later. But for now let's agree that creativity is a human attribute that is manifested in different forms in different cultures and is not notably absent among appropriately trained workers in even the poorest nations.

In any case, as we will see in Chapter 2, the role that creativity plays in the software industry has been greatly exaggerated. And certainly the incontro-vertible facts of the industry give the lie to the idea that Americans have a special lock on software-writing skills. Many other nations, not least some of the world's poorest, have demonstrated that they have what it takes to com-pete in the industry. Moreover, the know-how to enter the software business is amazingly easy for the developing world to acquire. And that opens up the possibility that American software workers will increasingly be undercut by low-wage workers abroad. In fact, as authors William Wolman and Anne Colamosca have pointed out in their book *The Judas Economy,* the threat of third world imports is potentially far greater in software than in hardware. The point is that thanks to breakthroughs in satellite communications, third world software companies can now deliver their products instantaneously and cheaply to customers anywhere in the world. By contrast, the third world is heavily handicapped in trying to export manufactured goods to the West because of abysmal local transportation systems, not to mention the high cost of shipping bulky goods to far-off overseas markets.

The conclusion, therefore, is that from the point of view of the American balance of payments, the shift to postindustrialism is double trouble. First, it weakens a nation's export strength. Second, it opens the United States to the prospect of rapidly increasing imports. That said, in the eyes of many Americans, the fact that postindustrial businesses do not do much for the balance of payments is an easy point to overlook. After all, the United States' huge current account deficits do not directly affect the quality of life within the nation—at least not in the short run. But in the long run trade matters—and matters fundamentally. The point is that a nation that allows its trade position to deteriorate too far for too long cannot expect to remain the world's leading economy forever.

In truth, almost anywhere you test the postindustrialists' case, it turns out to be more sizzle than steak. Having understood the New Economy's weaknesses, let's now review the case for manufacturing.

IN PRAISE OF HARD INDUSTRIES

As we have already noted, the most obvious advantage of manufacturing is that it creates jobs for a wide range of people. In fact, even in the most sophisticated areas of manufacturing, opportunities abound for the sort of blue-collar workers who are being increasingly marginalized in postindustrial economies. Take the most advanced areas of the steel industry. Many steel industry jobs have become simpler and easier to carry out as steelmakers have moved to ever-higher levels of automation over the years. In essence, in many manufacturing industries these days, so much knowledge can be built into the production machines that even a worker of less than average intelligence can operate them effectively.

As Bennett Harrison of New York's New School has pointed out, all conventional wisdom to the contrary, unskilled workers "barely off the farm" can readily be trained to operate computer-controlled presses and similarly sophisticated production machinery. In Harrison's terms, today's high-tech production machinery is not "skill-demanding" but "skill-enabling." Quoting a study by the economist David Howell, Harrison rebuts the widespread belief that a move to more advanced production techniques necessarily must result in the marginalization of workers of average intelligence. Referring to the trend for low-paid workers to suffer declining real wages in the United States in recent years, he comments: "If wages of poorly educated workers are falling, we need to look for explanations other than technology. After all, the same technologies have penetrated factories and offices in Europe and Asia, yet nowhere outside of the United States have low-end wages fallen so far and so fast."

Of course, high-tech manufacturing is necessarily very capital-intensive. To the postindustrialists, this seems like a major disadvantage. But they could hardly be more wrong. Remember that in general the more capital is invested in a factory, the higher its labor productivity rates are likely to be. And superior productivity is, of course, the royal road to high wages. Moreover, the fact that an industry is capital-intensive almost automatically elevates it beyond the reach of competitors in low-wage nations. And the truth is that many manufacturing industries are becoming even more capital-intensive all the time, thereby raising ever higher the barriers to entry for poorer nations.

Even quite mature manufacturing industries can be notably capital-intensive—and particularly, of course, the more advanced sectors of such industries. Take the textile industry. Although the production of textiles is generally regarded as labor-intensive, many of the textile industry's subsectors are highly capital-intensive and therefore tend to be dominated by rich nations. Spinning is a good example. As recorded a few years ago in the *Wall Street Journal,* the capital required in a state-of-the-art spinning mill these days can amount to as much as $300,000 per job. It is hardly surprising, therefore, that the world's most productive spinning mills are located in affluent northern Italy, not in dirt-poor India or Pakistan.

Perhaps the ultimate example of high capital intensity is the components side of the electronics industry. As we will see, the investment per job in some Japanese component factories can reach well over $1 million—or more than one hundred times the rate of capital intensity in some parts of the world software industry.

It goes without saying that in capital-intensive businesses, wages are likely to represent only a small proportion of total costs. They are dwarfed by depreciation, financing charges, royalties for intellectual property, research and development expenses, and other high overheads. Just how small the wage component of costs can be was startlingly illustrated in the case of a new cellular phone factory built by Motorola a few years ago. After looking at many alternative sites around the world, Motorola decided to locate the factory in ultra-high-wage Germany. Germany's high wage costs mattered little because wages accounted for only 3 percent of the company's total expected costs. In truth, from the point of view of an advanced manufacturing company, the need to pay superhigh wages is only a small price to pay for the many advantages of a German location. Whereas higher German wages add only slightly to total costs, Germany offers a world-beating manufacturing infrastructure complete with superb utilities, reliable delivery services, honest regulators, and a pleasant residential environment for expatriate executives. And, of course, there is also the advantage of Germany's well-educated and disciplined work force. As Norbert Quinkert, chairman of Motorola's German operations, pointed out, the advantage to the company of choosing a lower-wage location such as Britain was actually negligible in the larger scheme of things.

If capital intensity were the only advantage manufacturing had over postindustrial services, the case for manufacturing would be strong enough. But manufacturing boasts another key advantage: it enables incumbents in an industry to build up a huge endowment of proprietary know-how that gives them a wide productivity edge over would-be new entrants.

Some such know-how is explicitly protected by patents; but in many cases the most valuable know-how is unpatented proprietary production technology. Typically such know-how can only be acquired by dint of many years of learning by doing.

Just how formidable an advantage superior manufacturing know-how can be is best seen from the point of view of a would-be new entrant to an industry. Lacking the benefit of the incumbents' know-how, a new entrant is condemned to achieve notably poor labor productivity rates. Thus, even if he operates from a developing nation and therefore enjoys a big advantage in lower wages, his unit costs will start out considerably higher than those of the incumbents, and he will probably have to continue to absorb losses for many years as he struggles to catch up in know-how. In practice, the struggle is an unequal one—and unless he enjoys the full support of an extremely farsighted, nationally organized effort such as that mounted by the Japanese government over the last one hundred years, he will undoubtedly think twice about entering the field in the first place.

It is difficult to exaggerate what a big advantage incumbents typically enjoy in many areas of advanced manufacturing these days. Take a product like liquid crystal displays. Most familiar as the flat screens used in so-called notebook personal computers, these seem at first sight to pose no great manufacturing challenge. And in one sense this is correct. They are basically an adaptation of semiconductor technology and are made using similar manufacturing equipment. Thus, in theory at least, many companies around the world could enter this extremely fast-growing business. But in practice few have done so, with the result that the world market for high-end screens is dominated by a handful of Japanese manufacturers. In fact Tokyo-based Sharp Corporation alone enjoys a world market share of close to 50 percent. Why such market concentration? The key to the mystery is something called "yield"—the percentage of flaw-free products in a given production batch. A liquid crystal display is flaw-free only if each of the countless "dots" that constitute its screen are fully functional. If even a single dot misbehaves, this will not only be noticeable to the human eye but may constitute an intolerable distraction. As each dot is controlled by a separate tiny transistor, the upshot is that every single one of hundreds of thousands of transistors must function as advertised. Given that, among other things, the tiniest contamination such as a microscopic speck of dust can render such transistors dysfunctional, the quality-control challenge involved in producing these devices is enormous. Thus, in practice a new entrant to the industry would be lucky to get a yield of good screens of as much as 10 percent. By contrast, the leading incumbents in the industry are believed routinely to achieve yields of 90 percent or more. Thus, differences in yield alone can give incumbents a nine-to-one productivity advantage over new entrants.

Of course, one obvious step a company can take to improve yield is to filter the factory air extremely carefully. But this is easier said than done, and even when a company takes all obvious precautions of this sort, it can still end up with a notably poor yield. In truth, many of the secrets of improving a factory's yield are highly elusive and can be discovered only by a careful, laborious process of trial and error.

Admittedly, not all manufacturing involves entry barriers as formidable as this. But even the manufacture of relatively simple materials often requires a great deal of valuable proprietary know-how that is difficult for would-be entrants to an industry to acquire. Take something as simple as adhesives. As an expert at the Shell/Royal Dutch oil group has pointed out, the exact chemical structure of an adhesive is often almost impossible for competitors to determine. In practice, a manufacturing company would need to have unrestricted access to its competitors' factories if it is to understand their production processes. In the nature of things, such access is generally denied; thus, in seeking to close the technology gap with more advanced competitors, manufacturing companies often resort to amazing—and often highly controversial—tactics. Take, for instance, some Japanese aerospace executives who wanted to acquire American aerospace know-how. As recounted by Larry Kahaner in *Competitive Intelligence*, these executives wore shoes with specially soft soles when touring American aerospace factories. Their objective was to pick up microscopic metal shavings from the factory floor, which were later analyzed for clues to the Americans' manufacturing secrets.

Of course, with reasonable luck, a security-conscious manufacturing company can keep most of its production know-how secret for years or even decades to come. Thus, even in mature manufacturing industries, proprietary know-how often provides incumbents with enduring protection against new competition. The photographic film industry provides a striking example. Because it is based on nineteenth-century breakthroughs in silver chemistry, it might seem like an easy industry for, for instance, the East Asian tiger economies to target. But in reality it has remained all but impregnable to them. Even the Koreans, for instance, are no more than a negligible force in the industry: although they make some film, they are highly dependent on inputs imported from Japan and the United States and do little exporting. A key problem for the Koreans, as for other would-be entrants, is that they cannot match the enormous endowment of know-how that the incumbents have built up over several decades of learning by doing.

The most recent major entrants to the business, Fuji Photo Film of Japan and Polaroid of the United States, got their start as long ago as the mid-1930s—and their story only serves to underline how high the entry barriers truly are. Fuji Photo, for instance, would probably never have got off the ground but for the fact that Japan's then-military government deemed photographic film an essential war matériel; thus, they spared no expense in establishing an indigenous source of supply ahead of Pearl Harbor. Meanwhile, Polaroid's rise was propelled by forces that were similarly unique: in this case, the enormous creativity of Edwin Land, one of the most brilliant inventors of the twentieth century. Yet, even with the benefit of Land's technological innovations, Polaroid never became more than a niche player, and by 2001 it had become so marginalized that it was forced to declare bankruptcy.

Thus, the fact remains that at the beginning of the twenty-first century, the global photographic film market remains dominated by just three companies: Eastman Kodak, Fuji Photo Film, and Agfa-Gevaert. Based respectively in the United States, Japan, and the European Union, these are all quintessential First World manufacturing employers. Admittedly, Eastman Kodak has been losing market share in recent years—but crucially, it is being challenged not by a low-wage competitor but rather by Fuji Photo, a Tokyo-based company whose labor costs are about 20 percent higher than American levels. In truth, making photographic film is a great First World manufacturing business.

The same pattern of large entry barriers is apparent right across the board in advanced manufacturing. In the circumstances, therefore, it is obvious that nations with a heavy orientation towards advanced manufacturing will enjoy a fundamental edge in world economic competition. Hence, for instance, the pattern we have already noted whereby manufacturing-oriented economies have shown strong income growth over the years. And the result is that wages in nations like Japan and Germany are now higher than in the United States.

Moreover, Japan, in common with such other advanced manufacturing economies as Austria, Switzerland, and Singapore, has generally enjoyed lower unemployment than the United States. Admittedly, one notable manufacturing-oriented economy has been doing less well in this regard. That country is Germany, whose unemployment rate was running at 8 percent as of 2000. Germany's problems, however, stem not from its manufacturing orientation per se but rather from the fact that its economy has been suffering continuing dislocation following German reunification (in the late 1990s, nearly a decade after reunification, unemployment in the territories of the former East Germany was still running more than double that of the rest of the country). An additional problem has been the increasing burden that Germany's leadership role in the European Union places on the German economy (in particular Germany suffers disproportionately from the fact that EU nations have been exporting unemployment to one another for decades). Germany apart, unemployment rates in most other high-wage manufacturing economies have remained notably low in the 1990s. Japan's rate, for instance, averaged less than 3 percent in the 1990s. Admittedly, it has shown a rising trend in recent years—in 2001, for instance, it averaged 5 percent. But the rise is a natural consequence of Japan's notably top-heavy demographic structure (Japan experienced a huge baby boom after World War II, and people of that generation are now being pushed out by Japanese employers). In any case, even at recent higher rates, Japan's unemployment level remains one of the lowest in the industrial world.

American press commentators sometimes suggest that Japanese unemployment figures are understated but, as research by both the U.S. Department of Labor and the Organization for Economic Cooperation and Development (OECD) has shown, this is a dogma-driven assertion that is unsupported by the facts. That there is no large hidden army of unemployed people in Japan is confirmed by the experience of foreign employers, who consistently complain of shortages of many types of labor.

If manufacturing merely delivered high wages and low unemployment, its contribution would be impressive enough. But it also delivers another crucial economic blessing: a powerful trade performance. This reflects the fact that manufactured goods are generally much more universal in appeal than services—a fact that is abundantly apparent in the consistently large current account surpluses that most of the successful manufacturing-based economies have achieved in recent years. Meanwhile, the two great postindustrial economies, the United States and the United Kingdom, have been running large current account deficits.

To sum up, whether judged by jobs, wages, or trade, manufacturing scores over postindustrial services.

THE FUTURE OF MANUFACTURING: AN HISTORIC CHALLENGE

We have seen that manufacturing industries are clearly highly effective in boosting the prosperity of many major economies today. But can manufacturing continue to deliver a superior economic performance in the decades ahead? The postindustrialists, of course, think not. Insisting that the world economy is already suffering from an acute excess of manufacturing capacity, they predict that this excess will get ever worse in the decades ahead. It is a frightening picture—but one that is based on a wholly mistaken reading of how the world economy works.

In reality, the long-term outlook for manufacturing demand is for expansion almost right across the industrial waterfront. Perhaps the easiest way to see how bright manufacturing's future truly is is to remember that about 90 percent of the world's population is poor. As the world's developing nations bootstrap themselves out of poverty, how will they spend their money? Do they ache to acquire such postindustrial products as personal home page software, databases of American newspaper clippings, or Wall Street's latest portfolio hedging services? Probably not. More than anything, what developing economies want is, of course, material goods. And they are not alone in this preference. Even in the most developed parts of the world, there are plenty of material wants waiting to be satisfied. In fact almost no one anywhere feels as affluent as he or she would like to be—and, asked to compile a wish-list of wants they would like to satisfy, most people would place more emphasis on material goods than postindustrial services.

Essentially, therefore, manufacturers face an enormous and highly exciting challenge. In the future, as in the past, they must aim to create even more goods—and in the process somehow use less of the earth's scarce resources. They must create ever greater abundance by developing more inexpensive materials and more efficient production technologies. The extent of the challenge can be summed up in just one sentence: if the rest of the world is ever to enjoy an American-style standard of living, the world's output of material goods will have to increase at least fivefold. It is a formidable challenge in itself—and is made more so by the fact that manufacturing will have to become much more environmentally friendly in the future than it has been in the past.

Of course, to many the idea that poor nations can ever hope to enjoy an American-style standard of living seems utopian at best. But is it? Certainly, there is no question that even with the best luck in the world, many nations will remain poor as far ahead as anyone can see. On the optimistic side, however, there is nothing utopian about assuming manufacturers will continue to improve the efficiency of their production processes and thereby spread prosperity ever farther around the world. This is exactly what manufacturers have been doing since the beginning of the Industrial Revolution, and it is a process that is clearly continuing apace in our own time.

One notable way in which manufacturers have been improving their efficiency—and boosting their output—in recent years has been in cutting down their use of expensive, rare materials and instead making ever more use of inexpensive, abundant ones. Whereas, in former times, many manufacturing industries consumed large amounts of expensive and scarce materials such as copper, zinc, and tin, they now use mainly abundant materials such as silicon and carbon. Take the telecommunications industry. In the old days it needed vast amounts of scarce copper to make telephone cables. These days, by contrast, it achieves far better results with an almost laughably cheap material—glass. Just seventy pounds of glass in the form of optical fibers can transmit as much telephone traffic as one ton of copper. Moreover, optical fibers require only one-twentieth as much energy as copper to produce. This is a classic example of how leading manufacturers are making more with less. The result is that the price of material products keeps falling in real terms and Western-style affluence is spreading ever farther into the developing world.

Another conspicuous example of how new technologies can spread prosperity is the development of the compact disk. Standard five-inch compact disks are only about one-eighth the weight of the old twelve-inch records they replaced. Thus, since both the vinyl in records and the polycarbonate in compact disks are derived from petroleum, there has been a reduction of roughly 90 percent in the call on the earth's resources. In essence, the CD revolution has enabled the world's music lovers to get ten times more music out of a barrel of oil.

The low manufacturing cost of CDs—they can be stamped out for as little as a few cents each—has helped spread abundance in formerly poor parts of the world. According to Peter Newcomb of *Forbes*, more than 11 billion CD disks had been sold as of 1998—equal to about ten disks for every household on the planet. Not surprisingly, therefore, CDs are a ubiquitous consumer item in many nations where twenty years ago records were a luxury beyond the reach of all but the richest citizens. Notable examples of such nations include South Korea, Malaysia, Thailand, Indonesia, and China.

At the same time, there has been a parallel miniaturization of CD players (many of which are less than one-thirtieth the weight of the trunk-sized record-players of the 1950s). This has yielded major savings not only in scarce materials such as copper and wood but in the machines' power consumption. Again the message is clear: manufacturers are making more with less, and in so doing they are helping spread prosperity ever further into formerly poor parts of the world.

For our purposes here, the key point is that the CD revolution has created a host of opportunities for some of the world's top manufacturers—most notably Sony Corporation, which, as we will see, dominates the world market in the key laser technology that has made the CD possible.

For as long as scientists and engineers continue to make new technological discoveries, the process of creating more with less is clearly set to continue; and it can be counted on to create similarly exciting opportunities for a host of other advanced manufacturers as the developing world increases its share of consumption of countless products the first world has long taken for granted—most notably consumer durables such as motorcycles, cars, refrigerators, air-conditioners, washing machines, television sets, cookers, heaters, telephones, and personal computers. Of course, many of the final assembly plants to produce these goods will be located in the developing world; but they will typically be owned by First World manufacturers and will certainly source most of their key materials and components from the First World's most advanced manufacturing nations.

More generally, as technological progress spreads prosperity into the developing world, First World manufacturers will enjoy major new markets for pollution control equipment, power-generation plant, telephone-switching gear, communications satellites, railroad locomotives, airplanes, medical equipment, scientific instruments, oil rigs, pipelines, bulldozers, excavators, and many other kinds of sophisticated capital equipment.

The expansion of world manufacturing opportunities will be accelerated by the high savings rates that characterize many parts of the developing world. A high savings rate enables a nation to invest heavily not only in private industry but also in public infrastructure. Either way the result should be a boost to total output, and particularly to exports. All this in turn enables a nation to increase its imports of foreign products. High savings rates look likely to prove particularly enduring in East Asia, where one nation after another has launched notably effective policies to buttress the savings habit in the last fifty years. In Singapore, for instance, workers and employers are required by law to invest an effective 34 percent of wages in the government's Central Provident Fund. Other East Asian governments have similar if less direct ways of promoting savings (typically with measures that directly suppress consumption).

Given high savings rates and the various other positive factors at work in the global economy today, the proportion of the world's population that will enjoy a full First World–style standard of living is likely to jump from about one-tenth today to nearly one-third by the mid-twenty-first century. At the end of the day, the success of the First World's most advanced nations in performing more–for–less alchemy in manufacturing industries will be the single most important force driving the world's increasing prosperity.

Thus, beyond the economic case for manufacturing, there is a crucial political one that has hitherto been overlooked by the postindustrialists: leading manufacturing nations enjoy enormous scope to project economic power beyond their borders. This power derives from control of production know-how—know-how that when transferred abroad can greatly improve other nations' productivity and by extension their income levels. Such know-how is so coveted that a great manufacturing nation can pick and choose which nations to bestow it upon and can insist on extensive favors from them in return.

Just how significant this sort of power can be was already apparent several decades ago when in the aftermath of World War II, the leading nations of both Western Europe and East Asia assiduously courted the United States for transfers of American production know-how. In return they were prepared to sign off on most of the United States' foreign policy agenda—including even such controversial geopolitical gambits as the Vietnam War.

Of course, these days the United States' ability to project economic power abroad has greatly diminished as it has withdrawn from one advanced field of manufacturing after another. But this means merely that other nations now hold the high cards. While the United States is, of course, still courted for transfers of production know-how, increasingly

nations like Japan and Germany are the focus of even more ardent woo-
ing. And the reason is clear: these nations now possess a huge fund of
valuable technologies that can be shared with other nations to considerable mutual advantage. Such sharing has clearly bolstered Japan's sway
around the world, particularly in East Asia. Equally, Germany's sway in
both Western and now Eastern Europe has been similarly bolstered as
other nations vie with one another for direct investment by German
manufacturing companies.

In the long run, therefore, the huge economic patronage that the great
manufacturing nations of the future will enjoy will serve as a powerful
counterweight to the United States' vaunted position as the world's "sole
remaining military superpower."

TRUSTING THE MARKET:
THE TYRANNY OF A TREACHEROUS IDEOLOGY

We have seen that the postindustrialists' case for the New Economy is a
tangle of misinformation and chop logic. But why do so many otherwise
intelligent and well-informed people fail to recognize the obvious holes
in their theories? Their basic problem is that they place a childlike faith
in the efficacy of free markets. They assume that as postindustrialism has
emerged first in the United States' avowedly free-market economy, it is a
self-evidently good thing. Essentially, they have been led astray by advocates of extreme laissez-faire, who, echoing Alexander Pope's admiration
for the work of the Creator, believe that in a free-market economy "whatever is, is right."

Admittedly, at first sight the idea that the rise of postindustrialism in
the United States reflects the superior efficacy of the American free-
market system seems sound enough. But to anyone who knows how far
economies of the United States' main competitors deviate from norms of
free-market dogma, an entirely different explanation of United States'
shift into postindustrialism is suggested. This is that, by dint of farsighted
economic policies, such competitors have been consistently preempting

the world's most exciting new manufacturing opportunities. Thus, the fact that so many American entrepreneurs have been lavishing their talents on postindustrialism is merely a passive adjustment to other nations' behavior. In essence, therefore, the United States' postindustrial drift is driven by foreign nations' industrial policies—policies that in many cases represent the very antithesis of laissez-faire. And, as we will see, these policies are highly effective thanks to the existence of complexities in the real economy that are utterly overlooked in the postindustrialists' simplistic laissez-faire model.

The basic error in the laissez-faire model is that it greatly overemphasizes the interests of capital over those of labor. This bias has always been there, of course, but in modern "globalist" conditions countervailing forces that in former times tended to curb it have now been largely eliminated. Hence the characteristic pattern of postindustrial society—large profits for a tiny elite and low wages for the broad mass of the work force. The postindustrialists, of course, argue that profits are a good thing. And up to a point, this is certainly true. But you can have too much of a good thing. And in the case of profits, this point is notably apparent in many parts of the Third World. After all, if a disproportionately heavy bias toward profits was really a formula for superior economic performance, we would expect nations like Mexico and the Philippines to be economic titans. By the same token, if low profits were a recipe for economic dysfunction, nations like Germany, Switzerland, and Japan would be paupers.

The most obvious way that the United States' competitors systematically preempt manufacturing opportunities is via subsidies. These are most apparent these days in "strategic" industries. Aerospace is a notable case in point. The spectacular growth of Europe's Airbus consortium, for instance, has been driven in part by subsidies. So successful has government support been that, after less than three decades in business, Airbus had drawn abreast of Boeing in market share in large commercial jets by 1998. Of course, subsidies are supposed to be banned under international trade rules these days—but, as the rules are largely unenforceable, subsidies are likely long to remain a factor in world economic competition (and certainly they are becoming an increasingly significant factor these days in such promising fields as renewable energy and fast-rail systems). One thing is for sure: Europe is unrepentant about using subsidies to build its aerospace industry: the reason, of course, is that, in its own eyes, Europe has merely been emulating the United States, which in an earlier era established a large lead in aerospace with an unabashed program of direct and indirect government supports.

Beyond subsidies, many nations use a plethora of less obvious devices to promote the growth of promising new manufacturing industries. Many nations, for instance, protect their home markets and, thereby, provide their manufacturers with a profitable sanctuary from which to attack foreign markets. Of course, in the view of laissez-faire advocates, trade protection is counterproductive because it featherbeds weak companies and bad managers. But while this is indeed sometimes true, there is another side to the story: where protection is structured intelligently with an eye to boosting the national interest as opposed to the sectional interests of individual businesses, it can serve powerfully to invigorate a nation's industries. The point is that so long as some appropriate system of rewards and penalties is in place to induce corporations to plow back their large domestic profits into improving their production technologies, worker productivity levels are bound to increase accordingly.

In any case, in many advanced economies these days, manufacturing companies enjoy much greater access to outside capital than their American counterparts. This reflects a fundamental macroeconomic fact: most advanced manufacturing nations now boast considerably higher savings rates than the United States. Of course, for believers in the simplistic logic of laissez-faire, the United States' perennially weak savings rate should no longer be a handicap for American manufacturers. After all, capital markets around the world have supposedly become "globalized" in recent years, thus, in theory, savings now flow freely from nations with a surfeit of capital to nations with a capital shortage. In the real world, however, things are different: even in these days when billions of dollars of capital can be moved across an ocean at the click of a mouse, most of the world's savings flows tend to be invested close to where they are generated. All this comes as a surprise to the postindustrialists.

Blinded by their laissez-faire models, they forget that, in the real world, bankers are people, not mathematical algorithms. And people have families and friends—factors that tend to encourage them to stay close to home. Even David Ricardo, that ultimate nineteenth century advocate of laissez-faire, considered it only natural that people should prefer to invest at home rather than abroad. As he pointed out, at bottom, investors like to keep a close eye on their money. They fear the unknown and are therefore naturally reluctant to invest in foreign lands where the rules and customs are not fully familiar.

Admittedly, the world has shrunk since Ricardo's day, but human psychology has not changed much in the meantime. After all, contrary to their globe-trotting image, modern bankers are no more likely than anyone else to enjoy living out of a suitcase. In any case, they like to deal with borrowers with whom they share strong cultural and, if possible, personal ties. And, of course, the closer these ties are, the smoother and more productive the banking relationship is likely to be. This is particularly the case in the high-saving nations of East Asia where networks of personal relationships, typically based on long-standing friendships formed at elite universities, hold borrowers to a standard of personal accountability that no mere legally binding contract can hope to equal. (That personal ties can be more effective in ensuring accountability than legal contracts is often disputed in the West, but few familiar with East Asia doubt it. The efficacy of personal ties is particularly apparent in the way that East Asian companies trade with one another without benefit of contracts yet consistently meet exceptionally high standards not only in the quality of their products but their punctuality in meeting delivery dates.)

It has to be added that the tendency for high-saving nations to invest close to home is generally bolstered by local financial regulation. Indeed, much financial regulation around the world is aimed at achieving precisely this result. For one thing, financial regulators tend to ensure that the lion's share of the local banking market is reserved for local banks. In Japan, for instance, Japanese banks enjoy a market share of fully 99 percent of the local savings deposits. Moreover, even where American banks have access to significant savings flows in foreign financial markets, they are under considerable regulatory pressure to lend the money locally rather than make it available to manufacturers in the United States.

A further factor that has tended to result in the relative decline of manufacturing in the United States is imbalances in the flow of trade secrets and other proprietary know-how. Here again is a factor that is utterly overlooked in the postindustrialists' laissez-faire models. If the postindustrialists think about these matters at all, they imagine that know-how flows freely in both directions. In reality, however, governments around the world try to ensure that the flow is almost entirely one way. On the one hand, they pry as much advanced know-how as possible out of the United States. On the other, they make sure that few if any of their own corporations' leading-edge technologies leak abroad. (Of course, as we have already noted, nations like Germany and Japan are increasingly transferring considerable amounts of know-how abroad—but such transfers almost invariably involve midlevel technologies that have already been superseded at home.)

All the evidence is that a well-organized nation can be highly persuasive in inducing American corporations to transfer their most advanced production technologies to factories within its borders. Its trump card typically is access to its markets. An American company will be presented with a choice. If it tries to export into these markets from its factory in the United States, it will probably face significant trade barriers. By contrast, if it chooses instead to manufacture within the nation concerned, it will not only enjoy privileged access to the local market but it will probably also be offered many other important benefits such as investment grants and tax concessions.

The really troubling aspect of this pattern for the American national interest is that in time the production technologies concerned may be entirely lost to the American economy. This is because once American corporations transfer their production technology to a foreign subsidiary, they may find it makes sense to concentrate all future production in this subsidiary. Such a decision typically is made when the corporation faces heavy investment costs in jumping to the next stage of the technology concerned. In such cases, it rarely makes sense to continue to maintain two production facilities turning out the same product. Thus, the obvious choice is to close the original American factory—obvious that is because American workers are much easier to fire than their foreign counterparts (who, thanks to tough labor regulation, usually enjoy considerable protection against layoffs). Thereafter, all the crucial learning-by-doing know-how that is the essence of advanced manufacturing will accumulate in the overseas subsidiary to the benefit of the productivity of its workers.

Why don't American executives fight harder against the pressure to transfer their production technologies abroad? Because they see little reason to do so. After all, they can assure themselves that they do not lose a technology merely because it migrates to one of their foreign subsidiaries. This is, of course, the spirit of globalism and almost everyone in corporate America's boardrooms these days is a true globalist.

From the point of view of American workers, however, things look very different. Not to put too fine a point on it, it is hard for American workers to achieve world-beating productivity rates if their employers do not equip them with world-beating production technologies.

The whole trend of wages over the last fifty years bears this out. In the 1950s, when the most advanced production technologies were typically deployed only within the United States, American workers were the world's highest paid—and they earned about six to eight times as much as their counterparts even in Japan and Germany. By the 1980s, however, Japan and Germany had caught up in production technologies. Wages in these nations duly passed American levels and have stayed ahead since.

In essence, as American labor is not represented in American boardrooms, the real losers from technological globalism have no say in the matter. Moreover, workers' interests count for so little these days that American corporate executives openly proclaim their commitment to utopian globalism without the slightest fear of embarrassment. The pattern was memorably exemplified a few years ago by an executive of

Colgate-Palmolive, who told *The New York Times:* "The United States does not have an automatic call on our resources. There is no mind-set that puts this country first." A similarly outspoken disregard for the interests of American labor was apparent in a remark by NCR President Gilbert Williamson some years ago, when he said: "I was asked the other day about the United States' competitiveness and I replied that I don't think about it at all. We at NCR think of ourselves as a globally competitive company that happens to be incorporated in the United States."

Many other examples could be cited of how far the real world diverges from the narrow world of the postindustrialists' laissez-faire models. Suffice it to say that the world is far from a level playing field in trade, let alone in finance or flows of technological information. And many of the distortions tend to promote manufacturing outside the United States, while the American economy, constantly propelled by the pursuit of short-term profits, drifts ever deeper into postindustrialism.

The worst part of it is that free-market dogma has tended to obscure from Americans how far the United States has been falling behind its principal competitors in recent years—most notably Japan. All press reporting to the contrary, Japan's highly distinctive economy, which defies laissez-faire dogma in almost every detail of its workings, did not collapse after its famous financial bubble of the late 1980s burst in the early 1990s. Far from it. As we will see, Japan has continued to gain on the United States in most of the ways that matter to top policymakers on both sides of the Pacific.

For now let's merely mention the crucial matter of trade, where Japan's performance has been stronger than almost anyone noticed. The result was that in the decade of the 1990s, Japan's current account surpluses came to 2.37 times their total in the decade of the 1980s.

When you remember that (a) Japan runs a large surplus in almost every tradable manufactured product, (b) Japanese manufacturers pay some of the highest wages in the world, (c) there have been virtually no American-style layoffs anywhere in the Japanese manufacturing industry in recent years, and (d) nations with lower wage costs like the United

States are rapidly increasing their trade deficits with Japan in high-tech goods, it is surely obvious that the Japanese economy is one of the strongest in the world—and is particularly strong judged by the yard-sticks that matter to Japanese policy-makers.

Essentially, the point is Japan's very different economy should be judged by Japanese objectives, not Western ones. And here we get to the crucial point: whereas the American economy is generally run to boost the short-term welfare of the American consumer, the Japanese econ-omy is run to boost Japan's ability to project economic power abroad in the long run.

Measured by this latter criterion, the performance of the Japanese economy since the Tokyo stock market bubble burst in 1990 has been little short of spectacular. Remember that every dollar of current account surplus a nation receives adds an extra dollar to its foreign assets. The truth, therefore, is that Japan has been growing its net foreign assets faster than any nation since the United States' golden years of expan-sionism in the 1950s. The result is that in the twelve years to 2001, Japan's net overseas assets nearly quadrupled. In the long run, this will be just about the only thing that historians will remember about Japan's progress in the 1990s—and it was the one thing American observers utterly overlooked at the time.

Before looking in detail at postindustrialism in following chapters, let's sum up the story so far. The argument of *Unsustainable* revolves around many points, but one is paramount: all conventional wisdom to the contrary, modern manufacturing industries are difficult to enter—thus, those nations that achieve early leadership in them are remarkably well insulated against future challenges from lower-wage foreign compe-tition. In truth, modern manufacturing industries require large amounts of both capital and proprietary production know-how—resources that are generally difficult for low-wage countries to acquire.

By contrast, postindustrial services are relatively easy to enter. For a start, they typically do not require large amounts of capital. Nor, all con-ventional wisdom to the contrary, do they require much proprietary know-how. Rather, most of the necessary know-how can be acquired from public or semipublic sources.

In sum, this book turns upside down the standard presentation of postindustrialism as a more advanced and economically desirable activity than manufacturing.

PART 2

POSTINDUSTRIALISM'S
DRAWBACKS

A HARD LOOK AT COMPUTER SOFTWARE CHAPTER 2

omputer software is the quintessential postindustrial business, and as such, it is undoubtedly the ultimate test of the postindustrialists' claims. After all, when postindustrialists cite examples of postindustrial opportunities, computer software is typically at the top of their list.

It has blossomed from a niche business that served just a few hundred mainframe computers in the 1950s to one that today is literally ubiquitous. While computer software is most familiar as the programs we run on our personal computers, it is also installed in everything from cars and telephones to video cameras, vacuum cleaners, and even refrigerators.

Looking to the future, the industry's potential to boost American prosperity seems to the postindustrialists to be almost limitless. So much for the hype. Now for the reality.

MICROSOFT'S SUCCESS:
A VERY SPECIAL CASE

For all the euphoria about software, the industry's image of fabulous success is remarkably narrowly based. In fact, this image is largely attributable to just one company, Microsoft. The enrichment of Microsoft's founders has powerfully supported the myth that the information economy is a latter-day El Dorado. The press seems to assume that, just as any young American boy or girl can aspire to become the president of the United States, any new software company can aspire to become another Microsoft. In reality, Microsoft is a very special company, one whose growth has been driven almost entirely by its monopolistic role in setting standards for computer operating systems. Microsoft inherited this role from IBM in the 1980s; as was abundantly apparent from IBM's famously fat profit margins in former times, the ability to set the computer industry's standards amounts to a license to print money. In the words of the American consumer activist Ralph Nader, Microsoft's position is the functional equivalent of "owning the alphabet."

By contrast, other software companies enjoy no such all-embracing franchise—and no such license to print money.

In any case, the Microsoft story is misleading in another way. Although the company is portrayed as a Leviathan, it is still a relatively unremarkable business in most respects. In fact, it counts as a giant on just one rather dubious measure, its stock market valuation. Measured by its peak stock price at the end of 1999, Microsoft was worth more than $600 billion—and even in mid-2003, after a painful stock market crash, it was still worth $260 billion. This latter figure was more than the annual gross national product of Switzerland! Its stock valuation apart, Microsoft is no colossus by most other measures. In fact, ranked by sales revenues, it is little more than a middleweight in *Fortune* magazine's league table of the world's 500 largest companies.

On the crucial yardstick of jobs, Microsoft compares even worse. As of 2003, its total workforce came to just 50,500. This was just one-seventh those of both Ford and General Motors. It should be added that the latter two companies as of 2003 were a fraction of their former selves in employment terms. By comparison in the early 1980s, before the fashion for postindustrialism took hold (and before the American auto industry was gutted by Japanese imports), Ford employed more than 500,000 workers and General Motors more than 850,000.

Perhaps the most telling indication of Microsoft's relative economic insignificance is that its workforce accounts for only about 2 percent of all employment in the American computer software industry. Thus, when the media talk about the famously large compensation levels at Microsoft, one should remember that 98 percent of the industry's workers work for less successful employers.

THOSE WELL-PAID SOFTWARE JOBS:
ONLY THE BEST NEED APPLY

Judged by the amount of cyberpower in the room, it was a press conference to end all press conferences. There, in plain view, were Bill Gates of Microsoft and Andrew Grove of Intel. Other notable "digerati" who turned out included Eric Schmidt of Novell, Gordon Eubanks of Symantec, and Carol Bartz of Autodesk. They were present as leading supporters of the Business Software Alliance, a Washington-based industry group. With a mission to increase the industry's lobbying clout in Washington, the digerati and their helpers were intent on doing their damnedest to underline the software industry's importance to the American economy.

Their strongest card was jobs. The industry, they maintained, was not only one of the nation's largest employers but one of the best. Citing survey results, they stated that the industry's sales in 1996 totaled $103 billion. On a value-added basis, therefore, software ranked third among American industries after automobiles and electronics—up from fifth place in a 1995 study. Thus, in the space of just two years, software had leapfrogged two major industries—aircraft and pharmaceuticals.

Between 1990 and 1996 the industry had grown at an annual rate of 12.5 percent, nearly two and a half times faster than the American economy as a whole.

The Business Software Alliance went on to emphasize the industry's contribution to the U.S. job base. Measuring indirect as well as direct employment, the industry was already employing 2,065,000 by 1996 and was projected to boost its contribution to the U.S. job base by 66 percent to account for nearly 3 percent of the entire American workforce by 2005. And the best part of it was the pay levels. People employed directly in the industry earned $57,300 a year on average. Workers in the packaged software section of the industry did even better, averaging $64,500.

"The average wages are phenomenal," said Robert Damuth, director of policy studies for Nathan Associates, which conducted the survey on behalf of the Business Software Alliance. "The incomes are extraordinary because software is a knowledge-intensive industry that is thriving and workers are getting compensated for their skills."

Rarely has the case for the software industry been better made. And even after the stock market crash of 2000–2002, that case seems to many American observers to be well founded. So what can possibly be wrong with this picture?

First, let's be clear. There is no question that there is much to be admired in the American software industry. Its achievements are legion. That said, the industry's contribution on the jobs front is distinctly double-edged. The software industry's high wages, for instance, are just the obverse side of the most obvious drawback of postindustrialism— exclusionist hiring. The industry recruits from the cream of the intellectual crop, and Bill Gates for one is not shy about saying so. Gates has publicly confessed that he is "very elitist" in hiring only engineers with extraordinarily high IQs. Of course, few other software companies can afford to be quite so choosy as Microsoft in hiring people who—in *Fortune*'s words— are "geniuses or near-geniuses," but the industry's message to job seekers is brutally blunt: workers of average intelligence need not apply.

In the circumstances, the surprise is not that the industry pays high wages but that its wages are not even higher. Although software workers rank well up among the intellectual elite, their wages are typically only slightly more than the average Japanese wage of $21.01 an hour.

So what are we left with? The industry recruits bright people and pays them wages that are not overly generous compared to their intellectual capabilities. Meanwhile, less intelligent workers who cannot make the grade are left out in the cold. Given the increasing polarization of American society in recent years, the software industry's elitist job structure is clearly not helpful.

And this is just the beginning of the problems with the software industry.

CULTURE, PIRACY, AND THE PURSUIT OF EXPORTS

As we have already noted, the software industry is a surprisingly weak exporter. In truth, there are good reasons for this.

For a start, there is the problem of piracy, which deprives software companies of a large share of their rightful revenues in many foreign markets. Piracy is so widely accepted in China, for instance, that popular Western computer software programs such as Microsoft's Windows are sometimes illegally copied in computer stores in full view of the customer. Bootleg copies of Windows are also much in evidence in Taiwan, Russia, Thailand, and many other potentially important markets.

Many other American software products suffer similarly curtailed export revenues because of piracy. According to figures supplied by Microsoft in 2003, the global piracy rate was running at 36 percent and accounted for $11.75 billion in lost revenues each year. Of course, software piracy is a pandemic problem even within the United States, but it is a far bigger one in many overseas markets. As of 2003, the piracy rate was reported to be running at 94 percent in China, for instance—compared to a rate of just 24 percent in the United States.

There is a deeply rooted unwillingness by consumers almost everywhere to pay up for the authentic product—not just in the Third World but even in some of the world's richest regions. Take super-rich Hong

Kong, where per capita incomes rival those of the United States. In the late 1990s, Hong Kong's top intellectual property official washed his hands of the software piracy problem, saying that any effort by the Hong Kong government to shut down stores that sold bootleg software would not be supported by the general public.

Also undermining software's export potential are various cultural barriers. These are problematical in many of the most visible types of software, not least in "shrink-wrap" personal-computer software, which often needs considerable adaptation to take account of local cultural norms in different markets around the world. In general, the more user-friendly a personal computer program is, the more heavily it needs to be adapted to sell in foreign markets. Known as localization, this adaptation process is often a managerial and cultural nightmare. For the Indian market alone, Microsoft recently produced its products in eight different languages!

American software companies usually do their localization outside the United States, typically in the foreign market concerned. Thus, the costs of localization can dramatically cut the exporting company's net foreign exchange receipts—and by extension U.S. export revenues.

In any case, American software developers find that the struggle to penetrate foreign markets is often an unequal one. For one thing, local software developers often reverse-engineer—that is, emulate features from—leading American versions of popular programs, and because they are faster at getting these features into the local market, they can maintain their market share for years against strong American products. Reverse-engineering, which is generally legal, is pandemic in the industry.

In fact, legal protection for software ideas is so poor that many of the greatest U.S. software inventions—what Ann Wells Branscomb has rightly described as "the crown jewels of the information economy"—have proven impossible to patent effectively. Not only are they unprotected in foreign markets, but they cannot even be protected in the American home market. The industry's history is full of great ideas that were "borrowed" by rival companies. IBM in particular has suffered from this sort of borrowing. Take the "relational" software structure that is now almost universally incorporated in database programs. This structure, which enhances speed in searching, was invented by the IBM researcher Edgar Cobbin in the late 1960s but was quickly commercialized by other companies, most notably Ingres Corporation and Oracle Corporation. Now it has been widely copied by software developers around the world—and for the most part, such foreign usage of the concept yields no royalties or other revenues to the United States.

Another American company whose pioneering software work has been enthusiastically plundered by software developers around the world is Xerox. Xerox is credited as the ultimate source of, for instance, the font software that controls the look of the alphabetical characters used on computer screens and in printouts. Xerox was also the source of various revolutionary ideas that propelled the growth of Apple Computer. These ideas included screen icons, mouse-activated pull-down menus, and over-lapping windows of onscreen text. Of course, Apple's ideas have in turn been reverse-engineered by countless other software companies, most notably Microsoft. In fact, Bill Gates once acknowledged the ultimate source of the ideas behind the Microsoft Windows operating system in a famous witticism. Gates joked that both he and the founder of Apple, Steve Jobs, had lived next door to a rich neighbor called Xerox, and when he broke in to steal the television set, he found that Jobs had already taken it! Of course, both Microsoft and Apple are American companies, so there was no net loss of revenues to the American economy as a whole from this "theft." Less visibly, however, many foreign companies have also exploited Xerox's innovations without paying a penny in royalties to the United States.

American software developers are now pressing hard for tougher intellectual property laws to protect their world-beating ideas. But they have a long battle ahead of them. In the meantime, the world will continue to help itself for free.

All this explains why the software industry is a notably disappointing contributor to U.S. export revenues. But this fact is less well understood than it should be because press reporters often talk airily about the industry's supposedly superlative export performance without checking the facts. The press rarely quotes specific numbers for U.S. software exports, and when it does, its estimates are often exaggerated. In fact, the press often conflates the American industry's exports with something quite different: overseas sales. There is a crucial distinction here: overseas sales include sales of products that are made largely or entirely abroad. Although there may be a flow of dividends and royalties back to the parent company in the United States, most of the revenues generated by such "made-abroad" products stay in the markets concerned.

Microsoft provides a good example of the distinction. Its exports from the United States accounted for only about one-quarter of its total sales in the latter half of the 1990s. This no doubt will come as a surprise to many Americans, who are under the impression that Microsoft's exports are much larger than this. They confuse Microsoft's overseas sales with its exports. As of 1996, its overseas sales contributed more than 60 percent of total sales. But more than half of such sales came from added value generated largely in its overseas subsidiaries. Only a small proportion of the resulting revenues flows back to the United States. Most of the money goes to pay salaries and other expenses in the overseas subsidiaries. (Workers employed outside the United States account for about one-third of Microsoft's total workforce.)

In any case, as we have already emphasized, Microsoft is a truly exceptional company, and few other software companies enjoy even remotely as advantageous a position in global markets. For the American industry as a whole, exports represent a low proportion of total sales revenues. No reliable official figures are available, but a reasonable guesstimate is that exports represent less than 10 percent of the industry's total revenues.

In sum, it is clear that the perennially troubled American balance of payments is getting a poor return from America's most brilliantly successful postindustrial businesses. It is little short of tragic that so many talented people are engaged in an activity that does little to advance America's long-term position in global competition. And then there is the problem of rising software imports.

THE FAST-DEVELOPING THREAT TO AMERICAN SOFTWARE JOBS: IMPORTS

If culture limits America's opportunities to export software, doesn't it, by the same token, protect the United States from imports? Hardly.

For a start, though many software products are indeed highly culture-specific, many others are not. Major software projects conducted on a contract basis for specific large corporate customers, for instance, generally entail a relatively small proportion of culture-specific work. Even such culture-specific software as the applications programs sold in American computer stores can be written in part by foreign programmers. In fact, the only element of such programs that requires detailed cultural knowledge is the design of the user interface. Most of the rest can be parceled out to skilled programmers anywhere in the world.

Given that programming wages are generally lower abroad than in the United States, American software companies have a clear incentive to rely more and more on foreign labor, and in so doing, they inexorably add to U.S. import bills. In fact, this incentive increases all the time thanks to a technology-induced sea change in the industry's economics. For one thing, cheap personal computers have replaced expensive mainframes as the main tools for developing software. At a stroke, therefore, the industry has swung from being a highly capital-intensive industry to a highly labor-intensive one. In fact, the capital required to establish a new software business these days is minimal. Virtually the only equipment needed is desks, telephone lines, and personal computers. Thus, for a software entrepreneur in a low-wage country, the capital cost per job can be as little as $10,000, a reduction of more than 90 percent from the mainframe era. This figure is well within the reach of software subcontracting companies in low-wage countries—and far less than is needed to get started in even the least sophisticated areas of manufacturing.

Another factor that has powerfully boosted the competitiveness of foreign nations in exporting software to the United States is the big fall in international telecommunication costs in the last twenty years. This drop has opened the door to many cross-border collaboration projects in which leaders based in the United States can coordinate large teams of programmers working in one or more low-wage foreign countries. Ominously for American software jobs, the impact of modern communications has been particularly dramatic in Third World countries, where satellite communications and cellular phones have suddenly liberated local software contractors from the acute limitations of primitive terrestrial telephone services. Given that as of the late 1990s at least half the world's people still lived more than two hours' travel time from the nearest telephone, we are as yet in only the early stages of a major proliferation of opportunities for the developing world to expand its software exports to the United States.

But how good can a programmer in the developing world be anyway? The answer is very good indeed. As we pointed out in Chapter 1, there is no reason to believe that citizens of poor nations are inherently lacking in the sort of creativity needed to succeed in postindustrial services. But in any case, creativity is not the most important mental faculty required in routine programming of the sort that accounts for most of the software industry's jobs. Rather, as the author Robert X. Cringely has pointed out, the key faculty is merely an excellent short-term memory— the ability, for instance, to remember long strings of numbers. Whereas most people can memorize a seven-digit telephone number, good software writers have the sort of memory that can readily memorize strings of fifteen or more digits.

Microsoft's Bill Gates himself exemplifies in high degree the sort of mind that succeeds in the software industry. He reportedly can recall the telephone extension numbers and car license plate numbers of countless Microsoft employees. According to the authors James Wallace and Jim Erickson, even as a child he displayed amazing memory skills. In particular, he won a local parish contest by memorizing and reciting the entire Sermon on the Mount. The passage is the equivalent of nearly four standard newspaper columns of type. Among the hundreds who participated in the contest over the years, Gates, who was then only eleven, was the only challenger who ever succeeded in reciting the entire passage without stumbling or missing a line.

Recall of this sort is rare, but it is clearly a God-given talent, not a uniquely American cultural attribute. There is no reason that other nations can't boast as high a ratio of talented software engineers as the United States.

Of course, the idea that other nations are capable of going head to head with the United States in software seems to be belied by the evidence of the American software market. After all, as even the most casual observer can see, virtually all the software in American computer stores is home-grown. But this actually proves little because personal computer software is a specialty in which cultural factors happen to be particularly important in protecting American software makers from foreign competition.

Even the fact that most of the world's computers now run on operating systems produced by an American company—Microsoft—rather than, say, a German or Japanese one offers little support for the idea that Americans enjoy a special franchise in the software industry. The fact that an American company proved dominant in operating systems was more or less preordained given that the United States enjoyed unquestioned leadership in hardware when the IBM personal computer was launched in 1981. By the late 1980s, when it became apparent that computer users and hardware manufacturers worldwide wanted a single world standard to ensure global compatibility, Microsoft's huge installed base ensured that its operating system was the obvious choice.

One thing is for sure: all talk of a special American edge in software to the contrary, other nations assuredly can make good software. Take the Japanese. Although the postindustrialists often maintain that the Japanese cannot write software, this is contradicted by the fact that thousands of Japanese software engineers work in Silicon Valley and are indeed highly prized there for their talents. Among the more notable admirers of Japanese software writing talents is none other than Microsoft Chairman Bill Gates. In his search for world-beating software talent, he named six Japanese universities among twenty-five top universities worldwide on which Microsoft should concentrate its recruiting efforts. Gates should know about Japanese software talent given that one of his closest friends and confidants in his early days was the Japanese software engineer

Kazuhiko Nishi. Before they had a falling-out in the mid-1980s, Gates described Nishi as "my best guy ever."

Not only are individual Japanese citizens noted for their software skills, but Japan-based software companies also are no slouches in the industry. They are particularly active in producing software that leverages Japan's strengths in manufacturing. A good example is computer games, in which the Japanese have had no difficulty developing superb software to go with their ultra-fast hardware. Although not all such software is written in Japan (much of it is written in the United Kingdom, where wages are much lower than Japanese levels), the process is directed from Japan, and much of the most creative thinking is done there. The Japanese are also in a league of their own in writing automation software for their factory robots. Their skills are readily apparent, too, in the elegant and foolproof "imbedded" software that guides the operations of Japanese electronic products. Such software is often highly complex: a Sony Handycam, for instance, contains as much software as a 1960s-era mainframe computer—and infinitely fewer bugs.

Another nation whose software prowess has also been absurdly underestimated by postindustrialists is Germany. Granted, like Japan, Germany does not export much personal computer software. But it has achieved great success in areas where it has a clear shot to compete on equal terms with the Americans. An example is SAP, a sophisticated software house based in Walldorf near Heidelberg. Founded by former executives of IBM's German subsidiary, SAP makes so-called enterprise resource planning (ERP) programs, which enable major corporations to integrate their worldwide accounting, marketing, and production operations into one seamless system. On the strength of serving the global software needs of hundreds of giant European, American, and Japanese corporations, its sales grew by 30 percent a year in the late 1990s and by 1998 it ranked among the world's five largest software companies. As of 2002, it boasted sales of more than $8 billion, broadly comparable with Redwood City-based Oracle Corporation, one of America's most successful software companies.

Perhaps the ultimate symbol of its leadership is that its products have been selected by many software-savvy computer companies as the backbone of their global administrative systems. Companies that have invested heavily in SAP products include IBM, Motorola, Texas Instruments, Intel, Hewlett-Packard, and—accolade of accolades—Microsoft.

That said, the Germans and Japanese obviously pose no great threat to American software jobs, for the simple reason that their wages generally exceed American levels. In any case, the governments of both Germany and Japan are clearly more interested in promoting manufacturing activities than software and other postindustrial services.

But the story is very different for many low-wage nations now breaking into the software business. In truth, lower-wage nations are full of potentially highly capable and productive software workers—workers who need only an appropriate technical education to compete successfully in the world market for software labor. They don't even need to have received any prior training in writing software given that in recent years more and more software employers around the world are happy to provide comprehensive on-the-job training for raw recruits. Moreover, it should be noted that even in some notably poor Third World countries, the appropriate education—in mathematics or science—is readily available to the middle classes, and the standard of educational achievement in those countries often compares surprisingly well with that of the United States.

With the spread of personal computers around the world, the opportunity to acquire hands-on experience in programming is now widely available even in many poor nations. Moreover, the rise of the Internet has made it possible for software engineers in the Third World to learn of the latest American software-writing techniques just as quickly as their counterparts in the United States. In fact, virtually all of the most important know-how needed to make good software can be transmitted around the world quite legally in informal Internet communications.

The speed with which software know-how leaks out of the United States these days is hard to exaggerate. As William J. Holstein has pointed out, many American software innovators hold an "ardent belief" that pioneering work should be widely disseminated in Usenet groups and Internet chat rooms. Writing in *U.S. News & World Report*, Holstein cited university researchers who had been engaged by a software company to help develop an important new program. Not only did these researchers not guard the resulting intellectual property from competitors, but they published full details of their work on the Internet before the company could bring the program to market.

One thing is certain: the software business is already a remarkably cosmopolitan one. Between 1994 and 1999, the US "imported" 124,000 Indians, 68,000 Chinese, 57,000 Filipinos, 49,000 Canadians, and 42,000 British holders of higher education degrees. A large proportion of them went into information technology jobs. In fact, of the five million people employed in the American information technology industry, about one million are foreign born.

Even at the top of the American software industry, foreign-born engineers are now much in evidence. Take 3Com, a Santa Clara–based networking software company: its chairman is the Algerian-born Eric Benhamou. The founder of Raza Foundries is S. Atiq Raza, a native of Pakistan. Indians constitute probably the most visible nationality of all; in some estimates, they account for nearly one-fifth of all the world's programmers. According to research some years ago by Raman Mishra of MIT, more than 5,000 Indian-born engineers were already then working for Microsoft alone. In fact, the core team that created Microsoft's Windows 98 operating program was largely composed of Indian-born engineers. About 30 percent of software engineers in Silicon Valley are reportedly of Indian origin, and many more came from China.

The point is not just that engineers from low-wage countries can play to win within the American software industry; it is also that more and more social networks are in place that help low-wage nations increase their software exports to the United States. After all, many key foreign executives now holding down high-level jobs in the United States retain links with friends and college classmates in their home country, and such links not only help low-wage nations to keep in touch with the latest

American software trends but give them an inside track in bidding for the American software industry's outsourcing work.

The significance of such links is notably apparent in the case of Ireland. Formerly an agriculture-based economy, Ireland in recent years has built up an important software export business, and increasingly it is exporting to the United States. Ireland has benefited in several ways from the fact that many Irish engineers moved to Silicon Valley in the 1970s and 1980s. This subsequently resulted in a reverse brain drain in which Irish-born software engineers increasingly returned from the United States to put their talents—and perhaps more important, their contacts— to profitable use within the Irish software industry.

Ireland's official economic development agency has stimulated the trend and used it to persuade several American corporations to establish important software operations in the country. Among the most notable of these have been Microsoft, IBM, Novell, EDS, Oracle, Motorola, and Symantec. These operations in turn have trained countless more engineers, many of whom have broken away to establish their own software start-ups in Ireland in recent years. One notable example is Iona Technologies, which started with just one full-time employee in 1991. By 1997, it was listed on the NASDAQ market, and by the end of 1999 it enjoyed—all too fleetingly, as it turned out—a market capitalization of more than $2 billion. As of its 2003, in the wake of the tech crash, its market capitalization was down to less than $70 million—but, with a work force of more than 600 at last count, it was still by the standards of the small Irish economy an important source of prosperity.

Another small nation whose software industry has also benefited greatly from its citizens' personal ties with the United States is Israel. Such major American corporations as IBM, Intel, Motorola, and 3Com have located important software operations there. Israel is also noted for its strong indigenous software companies, many of which are world leaders in communications. Some, for instance, have made important breakthroughs in asynchronous transfer mode, which is a high-speed, wide-band standard for data communications. Others are leaders in a technology known as wireless LAN (local area network), which, among other things, enables a company's notebook computers to communicate with one another by radio or infrared signals. Still others are advanced in video compression, a key technology in digital television. As of 1997, four Israeli makers of Ethernet switches had won the highest rank accreditation by the United States-based National Software Testing Laboratories, a prestigious testing organization.

As a result of successes like these, it is hardly surprising that Israel, even more than Ireland, has become an important exporter of software to the United States. Of course, because these countries are small and their wages are not much below American levels, their export growth has done little to undermine American software jobs. But they are the thin end of what could prove to be a very large wedge. Certainly, their success in exporting to the United States and other leading economies has not been lost on many larger nations, not least such low-wage nations as India, the Philippines, and Malaysia.

Today these new contenders generally participate in the world software industry merely as sources of cheap labor for local subsidiaries of American software companies. But in the long run, their own indigenous companies may grow to become major players in the global software industry.

A key point here is that the managerial challenge of running a software company is not nearly as daunting as is generally imagined, and it is certainly modest compared to running an efficient manufacturing business. Whereas the production flow in a modern First World factory may have to be coordinated on a split-second basis (think of the just-in-time inventory control system in the automobile industry), software work generally involves few truly critical deadlines; typically there is just one: the deadline by which the entire program must be finished. Thus, although the success of top manufacturing companies like Toyota and DaimlerChrysler stems in large measure from a sophisticated management culture that has taken several decades to hone, software firms need no similarly deep management tradition to succeed.

In short, as the Silicon Valley venture capitalist Donald Valentine has pointed out, software is "a simple business." Given that Valentine helped create such phenomenally successful ventures as Cisco Systems, Oracle, and 3Com, he should know. Speaking of his habit of investing large amounts of money in software start-ups run by untried young entrepreneurs, Valentine says of the software industry: "Twenty-three-year-olds can figure it out. If it were a complicated business like a steel mill, with unions and all this material coming all the time and two shifts, I might want older people with experience."

Even Microsoft, big as it is by software-industry standards, illustrates the point. According to Michael A. Cusumano and Richard W. Selby, authors of *Microsoft Secrets,* Microsoft operates on remarkably simple management structures that are reminiscent of the administration of the Roman army. Microsoft ensures that interdependent aspects of a program are kept to a minimum, thus enabling software development managers to function like Roman centurions who "go off on their own and report back only occasionally." What the Roman army could do two thousand years ago, many software start-up companies in the developing world can undoubtedly emulate today.

In fact, a rapidly increasing proportion of software used in the United States is already being imported from low-wage countries. CrossComm of Massachusetts, for instance, has been sourcing important software from Poland.

Among other East European countries that are exporting to the United States, Russia is a major player. As of the late 1990s, highly advanced data encryption software developed in Russia was being distributed in the United States by Sun Microsystems.

Perhaps the ultimate accolade for Russia's prospects as a software exporter has come from Microsoft's Bill Gates. Speaking to reporters in Moscow in 1997, Gates said that a strong education system positioned Russia to become one of the world's three largest software exporters. He added, "Russia has a very bright future as a country developing software, and we are definitely seeing the beginning of that."

Even mainland China is now targeting software as a major export industry. It has already scored a spectacular success with Founder Group, a firm that makes typesetting and desktop publishing systems for East Asian users. Launched in 1976 by a husband-and-wife team of mathematics professors, Founder had by the late 1990s captured 80 percent of the market worldwide for Chinese-language typesetting software. The company serves large publishing companies in Hong Kong, Malaysia, and Taiwan. The company has also developed a system for the Korean language and is participating in Malaysia's ambitious plan to build an export-oriented software industry in the so-called Multimedia Super Corridor near Kuala Lumpur. As of 2001, its sales had hit $214 million and were growing by 20 percent a year.

As yet, China has done little exporting to the United States, but that may be changing. The recent trend of software programs being designed as a series of discrete components has been helping Chinese software companies overcome cultural barriers in exporting software to the West. By the late 1990s an IBM affiliate in China was showing the way. The firm, Advanced Systems Development Corporation, a joint venture with a top Chinese science university, was developing a sophisticated range of component software called Java Beans. These were a series of interchangeable software modules designed for commercial users of the Internet. Thus, Chinese programmers could develop software for, say, a clinic in the United States without knowing anything other than the end-user's basic requirements. Perhaps the most surprising—and for American software workers, the most ominous—aspect of IBM's Chinese affiliate was that it pioneered a new work shift system linking several low-wage countries. When the Chinese programmers finished each evening, they passed their work on to Latvia and Belarus, where other IBM engineers continued working on the modules during the Chinese night.

No wonder Bloomberg News commented, "The tilt in software design towards more basic, interchangeable products is good news for countries like China with armies of talented programmers." Given that IBM has laid off thousands of programmers in the United States and other Western countries in the last five years, the message could hardly have been clearer: the software industry's spread into the Third World had already begun—and a challenge to the West's software job base is imminent. In the event, one of the most important real-economy effects of the tech crash of 2000 was that tens of thousands of American software workers were laid off as their work was increasingly assigned to low-wage nations, many of them in the Third World.

Probably no nation has illustrated the strength of that challenge more vividly than India, which, as we will now see, emerged from nowhere in the 1990s to become one of the world's great software exporters.

MORNING IN MADRAS:
THE RISE OF THE INDIAN SOFTWARE INDUSTRY

In their book *The Judas Economy,* William Wolman and Anne Colamosca tell a provocative story of how a top executive of the Caterpillar bulldozer company once pulled rank in negotiations with some Indian officials. In an effort to underline India's deficiencies in manufacturing, he flung a cigarette lighter across a conference table with the comment, "When you guys can make one of these things, let me know about it."

Although in the thirty years since this incident took place, the Indians have made no noticeable progress in manufacturing cigarette lighters, it is hard to imagine any American executive displaying such hubris these days. For all its shortcomings in manufacturing, India has made remarkable progress in an industry that to most Americans is more impressive than manufacturing—and that industry is, of course, computer software.

In fact, since India began targeting software as a key element of its economic growth strategy in the mid-1980s, its software exports have been growing at a compound rate of more than 40 percent. Of course, India started from a tiny base and is still a relatively minor player in the global industry. Moreover, it remains an easy country for foreigners to underestimate. For a start, there is the problem of India's overly bureaucratic style of administration. In contrast with Northeast Asian governments, which have generally played a positive role in their nations' economic development, the Indian government can't seem to get out of its own way—or anyone else's.

India's image problem is not improved by the poor quality of official promotional brochures handed out to would-be foreign investors in the Indian software industry. Such brochures are typically printed on cheap glossy paper that betrays a grayish/brownish tint. The typefaces are unfashionable, and the pictorial content consists mainly of faded photographs of satellite dishes in dusty, not overly scenic locations.

Various Indian regions competing for direct investment from foreign software houses add to the amateurish tone with their slightly ridiculous jockeying for attention. As reflected in an official press pack sent out in the late 1990s, no fewer than three Indian states—Karnataka, Gujarat, and Orissa—made mutually contradictory claims to the title of "India's Silicon Valley."

The less than sophisticated image is not surprising given that, with a per capita income of just $474 a year at last count, India remains one of the poorest countries on earth. Little wonder, therefore, that when the government first targeted the software industry, few in the United States took notice. As Dewang Mehta, executive director of the Indian software industry's trade association, has admitted, even Indians themselves originally scoffed at the idea of their country becoming a software powerhouse.

The software industry, however, is a natural choice for India in these days of ultracheap intercontinental telecommunications. "Improvements in the telecom infrastructure have meant that the United States and other developed markets are on India's doorstep, not on the other side of the globe," says Iain Allison of Marlin Partners, a Bombay-based consulting firm. "No other Indian industry has this factor favoring it."

India's prospects are also helped by the happy fact that the industry's capital needs are so modest. Just how modest is apparent in the case of Infosys, a software company founded in the mid-1980s by N.R. Narayana Murthi on an investment of less than $1,000. From that tiny acorn, Infosys has now grown into a world-girdling giant that has won important contracts from such notable American clients as AT&T, Nordstrom, Citibank, and General Electric.

Moreover, in targeting software, India enjoys an important fundamental advantage in its education system, which educates the middle class to a level broadly comparable to that of the United States and the United Kingdom. Indian schools tend to be particularly strong in mathematics, a fact that reflects a long tradition of mathematical scholarship dating back to ancient times. The concept of negative numbers, for instance, was used by the Hindu astronomer Brahmagupta in the seventh century—more than nine hundred years before its first recorded use in Europe. Moreover, our so-called Arabic numeral system has its ultimate origin in India.

Thus, India was positioned for takeoff in software even before the government began targeting the industry for growth in the early 1980s. In fact, the industry's true beginnings go back surprisingly far—to 1968, to be exact. That was the year when a firm called Tata Consultancy Services (TCS) was launched as a computer service offshoot of Tata Sons, a giant Bombay-based conglomerate that makes everything from steel to cosmetics.

For the first few years, TCS concentrated on the domestic Indian market, serving affiliates in the Tata group as well as other Indian-based clients. In the early 1970s, it began testing the water in export markets, and in 1975, it achieved a major breakthrough by securing a contract from a British-based subsidiary of the Burroughs Computer Company. After successfully completing that contract, TCS went on in 1976 to forge a continuing relationship with Burroughs.

Since then, TCS has been growing at a compound rate of more than 30 percent a year, and as of 2002, its workforce had expanded to include 22,000 consultants serving clients in 55 countries. Other major Indian software makers, such as HCL Corporation and Tata Infotech (which, like TCS, is an affiliate of Tata Sons), have enjoyed similar growth. The result is that India's exports of software and allied services totaled $9.5 billion in the year to March 2003. This represented an increase of 26 percent on the previous year. The performance was all the more remarkable for the fact that many software companies in the United States and elsewhere were suffering declining sales.

As India's software houses have grown, they have simultaneously honed their skills to the point where today they claim to do leading-edge work in many of the software industry's most important subdisciplines. They pride themselves, for instance, on the speed with which they have adopted such software-writing techniques as object-oriented programming. This is a technique by which programs are designed as a series of discrete modules rather than as one large whole. Indian software houses are also experts in CASE (computer-aided software engineering) and graphical user interfaces.

Recently, Indian software houses claim to have pioneered important new approaches to the management of software projects. In particular, they are proud of having introduced an element of forward planning into an industry that had previously been notorious worldwide for false starts and radical midway changes of direction. In an effort to underline their commitment to rigor and precision in the production process, Indian software leaders even talk about their companies as "software factories." As Shiv Nadar, chairman of HCL Corporation, has pointed out, the factory concept is intended to conjure up associations with Japan's highly organized mass-production approach in manufacturing.

> We have chosen deliberately to distance ourselves from the image of software development as a "creative activity." Instead, we see it as a process-driven activity. Creativity and problem-solving skills are encouraged during an initial period of "head-butting" or discussion by the project team. But once the project gets going, the teams go in for strict project management using mature development methodologies.

Other Indian software executives draw an analogy with the construction industry. Tata Infotech's Sreenivasan Mohanagopal, for instance, says:

> Our approach requires us to plan ahead, rather like an architect who plans the whole of a building before a single brick is laid. Builders do not alter the basic structure of a building halfway through the construction process; equally in our approach to software engineer-

ing, we do not make basic changes to the structure of a software
program midway through the production process.

All this is music to the ears of customers around the world because
it promises something they particularly value and all too rarely receive:
a surprise-free software product delivered on time. In the software
industry, surprises are generally unpleasant ones, and on-time delivery
is a rarity (even mighty Microsoft is noted for missing its own publicly
announced deadlines).

The proof of the pudding is in the eating, of course. How well does
the Indian software industry live up to its marketing promises? By all
accounts, quite well. Certainly, the industry has built a long list of satisfied clients in major overseas markets. The industry has been particularly
successful in the United States, which now takes fully two-thirds of all
Indian software exports. Delhi-based HCL alone boasts a customer list
that reads like a *Who's Who* of American business—names like Boeing,
AT&T, Citibank, Merrill Lynch, Novell, Cisco, Compaq, IBM, and
Sun Microsystems. Its customers also include many of Japan's most
prestigious companies, including NTT, NEC, Hitachi, and Toshiba.

As reported by the *Financial Times* of London, Indian software companies are particularly strong in applications for the transportation industry.
Indian firms created, for instance, the administrative systems of Swissair
and American Airlines, the train scheduling system for the London
Underground, and the reservation system for the Holiday Inn motel chain.

All such achievements pale, however, in comparison with the success of
Tata Consultancy Services a few years ago in a showcase contract for the
Swiss securities industry. The project involved creating a securities trading
system that would reduce the settlement time for trades from ten days to
just one. It was a contract of national importance for Switzerland—all the
more so because a few years earlier the massive task of writing the London
Stock Exchange's proposed new Taurus trading program had become so
bogged down in unmanageable complexity that it was never completed.

The Swiss project was developed and executed by Nirmal Jain, an
intense electrical engineer. Jain, who earned a doctorate from the

University of Hawaii in the 1970s, worked in the American electronics industry in Dallas before returning to India to work for TCS.

When Jain learned that the Swiss were seeking bids for a new trading system, he immediately recognized a chance for TCS to leap into the big leagues. Leaving nothing to chance, he dispatched a team of ten people to Switzerland for six months in advance of bidding on the contract. This move not only enabled him to develop an exceptionally detailed proposal but impressed the Swiss with TCS's seriousness. In the end, there were just two finalists, and TCS was one of them. The other was Chicago-based Andersen Consulting, one of the most trusted names in the world of software contracting. Then the word came through from Switzerland that TCS had beaten out Andersen. For the whole of the Indian software industry, it was a moment to remember. And for the American software industry, it was a watershed of sorts. The demanding Swiss had been persuaded that Third World India could deliver the relevant quality standards; thus, TCS's price, at reputedly little more than half of Andersen's, had been the clincher.

There is a special irony in the fact that this most prestigious of contracts was carried out in the southern city of Madras. Even by Indian standards, Madras is an unprepossessing location for a leading-edge business. There could hardly be a more telling illustration of how much more competitive Third World companies can be in software than in hardware, for Madras's success in exporting software to the West contrasts starkly with its distinctly limited export potential in manufacturing. Just how limited is that potential? One of the city's more notable manufactured products is rickshaws.

AMERICAN SOFTWARE JOBS:
THE SHAKEOUT REVISITED

Given the rise of vigorous software-exporting industries in India and other cheap-labor countries in the 1990s, a painful jobs shakeout was long in the cards for the American software industry. In the event, that shakeout began late in 2000, soon after Internet stocks entered on a painful bear market. According to the Chicago-based outplacement firm, Challenger, Gray and Christmas, nearly 600,000 U.S. technology jobs were snuffed out in the subsequent two years. As of 2003, the shakeout was continuing, albeit at a slower pace.

Although some observers issued timely warnings of the coming disaster (this present writer's warnings were issued in strong form in 1999, having been articulated less outspokenly as far back as 1995.), almost everyone was taken by surprise by the severity of the job cuts.

They should not have been. The palpable sense of invulnerability displayed by the American software industry in the late 1990s was based on wishful thinking.

Even at the time it was clear that many of the forces that drove the big increase in demand for software were quite temporary. First and most obviously, there was a question mark over the personal computer industry's ability to maintain its phenomenal growth rate. Although sales of personal computer software boomed in the 1990s, already as of 1995, Microsoft acknowledged that the industry had entered a mature phase. Many standard application packages had been around so long that further enhancements added remarkably little value.

Another factor that greatly added to the false sense of endless prosperity in the late 1990s was huge demand for software in the financial services industry. This demand was fueled in part by deregulation, which entailed a great deal of restructuring of financial services; one consequence was that vast amounts were invested in new computer systems, not only in the United States but in many other countries. But the trend toward deregulation had reached a mature phase in the late 1990s, and there may be little more milk in this cow.

The financial services industry's demand for software was further inflated by the introduction of the euro, the new pan-European currency, which required countless banks and corporations around the world to reengineer their information technology. According to Andersen Consulting, the cost for a typical multinational corporation worked out to the equivalent of between 1 and 3 percent of annual sales.

Germany's DaimlerChrysler alone reportedly spent $110 million on euro-related software.

As if the personal computer boom and the financial services boom were not enough, software demand in the late 1990s was further inflated by the infamous year-2000 problem—the problem of rewriting computer software to take account of the move to the twenty-first century. If the Gartner consulting group is to believed, the total worldwide cost was as much as $600 billion. Although this figure was inflated by costs that would have been incurred in any case in routine upgrading of computer hardware and software, it seems reasonable to believe that the millennium bug produced a windfall demand for software services totaling about $200 billion. Given that most of this money was spent on the remuneration of software engineers and consultants, the employment effect was evidently huge—creating enough work worldwide for perhaps 300,000 people for up to three years.

Once the backlog of late 1990s work began to clear, however, no similarly major new sources of demand emerged for American software labor. Thus, painful though the shakeout had been as of 2003, it was not at all clear that it had run its course. So far, much of the impact on American software jobs seems to have come from the so-called body-shop business. Body shops are recruitment agencies based typically in India that dispatch highly qualified engineers to the United States on short-term visas. Although these engineers work on the premises of American clients, they are often paid wages that are closer to Indian norms than American ones. Not surprisingly, therefore, body-shopping is regarded as a thinly veiled legal stratagem to pay Indian engineers working in the United States less than the American minimum wage.

But the truth is that the scale of the challenge from cheap software imports is massively larger than that from the body shops. After all, the body shops account for only a small proportion—probably little more than 10 percent—of all American software jobs.

This is clearly small by comparison with the potential impact when such low-wage software exporters as India, China, and Russia hit their stride. One indicator of how big the import challenge could grow has come from the World Bank, which has predicted that global trade in data processing and allied services will be twenty times higher in 2005 than it was a decade earlier. Given that software wages are several times higher in the United States than in the Third World, there can be little doubt about which nation will be doing the lion's share of the importing.

One thing is clear: many of the Third World countries now targeting the industry have the potential to ramp up their software workforces very rapidly. Take India. According to India's *Economic Times,* 1,700 Indian colleges and institutes were producing a total of more than 60,000 graduates a year in computer science and similar disciplines in the late 1990s.

Given the attractions of the industry to bright young Indian graduates, we can expect a rapidly increasing number of them to choose a career in software in the future. The main attraction is, of course, pay. Although pay rates in the Indian software industry do not seem high by Western standards—they run only about one-third of American levels—they are sensationally high by comparison with other sectors of the Indian economy. In round numbers, a typical Indian software engineer earns about twenty to thirty times the national average wage. In the longer run, the potential for India to increase its share of the world software market is almost limitless, given that it boasts an educated class of nearly 200 million people.

The point has not been lost on the Indian software industry. Speaking in 2003, Som Mittal, head of an Indian software industry association, predicted that Indian software exports would reach $50 billion by 2008. That would represent fully sixfold growth on 2001.

All this helps explain why one American software industry expert, Christian Byrnes, has suggested that India is on the way to becoming a software superpower. Byrnes, an executive of Meta, a Connecticut-based consulting firm, said: "Just as the Japanese took over America's leadership in manufacturing through superior quality processes, the U.S. must now face the challenge of India becoming the world's number one software producer in the next decade."

Perhaps the ultimate irony here is that even for India, the long-term rewards from developing a major software export industry may prove disappointing. As computers become more sophisticated, they may increasingly write their own software—and thus, pose a threat even to Indian software jobs. This point may not be that far off. If Bill Gates is to be believed, we may reach it as early as 2010. All in all, it is hard to see how the United States can retain its long-term competitiveness if it continues to bet so heavily on an industry whose long-term economics are at best so questionable.

SOFTWARE AND THE PRODUCTIVITY PARADOX

So far, our account of the economic fundamentals of the American software industry has been one of almost unrelieved gloom. But aren't we overlooking some important positive factors that should be entered into the balance? After all, the early rise of such a vigorous U.S. software industry has at least ensured that the United States has been consistently in the vanguard in applying the benefits of computerization throughout industry.

In the view of postindustrialists, this is self-evidently an unmitigated blessing. And at first sight, they seem to have an important point, given the computer's legendary ability to improve productivity in a host of industrial applications. But has America's early embrace of computerization really been such a good thing? Actually no. Far from it. In fact, a large body of evidence suggests that America's embrace of computers has been too hasty—so hasty, in fact, that it has proved a net *disadvantage* in competing with nations like Japan and Germany. These latter nations have generally been slower to computerize their industries, and they are often roundly scorned on this score. But what looks like "backwardness" to the postindustrialists should in many cases more correctly be seen as prudent caution. Where computers are concerned, the watchword in these nations has been "look before you leap." The truth is that early computerization involves many hidden pitfalls.

Thus, although postindustrialists often celebrate the fact that American businesses spend much more on software than their foreign counterparts, careful academic studies suggest that a large proportion of the huge investment involved is wasted. So marked is the tendency for business software to produce disappointing results that the phenomenon has become widely known as the computer productivity paradox. This paradox has been authoritatively documented by, among others, the Morgan Stanley economist Stephen Roach, the sociologist Paul Attewell, and the former Xerox computing chief Paul Strassmann.

That a good portion of the U.S. investment in computerization has been largely wasted is, of course, hotly contested by the postindustrialists. And every time U.S. productivity figures experience a temporary acceleration—as they did in 1997–99—the postindustrialists rush to proclaim that America's huge investment in computer software is finally producing large economic returns. But, invariably, subsequent events show that this was wishful thinking. Perhaps the most accessible account of the productivity paradox has come from Thomas K. Landauer, a top software designer. In his book *The Trouble with Computers,* he points out that the United States has suffered an acute case of diminishing returns as it has attempted to computerize more and more aspects of its economy. On the one hand, computers have generally been highly successful in the kinds of tasks they were first applied to in the 1950s and 1960s. They have been far less effective in later applications, however, and in some cases their performance has been so disappointing that, when all the costs are included, they have produced on balance a negative return on investment for society.

Typical examples of successful early applications—let's call them Type One applications—include the control of production machinery, the routing of telephone calls, and the automation of utility billing systems. Later applications—Type Two applications—include inventory control and general office administration programs. Type One applications are clear-cut and self-contained, whereas Type Two applications are flexible and open-ended. Most Type One applications require little interaction with human operators, and whatever interaction is necessary can generally be carefully choreographed in advance. Type Two applications, on the other hand, involve extensive, unstructured interaction with human operators and thus require that the programmer write a whole host of "if . . .

then" sequences to try to anticipate the general fallibility and almost infinite unpredictability of the human mind.

Type One applications are typified by foolproof programs that make full use of the computer's great fundamental advantages of speed, tirelessness, and accuracy. The result has been an impressive contribution to productivity in many industries.

Later attempts to extend the benefits of computerization to Type Two applications, however, have been stymied by the complexity of the tasks involved. The most obvious challenge has been to create user-friendly user interfaces. Unfortunately, user-friendliness is generally neglected in the software industry, and this tendency is exacerbated by the fact that the user interface is typically one of the last aspects of a program to be written. Its quality is therefore often sacrificed when software developers are racing to meet a tight deadline.

The result is familiar to every computer user; if a user interface is badly written, the program may hang or crash in response to minor keystroking errors. Confronted with complaints about such problems, the software industry typically adopts a "blame the customer" stance; the hapless user is scolded for not having read the user manual properly. But as Landauer points out, the fault lies not with the user, who cannot be expected to memorize the entire contents of a weighty user manual, but rather with the software developer, whose job it is to anticipate common user errors and provide appropriate safeguards against them.

Even just the everyday task of making sure that a corporation's various computer systems can talk to one another is often traumatic and typically requires heavy running costs in maintaining a large information technology department. Another hidden drawback is the need to keep buying program upgrades. If you don't buy the upgrades, you risk being left behind as your data are stored in an increasingly obsolete format. Yet, as Clifford Stoll has pointed out in *Silicon Snake Oil,* most upgrades provide poor value. They may, for instance, include many new commands that superficially add functionality but on closer examination turn out to be no more than marketing gimmicks. Unfortunately, new commands add greatly to a program's complexity because they tend to interact with one another in ways that increase the number of lines of programming code almost geometrically. The result generally is more bugs—and less user-friendliness. As Steven Levy has pointed out, the worst part of it is that program upgrades place heavy demands on users, who must constantly take time out from their busy schedules to keep current with the technology.

Another part of the explanation for the productivity paradox is that corporate America feels tempted to use the computer's dazzling capabilities just because they are there. Once a computer system is in place and all of a company's inventory, sales, and expense data are available for electronic manipulation, the opportunities for analysis are dizzying. Landauer comments, "Every manager now gets reports measured in stack-feet per month. Nobody can read it all or digest what they've read." The result is, of course, acute information overload. As Landauer points out, the information technology industry has found it far more difficult to provide the *right* information than to provide lots of the wrong information.

A major part of the problem is that corporate America's top executives have not been monitoring their information technology departments as closely as they should. As Paul A. Strassmann has pointed out, the millennium problem, for instance, was a stunning indication of "managerial laxity." Writing in the late 1990s, Strassmann commented, "There is absolutely no justification for allowing this condition to burst to executive attention at this late stage."

According to Strassmann, a former chief information officer of Xerox Corporation, the computer software industry should have started getting ready for the new millennium by the early 1970s, if not the mid-1960s.

Worse, the managerial myopia demonstrated in the millennium affair was, he maintained, only the tip of the iceberg:

> A typical programmer can make hundreds of such myopic decisions
> in each project. The only reason that the year 2000 "insufficiency"
> has attracted so much attention is that it is ubiquitous and has a
> deadline when its effects will become visible. There are millions of
> other bugs just as negligent as this, but they pop up randomly, one
> location at a time, to be squashed with as little publicity as possible.

Strassmann issued this prescient verdict: "Very soon the decades-long infatuation with spending money freely on information technologies will come to an end. It will become acceptable to admit that organizations were spending too much money because operating executives were afraid, unwilling, or untrained to manage it, while abdicating that role to technical experts."

Another notably double-edged factor driving the software industry's growth in the United States has been government regulation. As computer power has grown, government agencies have placed increasing demands on corporations to report ever more minutely on their compliance with regulations on pension fund administration, equal opportunity employment, environmental protection, and a host of other matters. Strassmann himself conducted a study that indicated that, in the 1994 tax year alone, tax-paying corporations incurred paperwork costs totaling $98 billion to pay taxes totaling $175 billion.

Perhaps the most ludicrously wasteful use of information technology has been in finance. As Landauer points out, the financial services industry has been second to none in its enthusiasm for information technology over the years. In particular, the industry has displayed an almost insatiable appetite for trading software. Thanks to heavy investment in computers and software, the financial services industry's investment per employee has risen sixfold in real terms since the 1950s. Yet the industry's record in boosting productivity in recent decades has been deplorable. In effect, the financial services industry has used computers primarily not to reduce its costs but to increase the complexity of its products. As we will see in Chapter 3, the end result has merely been to bamboozle customers in ways that tempt them to trade far more often than is necessary. This may do wonders for the financial services industry's profits, but clearly the implications for society as a whole are hardly positive.

The ultimate evidence against computers is in the overall U.S. productivity statistics. As the editor of *Challenge* magazine, Jeff Madrick, has pointed out, although American businesses have been increasing their investment in computers by more than 30 percent *a year* since the early 1970s, the rate of growth of productivity has fallen from an average of

2.85 percent a year in the decades before 1973 to about 1.1 percent a year since. No wonder the Nobel Prize–winning economist Robert Solow has commented: "You can see the computer age everywhere but in the productivity statistics."

Given that the United States has invested more than $4 trillion in computerization since 1960, the scale of the waste is staggering. The American love affair with information technology reminds one of Dr. Samuel Johnson's characterization of remarriage: the triumph of hope over experience.

CHAPTER 3

As we noted in Chapter 1, the financial services industry ranks second only to computer software in the extent to which it has been extolled by postindustrialists. Even the devastating financial crash of 2000–2002 did little to diminish the industry's standing in the pantheon of postindustrial businesses.

True enough, at first sight, the postindustrialists' enthusiasm for financial services seems to make sense. After all, pay levels in financial services are generally well above average. Moreover, many kinds of financial services have shown extraordinarily rapid growth in recent decades, not least in the two leading postindustrial economies, the United States and the United Kingdom.

But on closer examination, such apparent strengths turn out to be distinctly double-edged. Take the industry's high salaries and bonuses. These are simply a reflection of the fact that, like computer software, the financial services industry hires disproportionately from the cream of the intellectual crop. Given that many top financial professionals clearly possess superb entrepreneurial skills, it is not hard to imagine them enjoying similarly large rewards running high-growth companies in exciting new fields of advanced manufacturing. Their attraction instead to a career in finance deprives the manufacturing sector of vital leadership and thus undoubtedly contributes directly to the serious deterioration in manufacturing competitiveness that the United States has suffered in recent decades. In this respect, the United States is merely following in the footsteps of the United Kingdom, whose deindustrialization in the early part of the twentieth century was driven in part by a similar trend: the cream of the intellectual crop preferred careers in finance and other high-prestige service industries over manufacturing careers.

Now for the financial sector's growth. Clearly, seen in terms of its increasingly significant role in depriving the manufacturing sector of leadership, such growth is far from the unmitigated blessing the postindustrialists imagine. Worse, many of the financial sector's fastest-growing activities turn out to be utterly unproductive and even positively destructive from the point of view of the general public good. As we will now see, much of what the financial sector has been doing in recent years has been feathering its own nest at the expense of the great investing public. Growth of this sort is the economics of the cancer cell, and in praising it, the postindustrialists have made their biggest mistake of all.

FIRST, SOME FAINT PRAISE

Let's be clear at the outset: much—perhaps most—of what the financial services industry does even these days is of considerable value to society. Banks, for instance, make a vital contribution not only in facilitating the transmission of money (via checks and bank wires) but in providing a store of value (via savings accounts) and in financing business expansion. Insurance companies enable individuals and businesses to minimize their risk of loss from accidents and other instances of bad luck. Foreign exchange dealers facilitate trade between nations. Even the securities industry, whose many excesses we discuss in detail later, makes a vital and important contribution to prosperity to the extent that it facilitates *long-term* investment in stocks and other risk assets.

Yet for all the talk of the supposedly beneficial effect of financial innovation in recent years, the financial sector's economically productive services are almost all old-established ones that had already, in both the United States and the United Kingdom, reached a high degree of maturity more than a century ago. In fact, there really have been few truly useful major innovations in financial services since then.

It is chastening, therefore, for today's financial professionals to look back to that time. For it is an amazing fact that the financial sector preempted vastly less labor then than it does now. Even the London financial services industry got through the day with a total of no more than 30,000 clerks, scriveners, and messenger boys—less than half the workforce of a single major Wall Street firm today. Yet London was then by far the world's largest financial center, functioning as it did as the clearinghouse not only for the United Kingdom's internal finances but for most of the world's international transactions. Today, by comparison, the London financial services industry needs more than 500,000 people to conduct a much smaller share of the world's financial transactions.

A question arises. Why do financial services preempt so much more labor today than in former times? A large part of the answer is, of course, that fundamental demand for financial services has soared in step not only with expanding world trade but with increasing personal wealth, and rising populations. Meanwhile, various minor but highly useful new services, such as credit cards and travelers' checks, have also contributed to the growth.

But there is something else going on here beyond an increase in demand for useful services—something that is best called financialism. The term refers to the increasing tendency for the financial sector to invent gratuitous work for itself that does nothing to address society's real needs but simply creates lucrative jobs for financial professionals. The financial sector can get away with this because the people ultimately paying the bill usually don't know they are doing so. The beneficiaries of big pension funds, for instance, rarely have any knowledge of, let alone control over, how their money is invested. Financialism has probably always been with us, but it has grown rapidly in recent decades, in step with the progressive deregulation of financial markets. In painting a euphoric picture of further fast growth in financial services, the post-industrialists are in the main merely projecting forward into the future the continuing proliferation of wasteful financialism.

THE ESSENCE OF FINANCIALISM: TRADING FOR TRADING'S SAKE

Probably the greatest factor driving the financial sector's growth in recent decades has been an explosion in financial trading. It has also been probably the most undesirable; as such, it is the very essence of corrosive financialism.

It is difficult to exaggerate the scale of the trading explosion. In aggregate, financial trading in the United States grew more than thirty-fold in real terms between the early 1970s and the mid-1990s. And in some specialist areas, the growth has been even more spectacular. In the last quarter of the twentieth century, the growth in U.S. trading in foreign securities was one hundred times faster than that of the American economy as a whole. Of course, after Wall Street crashed in the first years of the new century, trading volume declined substantially compared—but, even so, it was running at levels that were unheard of before the mid-1990s.

The major driver of the growth in trading has clearly been deregulation, which, in turn, has been driven by the widespread belief among conventional economists that the freer a financial market is, the more "efficient" it is—that is, the more accurate it is in valuing financial assets. Such accuracy is important to the general health of the economy in that it serves to ensure that capital is channeled to those uses that are most likely to result in high economic growth.

The problem is that there is no evidence that deregulated financial markets do in fact value assets more accurately than regulated ones. Rather, the reverse may be true: the evidence is that as deregulation has proceeded, markets have become increasingly volatile and are therefore valuing assets more and more irrationally. Certainly, this seemed to be the message of the implosion in Internet stocks in the first years of the new century. Within the space of little more than a year, many such stocks lost more than 90 percent and in some cases more than 95 percent of their value.

The all-time classic example of how deregulation has served to increase market volatility was the New York stock market's infamous "Black Monday" plunge of 22.6 percent on October 19, 1987. If share prices are supposed to reflect a rational consensus on the future prospects for corporations, this move was utterly inexplicable. There was no significant development in the real economy that day that presaged serious trouble ahead for American business. In fact, as the Yale economist Robert J. Shiller has pointed out, the only significant economic news on Black Monday was the news of the crash itself. Based on a survey of nearly 1,000 investors soon after Black Monday, Shiller concluded that the collapse was an utterly irrational outbreak of crowd psychology in which 40 percent of institutional investors experienced "a contagion of fear from other investors." This conclusion was handsomely vindicated in the following year, when not only did the American economy boom but New York stocks bounced back spectacularly to recover all their losses, and more.

The important point for our purposes here is that the Black Monday crash—the biggest one-day fall ever—took place in what free-market theorists considered the most "efficient" market the world had seen up to that time. Thanks in large measure to deregulation, countless new financial instruments had been introduced in the previous decade that had dramatically increased trading volume—and thus were supposed to forestall precisely the kind of monumental irrationality so apparent on Black Monday.

Among these financial instruments, perhaps the most devastatingly counterproductive was so-called portfolio insurance. Portfolio insurance is a system of program trading in which an investment fund automatically sells more and more of its holdings as share prices drop. In principle, it closely resembles the "stop-loss" orders favored by many unsophisticated small-time stock speculators. Stop-loss orders are widely considered by intelligent investors to be a loser's strategy, and for good reason: they run directly counter to the basic logic of sensible long-term investment, which is, of course, to buy low and sell high. According to the Brady Report, an official inquiry into the incident, between $60 billion and $90 billion of equities were subject to portfolio insurance in mid-1987 and were thus poised to be dumped as the market fell. The result was what Robert Kuttner has aptly described in his book *Everything for Sale* as "mindless freefall."

The tendency for increased trading to breed ever more irrational volatility has also been notably apparent in currency markets, where trading volume has been soaring at a compound rate of 20 percent annually in recent years. The irrationality has been particularly apparent in the case of the tempestuous relationship between the Japanese yen and the American dollar. By the standards of conventional economics, the yen-dollar market should be one of the world's most efficient and, by extension, one of the most stable. After all, the fundamental determinant of exchange rates is each nation's relative competitiveness in tradable goods. Given that divergences between different nations' levels of competitiveness change only very slowly over the years, the yen and the dollar should probably move within a band of no more than a few percentage points against one another in any one year.

In practice, however, the yen-dollar exchange rate has become ever more irrationally volatile since the mid-1980s. In that time the yen has doubled in dollar terms on two separate occasions—first in the mid-1980s, and again in the first half of the 1990s. Then, in the second half of the 1990s, it was the dollar's turn to soar: between the spring of 1995 and the summer of 1998 it jumped more than 80 percent against the yen. To cap it all, the market then immediately reversed itself, with the yen soaring more than 30 percent in less than two months, one of the fastest recoveries in currency market history. For several years thereafter, the yen-dollar rate remained fairly stable but, as of this writing in

2003, new turbulence seemed on the horizon as fears about America's massive trade imbalances roiled the dollar.

There might have been a modicum of method in all this madness if each currency had risen or fallen as its home economy's fortunes waxed or waned. But if anything, the pattern of the last twenty-five years has demonstrated the opposite principle. Several times when the American economy has done badly, the dollar has soared on currency markets—most notably in 1980, 1982, 1990, and 1991. Similarly, in several years when the Japanese economy has done badly, the yen has soared—most notably in 1986, but also between 1992 and 1995. Conversely, in 1996, a year when Japan recorded the best growth of any major nation, the yen lost more than 9 percent of its value.

It is hard to see any purpose in all this financial churning—other than, of course, to create lots of jobs for currency traders. The consequences are doubly negative for society as a whole: not only are such traders' talents wasted on a useless activity, but the volatility created by the trading explosion generates dangerously misleading signals for business executives trying to plan ahead. In the early 1980s, when the dollar was wildly overvalued, American business executives made major decisions to move production offshore—only to find that with the subsequent fall in the dollar, these decisions looked distinctly questionable. Perhaps the most farcical example was a decision by IBM in the early 1980s to initiate a major expansion of its production operations in Japan to take advantage of the then-low exchange rate for the yen. In pursuit of that strategy, IBM moved hundreds of key American and European executives into Tokyo in 1984 and 1985. Most of these executives had families who had to be transplanted to Japan at vast expense in terms of moving costs, real estate commissions, and initial charges for joining exclusive Tokyo clubs. Yet, no sooner had the expenses been incurred than the yen suddenly rocketed on foreign exchange markets, thereby pulling the rug out from under the entire plan. Within three years the yen had doubled—and an embarrassed IBM was forced to sound an ignominious retreat, in the process incurring additional large expenses extricating the bemused families from Tokyo!

If the irrational volatility of financial markets were the only evidence we had to indict the trading explosion, our case would be damning enough. But there is much more. Take, for instance, the contribution of the ever-growing army of well-paid analysts and other "experts" whose views drive so much trading these days. When Wall Street analysts turn positive on a stock, institutional investors rush to buy. Then, a few months later, when the analysts inevitably turn cool, the institutions dump the stock by the millions.

For Wall Street securities firms, this is a wonderfully profitable merry-go-round—which is, of course, the whole point. But for society at large, the vast amount of intellectual energy expended on all this churning is almost entirely wasted. For the fact is that Wall Street securities analysts are notoriously unreliable. In a study in the late 1990s, David Dreman and Eric Lufkin found that Wall Street analysts' forecasts of corporate earnings were "written in sand." In the first seven years of the 1990s, a typical analyst's forecast of corporate earnings was off by a shocking 48.7 percent—an even worse performance than was revealed in similar surveys carried out in the 1970s and 1980s. Writing in *Forbes* magazine, Dreman issued this resounding condemnation: "The inaccuracy of these forecasts shows how dangerous it is to buy or hold stocks on the basis of what analysts predict for earnings. In a dynamic, competitive worldwide economy, there are just too many unknowables for such pretended precision."

So much for the securities industry's efforts to predict corporate earnings. Some of its other efforts to provide investment advice are even less intellectually respectable. Take, for instance, the activities of Wall Street's "chartists." These are analysts who ignore corporate fundamentals such as earnings trends and instead try to predict future stock price movements based merely on studying a stock's past trading patterns. Yet, for all the millions of man-hours the chartists expend on analyzing stock charts, it is a well-known fact, proven in careful academic studies, that chart-reading simply does not work. The ultimate indictment of the chartists has come from the economist Burton Malkiel, who in a famous study many years ago asked students to construct bogus stock charts based on flipping coins.

He then presented these charts to several chartists. Sure enough, the chartists professed to read into the random zigzags significant patterns that they believed would help them make money on future price movements of the "stocks" concerned.

Given advisers like these, it is clear that most fund managers are adrift in a sea of make-believe and self-delusion. And the proof is in the pudding. All the evidence is that fund managers in aggregate consistently fail to match the performance of the market averages. In fact, the shocking truth is that American portfolio managers, aided as they are by an army of advisers, a globe-girdling network of computers, and a cornucopia of new financial instruments, are likely to underperform the random choices of a chimpanzee throwing darts at the stock pages.

As reported by Edward Wyatt of *The New York Times*, barely 10 percent of all diversified mutual funds outperformed the Standard & Poor's 500–share index in the five years to 1998. Nor was this an unrepresentative period. As far back as 1968, Michael C. Jensen showed that mutual fund managers failed to outperform relevant market indexes. According to a survey in 1992 by Ravi Shukla and Charles Trczinka, no less than 200 subsequent studies generally supported Jensen's conclusions.

A detailed analysis by John C. Bogle, chairman of the Vanguard group of mutual funds, has shown that in the ten years to 1995, the annual return on diversified funds lagged the index by fully 1.8 percent a year. Yet, to produce this disappointing result, the mutual fund industry had employed a veritable army of highly paid portfolio managers in identifying and buying stocks believed to enjoy better-than-average prospects. As a result, the funds incurred expenses totaling about 1.7 percent of total assets each year.

The conclusion is that portfolio managers are engaged in what is at best a zero-sum game; to the extent that they incur any significant expenses, it becomes a negative-sum game. Not surprisingly, therefore, most first-rate independent advisers tell savers to steer clear of the standard heavily advertised mutual funds and invest instead in so-called index funds, whose portfolios mirror the makeup of a relevant market index and therefore guarantee a performance close to that of the index. As index funds require virtually no ongoing trading or stock-picking, they can therefore promise to keep expenses to as little as 0.2 percent of total assets under management.

Of course, this is not to deny that *some* investors can beat the market. But all experience shows that such people are rare, and not unnaturally they prefer to apply their talents to managing their own money—or at least to managing investment vehicles in which they themselves are major investors. In essence, the typical run-of-the-mill investment manager who runs mutual funds and other widely marketed investment vehicles is wasting his time. One is reminded of the old adage, "Those who can, do; those who can't, teach." In the matter of picking winning stocks, those who can, make profits for themselves; those who can't, lose money for other people.

Perhaps the ultimate irony is that some of the world's most successful investors are outspokenly scornful of both the recent explosion in financial trading and the deregulation that has spawned it. Take, for instance, the speculator-turned-philanthropist George Soros. Having built a fortune of several billion dollars by taking advantage of the irrationality of other investors, he can probably claim to understand better than almost anyone how *inefficiently* today's deregulated markets value financial assets. In recent years he has become a vociferous advocate of a move back to greater regulation of financial markets as a way to "stop the market destroying the economy."

Perhaps even more devastating for the postindustrialists is the testimony of Warren Buffett, the Omaha-based stock investor who is ranked by *Forbes* as second only to Microsoft founder Bill Gates among the world's richest individuals. Buffett never tires of mocking the proliferation of new financial services. His message is that those Wall Street gurus and advisers who come up with new techniques for evaluating shares and other financial assets are—not to put too fine a point on it— snake oil salesmen.

As for new financial instruments, he flatly rejects Wall Street's self-serving view that these do the work of Adam Smith's "invisible hand." Rather, in Buffett's view, such instruments are "an invisible foot kicking society in the shins." He sees traded stock options as gimmicks that do nothing to create real wealth but merely ensnare financial professionals in playing futile zero-sum games with one another. He has been particularly scornful of portfolio insurance, labeling it an "Alice-in-Wonderland practice," and he has been perhaps the single most influential voice in blaming it for the Black Monday crash of 1987.

The ultimate tragedy is that all the money to keep this charade on the road comes from millions of ordinary American savers. They pay high fees for the management of their pension and mutual fund assets, and less visibly, they pay the stockbrokers' commissions and other costs incurred in the ever quickening pace of financial trading.

A key to understanding why this charade continues unchecked is marketing. Mutual funds and other investment products are sold, not bought. The more an investment company spends on marketing, the more business it can expect to garner. Various techniques have been honed over the years to take advantage of savers' emotions—and particularly their gullibility and greed. The time-honored method of catching unsophisticated savers, for instance, is persistent foot-in-the-door salesmanship. At a higher level, the formula that works is more subtle: mahogany-paneled offices, Persian rugs, British hunting prints, and an army of well-tailored sales executives drawn mainly from the upper ranks of society. But either way, what wins business is the right marketing strategy, not the best investment record. This is abundantly apparent in, for instance, the fact that, as recorded by the investment columnist James K. Glassman, those fund management houses that charge the highest fees actually produce by far the worst investment performance. The simple truth is that such houses don't have to perform well so long as they can continue to charge the hefty fees that fund their vast ongoing marketing efforts.

The end result of all this excessive marketing and trading is that the American investment management business is costing the United States probably at least $50 billion a year more than it should. This represents enormous waste by any standards. Yet in large part because the workings of the modern financial services industry have been so enthusiastically endorsed by the postindustrialists, it has never been subjected to any serious reality-checking.

AMERICAN FINANCIAL EXPORTS:
MYTH VERSUS REALITY

American savers are, of course, not the only potential customers for the American financial services industry. There is a whole world of foreign savers out there, many of whom have huge amounts of money to invest. This point has encouraged the postindustrialists to imagine that the United States can make a fine business exporting its financial services to "less financially sophisticated" nations around the world.

At first sight, this seems to be one of the postindustrialists' stronger cards. After all, to the casual observer it would appear that American financial companies are already huge exporters. In fact, in their public relations activities, American financial organizations never tire of boasting about their "global reach." As any American who travels on business can testify, American financial organizations seem to have long ago appropriated much of the prime office space in such important foreign financial capitals as London, Hong Kong, and Tokyo.

But how globalized are American financial organizations really? The truth is profoundly disappointing for the postindustrialists.

Take a look, for instance, at the operations of a typical "globalized" financial firm such as Merrill Lynch. To judge by its self-evaluation, Merrill Lynch is the sun around which the world's financial system revolves. Rarely has this message been more powerfully conveyed than in the pictures that adorned the firm's annual report a few years ago. As one leafed through the pages, the clichés of financial globalism fairly tumbled out. The report opened with a parade of picture-postcard views that would do justice to a travel agent's brochure: a camel seated in front of an Egyptian pyramid, a fleet of Neapolitan gondolas, a little Japanese girl in a traditional kimono, a turbaned Indian boy, a troupe of African dancers. Later pages were decorated with a snowstorm of exotic foreign banknotes, plus enough national flags to outfit a Miss World contest.

The report made much of various awards the firm's international operations had received in the year under review: "Best Debt House in Asia," "No. 1 Latin American Research House," and five other similar mouthfuls that in their grandiloquent territorial claims would do justice to Ozymandias himself.

In view of the apparently vast scope of Merrill Lynch's foreign activities, one would have been forgiven for assuming that the firm was a major contributor to America's invisible exports. A look at the fine print, however, showed that its contribution was actually negligible. In fact, for all the globalism of the firm's annual report, fully three-quarters of its revenues were generated within the plain old United States of America. Moreover, little of the 24 percent of revenues generated abroad constituted American exports. Remember that for a service to count as a U.S. export, it must not only be paid for by foreign customers but be performed within the United States. Most of Merrill Lynch's foreign revenues, however, arose from services performed offshore by foreign personnel working in foreign offices. After deductions for foreign salaries and other foreign expenses, there was little left to be remitted to the United States.

Take, for instance, a typical service provided by the firm's Tokyo branch—a purchase order from a Japanese client for stock in a Japanese company. Typically, such a trade is handled by a Japanese employee working in a Japanese office. The employee's salary, the office rent, the telephone bill, and countless other expenses are paid in yen and represent value added that accrues entirely to the Japanese economy. In fact, the American economy's balance of payments is likely to benefit only to the extent that the Tokyo branch makes a profit on the trade.

In reality, the aggregate amount of profit remitted to the United States by Merrill Lynch's overseas subsidiaries is tiny and probably represents less than 3 percent of the firm's total revenues in a typical year.

Similar analysis shows that other supposedly globe-girdling American financial services companies make equally disappointing contributions to the U.S. balance of payments. Take American Express. In many ways, it is better equipped than any other important financial services company to compete in foreign markets. After all, having introduced the traveler's check in 1891, it was a highly globalized company before World War I, and with the subsequent development of the American Express card, it went on to establish a network of offices in more than 160 countries. Thus, American Express enjoys probably a greater global reach than any other financial services company, and it certainly boasts one of the strongest brand names in the global financial services industry.

That said, American Express's contribution to the U.S. balance of payments is quite disappointing. As of the late 1990s, little more than one-quarter of the company's business was done abroad. Yet fully 40 percent of its workforce—a disproportionately large share of the total—was employed outside the United States, and many of the company's other foreign expenses were also correspondingly large. When the company's various foreign expenses were deducted, the company's net contribution to the American balance of payments was probably less than $500 million a year—or about 3 percent of the company's total revenues.

Clearly, from the point of view of the American balance of payments, a fundamental problem with financial services is precisely that they are services and thus for the most part must be performed close to the customer. But this is far from the only reason financial services tend to make a poor contribution to a nation's export prowess. Another key reason is that almost all the world's financial markets are tightly regulated in a way that inevitably limits opportunities for great American financial institutions.

This is particularly true in East Asia, which happens to be precisely where the great bulk of the world's savings surpluses arise these days. The financial markets of most continental European countries also offer disappointingly few export prospects for American banks. Take Germany. As the world's third-largest economy after the United States and Japan, Germany could be a lucrative market for American banks. In reality, the vast German banking market remains a secure fiefdom of Germany's Big Three banks, Deutsche Bank, Dresdner Bank, and Commerzbank. In particular, Germany's great industrial corporations generally entrust the Big Three with most of their banking business. This is not an accident:

much of the stock in major German industrial corporations is owned or controlled by the Big Three.

Opportunities for American banks are similarly curtailed in most other parts of the developed world. In truth, banking is considered almost universally by government officials to be a "strategic" industry that wields potentially enormous power to shape a nation's economy. Thus, nations naturally prefer that their bank industry stay under the control of their own nationals.

But even in areas of the financial services industry where politics is less likely to be a major concern than in banking, American players are still firmly blocked in their hopes of expansion abroad. Take the American discount brokerage industry. In theory at least, its services ought to be of great interest to countless investors around the world. After all, the industry's low commission rates make American discount brokers highly competitive compared to brokers in other parts of the world. Take a typical example, a purchase order for one hundred shares of Microsoft. As of the late 1990s, this would have cost a Japanese investor around $500 in brokerage and other transaction costs if it were carried out in Tokyo, but as little as $3 if carried out over the Internet by an American discount broker.

Yet Japanese investors do virtually no business through American Internet brokers. The reason, of course, is that there are many barriers blocking the expansion of American Internet brokers around the world. One obvious obstacle is the requirement that American brokers obtain local regulatory permission to advertise their services in foreign markets. As John Tagliabue of *The New York Times* has pointed out, such permission is generally withheld when a brokerage firm provides its services from a location beyond the reach of the financial regulators of the nation concerned. The inability to advertise may seem like no more than a minor hindrance, but in practice it is a major barrier because investors tend to prefer to deal with organizations whose names are well known to them.

Even English-speaking nations known for their strong support for the theory of globalization are notably inhospitable to the American discount brokerage industry. Take Canada. Before it allowed E*trade, a

California-based online broker, to do business within its jurisdiction, it insisted that the firm set up a branch on Canadian soil. Australia and New Zealand also set similar conditions. As *The Economist* pointed out, such conditions tend to negate the basic advantage of online trading, which is that it obviates the need to maintain the costly physical infrastructure necessary in precyberspace days.

Perhaps even more startlingly, the United Kingdom has given U.S.-based Internet brokers a chilly reception. Again, E*trade's experience has been instructive. When E*trade first applied to do business in the United Kingdom, British regulators insisted that, among other things, it locate its computers on British soil. In the end, E*trade finessed the problem by announcing plans to provide its services through a British partner—but this arrangement, of course, meant that the service would be performed largely or totally by workers in the United Kingdom, not by U.S. workers. The contribution to the U.S. balance of payments is therefore likely to be negligible.

The most significant aspect of the United Kingdom's attitude is that it is likely to provide cover for other nations that have consistently dragged their feet about opening their financial markets. If even the enthusiastically globalist United Kingdom is not prepared to exempt American online brokers from local regulatory oversight, few other major nations are likely to roll out the red carpet for them.

To apologists for postindustrialism, the fact that so far most foreign financial markets are largely closed to American financial organizations represents no more than a temporary problem. In their view, other countries have merely been a little slower than the United States to recognize the supposed win-win advantages of deregulation and globalization. Thus, the apologists confidently look forward to the day when other nations will deregulate and therefore open themselves to the American financial services industry. This expectation, however, overlooks the strategic view that other nations take of their financial systems. For a start, most other nations see tight financial regulation in part as a vital tool in deterring their wealthier citizens from hiding hot money in foreign bank and brokerage accounts. Moreover, governments tend to regard their nations' savings as a national resource that should be applied in the first instance to boosting their own industries and jobs. Even the supposedly open financial capital of Singapore insists that its citizens put much of their long-term savings money in the government-controlled Central Provident Fund. Needless to say, this fund favors Singaporean jobs in its investment policies. A similar, if much more subtly expressed, concern that national savings be mobilized for the benefit of local job creation can also be discerned in several rich European countries, most notably Germany and Switzerland.

U.S. aspirations to sell financial services abroad are further frustrated by a fundamental weakness of the modern American economy—a low savings rate. In the space of a single generation, the United States has gone from being the world's biggest exporter of capital to the world's biggest importer. Since capital is the scarce raw material of financial services, the hidden leverage that the United States once enjoyed over world financial markets has long since disappeared. The unfortunate truth is that the United States no longer sets the rules of world finance.

A QUESTION OF ETHICS:
FINANCE AS ROTTEN APPLE

If the expansion of financial services in recent years resulted merely in the frittering away of the talents of many top Americans on a negative-sum game, it would be bad enough. But another lamentable dimension to the financial services explosion cries out for attention: the deterioration it has fostered in the nation's ethical standards.

This deterioration was already starkly apparent to some observers, not least the present writer, in the late 1990s. It took the Wall Street crash of 2000–2002, however, to bring into general view the full, appalling state of American financial ethics. One of the first hammer blows was the scandalous collapse of Enron. Soon, similar stories of accounting scandals and financial misdemeanors emerged at many other companies, most notably Worldcom, Tyco, and ImClone. Meanwhile, shocking revelations emerged about the role key Wall Street analysts such as Henry Blodget of Merrill Lynch and Jack Grubman of Salomon Smith Barney had played in the stock bubble of the late 1990s.

The truth is that Wall Street's ethics had been in decline for many years. As turbo-charged new investment vehicles such as derivatives had proliferated in the 1980s and 1990s, illicit opportunities for financial criminals to enrich themselves at the expense of the general public increased dramatically. Perhaps even more important, the risk of detection was perceived to be decreasing all the time. In truth, in a world of deregulated financial markets, it is easy for miscreants to use the secrecy of foreign bank accounts to hide their frauds in a dense thicket of complexity while concealing their gains in secret foreign bank accounts.

At issue here are not the cruder forms of financial crime, such as selling worthless penny stocks to elderly widows and other vulnerable members of society. Today, as in the past, heartless villainy of this sort is practiced by only a tiny minority. At issue instead are much more subtle practices that evidently prove tempting to a much broader range of financial professionals, most of whom would never stoop to the bare-faced blackguardism of the penny-stock promoters.

One such practice is insider trading, which, if the Securities and Exchange Commission's caseload is any guide, has grown dramatically in recent years. Already in 1997, as reported by Paul A. Gigot of *The Wall Street Journal*, the SEC was investigating more than twice as many cases as it had been a decade earlier. Moreover, given that financial scams were more difficult to detect than ever before, the SEC's caseload was probably no more than the tip of the iceberg.

One of the fastest-growing financial crimes is a maneuver known as "front running," which involves buying a stock ahead of a major buying program by a big fund management house. A few days later, after the buying program has sent the stock price soaring, the front runner can hope to cash out at a handsome and almost risk-free profit. Another form of insider trading that has burgeoned in recent years has been illicit buying by influential stock analysts for their own accounts before they issue a bullish view on a stock.

Other financial crimes can be a lot more subtle. Take, for instance, a technique known as selective allocation. The key to this is that many portfolio managers act for several different portfolios in their stock-purchasing activities. They often allocate their purchases to their various portfolios only at the end of each day—by which time many trades may already be showing significant profits while others will be showing losses. By selectively allocating the profitable trades to some portfolios and loss-making ones to others, they can greatly favor some beneficiaries at the expense of the rest.

As Steven D. Kaye has documented in *U.S. News & World Report*, favoritism in allocating winning trades can pay dividends for fund managers in many circumstances. In one blatant case uncovered by the SEC a few years ago, Kemper Financial Services (a firm now renamed Zurich Kemper Investments) allocated winning trades to an in-house account, while allocating less profitable trades to two Kemper mutual funds that managed money on behalf of the ordinary investing public.

In a less blatant version of the technique, fund management houses may allocate winning trades to portfolios run for large corporations and other sophisticated clients. Such clients are generally much more demanding than small investors in expecting good performance and are much faster to vote with their feet when the performance is subpar. Thus, a fund management house has a strong interest in keeping such clients happy, even if this means penalizing the mutual funds and other portfolios run for the benefit of small investors. Many variations are possible. In one example of alleged impropriety reported by the SEC, a California-based money manager was accused of allocating profitable trades to certain accounts that paid high management fees based on performance, while allocating less profitable trades to other accounts that paid no special reward for good performance.

The development of increasingly complex derivatives in recent years has been a particular boon to financial criminals. In a typical pattern, securities firms deliberately concoct instruments that are so complex that most institutional investors cannot fully understand them. Moreover, the market in any particular type of instrument is typically extremely thin, and thus prices can be readily manipulated by the securities industry. Devastating accounts of Wall Street's profits from the derivatives game have been written by, among others, the former Salomon Brothers executive Michael Lewis and the former Morgan Stanley executive Frank Partnoy. Partnoy in particular has been coruscating in his criticisms of the securities industry's practices. After alleging in his book *F.I.A.S.C.O.: Blood in the Water on Wall Street* that Wall Street makes huge profits by "trickery and deceit," he adds for good measure: "Everyone I knew who had been an investment banker for a few years, including me, was an asshole." Referring to his time as a derivatives salesman, Partnoy commented: "The way you earned money on derivatives was by trying to blow up your client."

Of course, the securities industry has never been famous for its high ethical standards. But the problem today is not only that the scale of the finagling is larger than before but that its ethical standards have been proving contagious. Prominent Americans in other walks of life see how money is made in a highly regarded industry and reckon that similarly opportunistic, if not illegal, tactics are acceptable in their own less exalted fields.

The contagious effect of Wall Street's low ethical standards is particularly apparent in, for instance, the increasingly manipulative way that industrial executives now use executive stock options to line their own pockets—often by engaging in short-term financial maneuvering that they know is damaging to their companies' long-term prospects. As early as 1989 the MIT Commission on Industrial Productivity reported that there was "no shortage" of executive incentive plans geared to a company's profit performance over just one year or even a mere six months. As the commission pointed out, a chief executive whose compensation is geared to such short-term measures is likely to take an even more shortsighted view than the stock market. The worst part of it is that short-term executive incentive programs tend to encourage outright gambling by corporate executives in their frantic efforts to manipulate their companies' profits. Such gambling is in fact a no-lose proposition for the executives themselves. On the one hand, if a gamble pays off, they can obviously cash out quickly at huge profits. Less obviously, but even more controversially, if the gamble fails, they always have another chance to play the game. And this time, because the stock price has undoubtedly fallen in the meantime thanks to the previous year's losing gamble, executives can reset the buying price for their options at a much lower level, thus putting themselves in line to benefit hugely from even the most modest recovery in their companies' profits.

All in all, it is clear that the financial services industry has played the role of pied piper in leading American society toward a general lowering of standards in the last thirty years. The consequences are hard to measure but are clearly significant for economic efficiency, not to mention for the general spiritual health of the nation.

The basic problem is that the financial services industry has forgotten that its function is to *serve* people. Instead the industry has come to regard itself as somehow superior to society—an attitude that the postindustrialists have clearly done nothing to discourage.

Our conclusion, therefore, is that finance is an essential service without which the economy could not function. But it should never had been raised on a pedestal above the rest of the economy. Still less should it be considered a driving force of the economy's future prosperity.

Stripped of rhetoric, most of the new financial activities the post-industrialists extolled in the 1990s fed parasitically on the rest of the economy. With the proliferation of financial services in the last three decades, what we have witnessed is not a goose that lays golden eggs but a different feathered vertebrate entirely: a cuckoo in the economy's nest.

CHAPTER 4

Besides computer software and finance, other businesses that are often regarded as important elements in the American postindustrial future include consulting, the media, direct mail, database information services, think tanks, and the management of "designer" brands. The story in these businesses is broadly similar to that of software and finance: most of these businesses make significant contributions to society, but their economic shortcomings in virtually every case are typical of postindustrial services generally—an unbalanced mix of jobs, a high degree of labor-intensity, poor export prospects, and little opportunity to build up a national reserve of proprietary know-how. In most cases, these shortcomings are so obvious that they need no elaboration. In concluding our look at postindustrial services, therefore, we will confine our comments to a few activities whose shortcomings are less obvious—activities, moreover, that figure particularly prominently in the hopes of postindustrialists.

First we will look at the communications revolution of the 1990s, particularly the Internet. Then we will move on to an analysis of the entertainment industry.

GETTING THE INTERNET INTO PROPORTION

As the 1990s wore on, the postindustrialists, like most other observers, came to see the Internet as an epochal breakthrough that promised almost boundless prosperity for the United States in the years ahead. Of course, not everyone agreed. A skeptical minority persisted in debunking the Internet as little more than a gimmicky, if amusing, system for transmitting "garbage at light speed." With the benefit of hindsight we can now see clearly that while the Internet boasts many dazzling, almost magical capabilities, such capabilities do not necessarily add up to an economic revolution.

One thing is certain: much of what the postindustrialists said in hyping the Internet was the sheerest nonsense. Take, for instance, the New Age guru Bran Ferren. Speaking in apocalyptic terms on ABC Television's *Nightline* program in 1997, Ferren rated the Internet as perhaps the human race's most significant discovery since hominoids first began to speak. It was a sign of the times not only that Ferren felt no need to elaborate on this extraordinary statement but that the presenter, Forrest Sawyer, felt no need to challenge him.

Or take Barry Howard Minkin, a futurologist who has predicted that 97 percent of all new jobs in the United States would soon come from "knowledge work." In his book *Future in Sight*, he waxed enthusiastic about the economic possibilities of the Internet and the wider telecommunications revolution it epitomizes. But exactly what benefits would this revolution bring? Minkin seemed notably short of ideas. He mentioned video telephones and home shopping—two applications that have been heralded for decades by previous generations of futurologists. But beyond these, most of his ideas were comically trite. Example: the Internet would, he averred, make it possible for sales people to make more polished presentations. Minkin saw this as particularly valuable to "smaller companies that need to create the impression that they are more substantial." He could have added that the Internet offers many other possibilities for people to pretend to be something they are not—but in pre–New Economy days, misrepresenting oneself was rarely considered a service to society!

Another Minkin idea was "blur-mercials"—hybrid video broadcasts that blend advertising and editorial content. He expected them to "flood the airwaves" and create "significant consumer demand." He foresaw, for instance, blur-mercial sequences combining information about "the how and why of exercise, food-making equipment, as well as ways to become a millionaire." Conspicuously absent from Minkin's vista was any mention of the damage the blur-mercial concept could do in undermining the media's editorial independence.

Minkin also enthused about the role that the telecommunications revolution would play in improving corporate America's labor relations. Corporations would increasingly use video instead of print, he believed, to communicate with employees. This would enable them to provide graphic video coverage of employee outings, including "softball game highlights" accompanied by choruses of baseball songs. Very entertaining, no doubt; but it did not seem to occur to him that what the American economy needed was not more ways to amuse office workers but higher white-collar productivity levels.

Did all this add up to the most jolting technological revolution since hominoids first started fine-tuning their vocal chords? Clearly not. In fact, the views of people like Ferren and Minkin constituted classic examples of the sort of nonsense that technology author Clifford Stoll—one of the few commentators to see through the New Economy hype at the time—derided as "silicon snake oil."

Before taking a closer look at the downside of cyberspace, let's first consider some of the more important positive developments promised by the ongoing telecommunications revolution. Certainly, the Internet has its uses. For many thoughtful Americans, its powers were nicely vindicated during the Iraq war of 2003, for instance. Suddenly, Americans had easy access to non-American sources of war news. Though many of these sources—*The Guardian, The Independent, The Financial Times,* and the BBC, for instance—happened to be British and therefore were to a large extent viewing the war through the same lens as the American press, they still offered a useful check on the standard sources Americans have relied on in previous wars. Still, the Iraq war proved only a fleeting opportunity for the Internet. Most of the time, after all, foreign media have little or nothing to offer most Americans.

Another important positive development made possible by the communications revolution is video telephony. Already mobile phones that transmit still images are a consumer reality in many nations, and the video telephone—featuring full moving pictures—seems set to follow by the end of the first decade of the twenty-first century. This clearly promises to add significantly to the consumer's quality of life, particularly for anyone wanting to keep in touch with far-flung friends and relatives. But for advocates of postindustrialism, this innovation is cold comfort because it represents an opportunity mainly for manufacturers, not for postindustrial businesses. After all, there are only two critical blocks to the wide use of video telephones: (a) the techniques for the mass-production of video telephone equipment have not yet been developed, and (b) the high-capacity telephone lines they require have not yet been laid. As manufacturers become more efficient in making the transmission infrastructure and receiving equipment, the price of video telephony can be expected to plummet. Then, in a pattern similar to the way earlier communications technologies such as radio and television were commercialized, demand will explode, bringing about further price cuts and increases in volume.

Video telephones apart, most of the late 1990s excitement surrounding the telecommunications revolution was clearly based on a false historical analogy. As the science writer Robert Pool has noted, countless Internet boosters draw an implicit or explicit parallel between the Internet and the invention of printing. They imagine that just as printing utterly transformed the world five hundred years ago, the Internet will work a similarly large economic miracle in the years ahead. The argument is superficially persuasive, but a moment's thought reveals that it is nonsense. Remember that, before printing, the task of replicating and transmitting written information was wretchedly slow and expensive. Just to produce a single copy of a book took a scribe—one of the most skilled and capable workers of his era—many months or even years. Then, with the invention of movable type, information-industry productivity suddenly soared several hundredfold. Within fifty years of Gutenberg's technological innovations, the total number of books in Europe had jumped from a mere 30,000 volumes to nine million. And this was only the beginning: cheap books, in turn, brought a sea change in the structure of society as more and more of the population acquired an education.

Those who imagine that a similarly historic transformation is afoot today forget that in its most economically significant applications, the Internet offers at best only a marginal improvement in productivity. Take, for instance, electronic mail. Used intelligently, email clearly offers cost and efficiency advantages over its nearest rival, the fax machine. But just as faxing did not really change the world very much (after all, before the fax machine became widely available, we could transmit urgent messages by telephone or telex), email has evidently had only a minor effect in boosting the economy's fundamental efficiency. By comparison with emailing, using a fax machine may seem cumbersome and expensive, but the savings offered by email are not significant compared to the total cost of the message (of which the sender's time is typically the major element). Commenting in the late 1990s in his capacity as head of MIT's computer science laboratory, the late Michael L. Dertouzos suggested that fully 95 percent of email activities and other computer-driven communications represented only a minor advance on the efficiency of the telegraphy age a century ago.

Moreover, the benefits of email are reduced by some notable drawbacks. Specifically, the convenience of email has generated an electronic version of Gresham's Law: frivolous and time-wasting users are driving out serious and welcome ones. The most talked about manifestation of email abuse is, of course, spam, the ever-rising torrent of unsolicited junk mail that is inundating everyone's mail box. As of 2003, fully half of all email was spam, according to Brightmail, the San Francisco maker of spam-blocking software. Moreover, spam in recent years has increasingly emanated from shady sources using false identities to sell everything from Viagra and other drugs to pornography and dubious investments.

The problem of coping with spam was estimated in 2003 to be costing American organizations fully $10 billion a year. Not surprisingly, people have been furiously working on techniques for reducing the torrent, but hitherto at least they have fought a losing battle. In any case, even if effective spam control devices can be found, there will remain a less controversial but still annoyingly costly proliferation of unnecessary email that no junk-mail filter can ever be expected to cope with effectively. Certainly, there is no question that, spam aside, much email that people receive from correspondents known to them is generated by nonessential users, among whom office comedians, self-publicists, pranksters, and other nuisances seem to be greatly overrepresented.

Writing in 1998, Michael Dertouzos sounded a note of outright despair: "Opening your door to e-mail is not far from opening the front door of your home and shouting to everyone: 'Come right in when you wish, and as you wish! I will see you and hear you out.'"

For many email recipients, there is no solution other than to resort to mass deletion of unread messages when in-boxes get overloaded. If a few grains of informational wheat must inadvertently be sacrificed in deleting all the chaff, so be it. In fact, so acute has email overload become that some people are beginning to automate the deletion process via so-called bozo filters. A pioneer in this regard has been Steve Ward, an MIT professor who decided to take drastic action some years ago after he began routinely receiving more than 100 email messages a day. He designed a filter program that automatically rated each message for relevance (based on such criteria as the sender's name, the number of people on the copy list, and the presence in the text of words of special interest to him). Senders whose messages failed to score high enough were automatically told that their message had been deleted and that if they wanted to end-run the computer's verdict they should contact Ward in person—via that miracle of nineteenth-century communications, the *telephone.* If the telecommunications revolution keeps racing ahead at this pace, pretty soon we'll be back to carrier pigeons!

Of course, the Internet offers more than a mere email service. It is extensively used, for instance, as a research tool. As such, it seems at first sight to provide a tremendously useful and efficient service. But does it? Certainly the Internet contains an embarrassment of information on virtually every topic under the sun. But when this information is judged on its *quality* as opposed to its *quantity*, its value is often a lot more debatable. By quality we mean, among other things, relevance. The truth is that much of the information turned up in an Internet search tends to be irrelevant. And the more specific and targeted your quest for information is, the less useful the Internet tends to be. If one is seeking a particular fact—even something as simple as, say, the address of a specific foreign company—the Internet can be a disappointing waste of time. The pattern is that it serves up everything but what you want. This writer discovered this the hard way when he was planning a business trip to Germany and urgently needed to establish which of the companies he had short-listed for a visit were located in which parts of the country. One of these companies was a much-publicized solar energy subsidiary of a major German electrical combine. Its address should have been easy to find, but after a fruitless ninety-minute search he was forced to throw in the towel. He then went back to researching the matter the precyberspace way. In a matter of five minutes (and at the expense of a local telephone call to the nearest marketing office of the German combine), he had turned up the information.

Perhaps this is an extreme example, but in general the Internet proves disappointing for seekers after truly useful business knowledge. It could hardly be otherwise. After all, if you think about it, the sort of information that businesses disclose to the public is almost by definition more chaff than wheat. The one exception is the financial disclosure that a corporation is required to make by law—but as many business researchers have long had easy access to such disclosures, the Internet provides little added value in this respect. As for other more general business information, corporations are naturally reluctant to release anything that would be of value to competitors. In fact, the more valuable a piece of economic information is, the more likely it is to be jealously withheld from the public. Think, for instance, of the formula for making Coca-Cola. It is very valuable information. How likely are you to turn it up in an Internet search? To ask the question is to answer it. In reality, of course, the Coca-Cola formula is so closely guarded a secret that it is kept in a vault of the Trust Company of Georgia.

A great deal of the business information one can download from the Internet is mere public relations material, and as such, it is designed to serve the provider's interests, not the recipient's. Known to the cognoscenti as "brochureware," such material generally conceals more than it reveals and is sometimes quite misleading or even mendacious. On the Internet, as elsewhere in life, you get what you pay for—and free information downloaded from the Internet is rarely worth more than the paper it's not written on!

Of course, not all information on the Internet is free. Surely in the case of paid-for information, the Internet provides an important service? Not really. Information sold over the Internet typically consists of newspaper clippings and other material that already exists elsewhere in the public domain and is thus easily accessible, for the most part, via a good business library. For almost anyone who has a serious need for business information, the Internet provides at best an element of convenience.

In any case, the value to business executives of information culled from the press is, to say the least, controversial. Such information is generally subject to spin and thus is often at best highly misleading. In fact, the press has a distinct habit of letting its readers down at precisely the moment when they most need reliable information. Any review of the record shows that the press has often been years or even decades behind the times in spotting trends that have crucially affected the American economy. Take, for instance, the rise of the Japanese steel industry. The press failed to spot the trend in the early days when an intelligent look at the Japanese industry would have sounded a timely warning for the complacent giants of Pittsburgh; instead, the press took notice only when the layoffs started. By then, of course, it was far too late for warnings.

Japan is, of course, a famously hard nation to read, but even in covering crucial developments nearer home, the American business press is often a treacherous guide for business executives. Take the press's generally fawning coverage of IBM in the 1980s. This was a time when journalists should have been alerting their readers to the near-fatal mistakes IBM had made in ceding to Microsoft and Intel control of the future of the personal computer industry—mistakes that in the 1990s redrew the map of power in the computer industry.

Even when press information is accurate and timely, its value to a busy executive may be highly debatable. Often, as the famed quality control expert W. Edwards Deming pointed out a few years ago, executives who spend too much time monitoring the media just exacerbate their already huge information-overload problems. In his book *The New Economics*, he commented:

> Many of us deceive ourselves into the supposition that we need constant updating to cope with the rapidly changing future. But you cannot, by watching every moment of television or reading every newspaper, acquire a glimpse of what the future holds. To put it another way, information, no matter how complete and speedy, is not knowledge.

Perhaps the ultimate comment on cyberspace as a source of information has come from the feminist author Germaine Greer. Writing in the *Guardian* newspaper, she delivered this resounding verdict on the Internet: "95 percent of what is on it is wrong, 3 percent is criminal and the other 2 percent is useful, if of course you can find it."

So much for the information revolution as seen by users of information. But how does the revolution look to information providers—the companies that stand to profit from the growing market for information? The truth is that for them, too, the Internet, so far at least, has been a distinct disappointment. In the words of Mark Landler of *The New York Times*, media companies have been "resoundingly unsuccessful" in squeezing a profit from the World Wide Web.

Beyond economic information, the Internet is a conduit of scientific information. Here, in contrast to business information, the Internet can be of great value. But even so, the Internet does remarkably little to benefit the American economy. To the extent that valuable technological information can be downloaded from the Internet, the main beneficiaries are America's foreign economic competitors. Leading American scientists and engineers have always worked within easy reach of first-rate scientific libraries that stock the relevant journals and papers, but their foreign counterparts have hitherto been greatly hampered by a lack of similarly comprehensive library facilities. For many Americans, the availability of scientific papers on the Internet at best merely obviates a pleasant ten-minute stroll to a campus library. For foreigners, by contrast, the ability to download American scientific papers via the Internet may save the time and cost of an intercontinental flight to the United States.

So much for the Internet's information potential. Perhaps its most important other possible use is as a new medium of commerce—a sort of global electronic shopping mall. Although this application has long been the subject of much heady discussion among New Age commentators, it has become clear in the first years of the twenty-first century that the prospects for electronic commerce were greatly exaggerated in the late 1990s. In fact, most business executives have been distinctly skeptical of the Internet's potential all along. Typical is Nathan Morton, chief executive of the Computer City superstore chain, who recalls that previous New Age marketing ventures have proven to be expensive flops. "Back in the 1980s, when the Home Shopping Network first came online, I can remember people on Wall Street saying, 'Retail is dead and everyone will be buying through their television sets,'" he told Saul Hansell of *The New York Times*. "Well, that has not happened."

Most shoppers still prefer to buy even computers from a traditional store rather than over the Internet. All through the bubble years of the late 1990s, online purchases accounted for only a negligible proportion of total shopping, and as recently as 2003, their share of total retailing was still less than 5 percent.

Of course, it is early days yet. But as Rupert Murdoch, among others, has suggested, to the extent that Internet commerce succeeds, it will cannibalize more traditional forms of marketing and distribution such as print advertising and direct mail. In the long run, the press in particular stands to lose. As the *Newsweek* economics commentator Robert Samuelson has pointed out, certain advertisers, such as innkeepers in holiday resorts, find that the Internet is an enormously more cost-effective way to reach prospective customers than advertising in newspapers and other traditional paper-based media. All this is good news for the world's dwindling forests. But otherwise, the rise of Internet-based marketing probably promises a lot less of an improvement in economic efficiency than the public has been led to believe. And as Samuelson, among others, has suggested, the tendency for the Internet to undercut more traditional forms of advertising could lead to a drastic reduction in the quality of the American mass media.

Some postindustrialists have postulated the possibility that American Internet merchants may be able to harness the medium's global reach to boost U.S. exports. To say the least, this idea seems premature. There are many practical barriers to be overcome before the Internet can ever serve as a major global marketing medium. For one thing, as former U.S. Trade Representative Charlene Barshefsky has pointed out, many U.S. trading partners are less than enthusiastic about making the necessary deregulation moves to enable their citizens to import foreign goods freely over the Internet. In any case, the many local distribution partners through which American exporters operate in foreign markets will use their deeply entrenched political and operational power to fight cross-border Internet commerce.

Besides these institutional and political barriers, there are also fundamental economic problems with Internet commerce. Many products need local service support, and this must generally be provided by a network of local distributors in foreign markets. In markets like Japan, such distributors are expected to meet extremely high standards in both quality of service and speed of response. All this has to be paid for—and the money comes from the higher prices generally charged in such markets.

As the Internet commerce expert Mary Cronin has pointed out, a wish to maintain different prices in different markets is a key reason why, as of the late 1990s, the long-predicted explosion of Internet-based international commerce had not happened. She cited the example of Millipore, an American company that supplies equipment to semiconductor manufacturers and scientific laboratories around the world. Noting that Millipore's website was being visited by 40,000 computer users every month, she commented that, on a superficial analysis, the company seemed to be a prime candidate to conduct international commerce via the Internet. Nonetheless, Millipore's website did not include pricing, product availability, ordering, or payment facilities—the so-called four horsemen of electronic commerce. In effect, Millipore's website was no more than an elaborate electronic advertisement. A key reason Millipore had balked at supplying price information was that its prices vary considerably in different markets abroad. Putting prices on the Internet would have stirred up a hornet's nest of problems with overseas customers and distributors. Moreover, the company did not want to disclose information on product availability to competitors. This concern is shared, of course, by many other companies operating in fast-moving markets.

Cronin reported that online payment ranked lowest among the services desired by customers in a survey of online commerce. She commented: "Despite the hullabaloo over E-commerce, customers may not even want it."

In the end, as *The New York Times'* Saul Hansell has pointed out, a fundamental problem for Internet commerce is that typical shoppers still want to see and feel merchandise before they buy it. There are exceptions, of course. As Amazon.com, for instance, has convincingly demonstrated, books can be sold with great success over the Internet. In fact, the Internet can provide enormous added value to many book buyers—particularly scholars and other discerning readers for whom the searchability and interactive capabilities offered by Internet-based bookstores are a vital aid in identifying exactly the right purchase. And as the New York–based publisher Jason Epstein has pointed out, Internet bookstores are a godsend for many publishers who have found that most traditional booksellers are ill equipped to sell specialized books that are of interest to only a small segment of the reading public. That said, even in the case of books, the Internet represents no more than an additional outlet; for as far ahead as we can see, the great bulk of books will probably continue to be sold in traditional stores, which should have no problem maintaining their competitive edge in ambience and the serendipity that has always been associated with book buying.

Books apart, many of the most conspicuous success stories of Internet commerce pack a distinctly double-edged message. Take electronic junk mail, which, according to *U.S. News & World Report,* was one of the first Internet businesses to start generating serious profits.

Then there is the notorious proliferation of sex-related sites on the Web. As estimated by the makers of Cyber Patrol, a software program designed to prevent children from gaining access to pornography on the Internet, there were already 20,000 sites unsuitable for children on the Internet as of 1997. By 2003, as reported by Internet Filter Review, the total number of pornographic sites had rocketed to 4.2 million. That was fully 12 percent of all Internet sites and they generated revenue totaling about $2.5 billion.

Another undesirable activity fostered by the Internet is medical quackery. The cyberspace has afforded crooks and charlatans a new way to prey on the gullibility and desperation of the sick. A basic problem is that those who seek medical help via the Internet often don't know who they are dealing with. Most cybersources are, of course, bona fide—but not all. The trouble is, it is often difficult to tell the difference. One problem is that many sites that give perfectly good advice have links to sites where the advice is self-serving or even dangerous. Thus, at the click of a mouse, the unwary Internet surfer can enter a medical twilight zone. In a 1998 *Fortune* account of cyberquackery, David Stipp told of the ordeal of a twelve-year-old Chicago girl who was dying from a rare type of bone cancer. With the help of an Internet search, the girl's parents had discovered an Iowa-based cancer advisory service, which in turn referred them to an alternative-medicine clinic in Mexico. When the clinic demanded an up-front fee of $2,000, the desperate couple paid up without a quibble.

After bringing their daughter to the clinic, however, they quickly concluded they were dealing with quacks. They promptly returned to Chicago, where their daughter died a few days later. The Iowa-based advisory organization refunded a $200 membership fee it had charged, but the couple never recovered the $2,000 fee paid to the Mexican clinic.

Another controversial industry that seems to have achieved more than average success on the Internet is gambling. According to the New Jersey–based consultant Frank Catania, there were an estimated 1,800 gambling sites on the Web as of 2003. That was up from just thirty sites as of 1997. These sites now offer gambling services ranging from casino-style games like video poker, baccarat, and roulette to wagers on sports events. Most such sites are based offshore in places like Australia, Asia, and the Caribbean, thus evading American regulations designed to ensure fair play.

According to Joseph Paravia of California-based Virtual Gaming Technologies, the early experience of Internet casino operators has shown that Web gambling can be "wildly successful." As of 2003, the internet gambling industry's worldwide revenues were estimated to be in excess of $4 billion.

Clearly, from society's point of view, such an explosion of online betting is a mixed blessing. For a start, business productivity may suffer if, as the Internet gambling expert Elio Masie has suggested, many workers are being induced to gamble during office hours. And of course, the lack of regulation of Internet gambling is a major concern. The state of Wisconsin in particular has been vociferous in condemning Web gaming as a "very bad bet." Jim Haney of the Wisconsin attorney general's office has commented: "You don't know who you are dealing with. You have no assurance that the games are fair and not manipulated. You don't know where to go if you are scammed."

Of the more useful businesses spawned by the rise of the Internet, most are still amazingly small. Even Amazon.com, the Internet bookstore regarded by many as the most successful example so far of an Internet-based sales organization, had sales of a little more than $4 billion as of 2003 and employed a mere 7,500 people.

Then there is Yahoo!, the most successful Internet search engine company. Thanks to the postindustrialists' hype, Yahoo! came to be regarded as a New Economy colossus in the late 1990s. Its stock market valuation had soared to $9 billion by mid-1998 and had exceeded $130 billion in the last wild months of the bubble in late 1999. Even valued at a more modest $17 billion as of mid 2003, Yahoo! was worth more than four times the old-established Dow Jones & Company. But the reality is that in 2003 Yahoo!'s annual revenues were running at only about $1.1 billion—or one-quarter less than those of Dow Jones. Moreover, Yahoo! employed only 3,600 people, little more than half of Dow Jones's payroll total.

Of course, to be set against their small size is the fact that many online businesses continue to outpace traditional businesses in sales growth. But even if the postindustrialists' most optimistic hopes are borne out, one point should not be forgotten: the Internet will require vast amounts of hardware to realize its potential and thus will provide a bountiful source of high-wage manufacturing jobs for the world's richest manufacturing nations.

THE UNIMPORTANCE OF BEING VIRTUAL

For many postindustrialists, one of the most exciting prospects promised by the telecommunications revolution is virtual reality. Certainly, virtual reality will have many interesting applications, but it is far from the panacea it is sometimes portrayed to be. For the most part, virtual reality will be confined to narrowly defined niches for many years to come. It will be useful, for instance, in enabling people to work by remote control in dangerous or inaccessible places, such as nuclear power stations, the ocean floor, outer space, burning buildings, and deep mines. It will also be an important tool in engineering, scientific research, and entertainment.

That said, much of what is expected from virtual reality is the sheerest moonshine. Take, for instance, the euphoric views of Newt Gingrich. In his book *To Renew America*, he suggested that the United States could harness virtual reality to become an export superpower in medical services. Noting that doctors may one day be able to operate remotely on patients in other countries via cyberspace, he predicted, "American doctors will be called upon to operate on people in India. We will be able to sell our services in every corner of the world. . . . We have a dramatic opportunity to increase our foreign exchange earnings."

Referring to the problems of the American health care system, Gingrich triumphantly added: "What we regarded as a huge liability may turn out to be our biggest asset. That is what comes from taking problems and turning them into entrepreneurial solutions."

Maybe, but to others, Gingrich's ideas seem less a matter of entrepreneurial solutions than of glib assumptions. First, Gingrich is on notably shaky ground in assuming that virtual reality will be widely accepted by surgeons, let alone patients. As the medical educator Austin Leahy has pointed out, the medical world regards virtual reality mainly as a potentially useful aid in teaching surgery. Virtual reality may soon, for instance, allow medical students to hone their fledgling surgical skills on imaginary patients in much the same way that would-be pilots safely learn to fly by using flight simulators.

One thing is certain: it will be a long time before patients come to trust virtual reality medicine. And if MIT's late Michael Dertouzos is to be believed, their reservations will be amply justified. Referring to virtual reality medicine in *What Will Be,* he commented:

> The reliability of complex systems that combine computer hardware, software, and communication links would be far too shaky to be trusted with people's lives. Even NASA's computers, designed for maximum reliability, are known to fail every few launches. . . . No matter how far technology advances, we should—and undoubtedly will—always feel free to exercise our human prerogative by saying "No."

In any case, even if by some technological miracle the risks of virtual reality medicine could be eliminated, there are other fatal problems with Gingrich's vision. For one thing, he blithely assumes that other countries' health regulators will throw their markets open to the American medical profession's virtual-reality exporters. To say the least, this seems unlikely.

After all, national regulators regard it as one of their most important duties to control entry to the medical profession. The task of checking out the credentials of their own nationals is daunting enough without having to check out the credentials of countless cyberspace practitioners operating outside their jurisdictions. Moreover, any effort by cyberspace practitioners to globalize the medical services industry will be opposed by national medical guilds, whose express purpose is to minimize competition for their members.

Perhaps the most devastating flaw in Gingrich's logic is an economic one: he overlooks the simple fact that trade is a two-way street. If the United States is to sell medical services to the rest of the world, the rest of the world will want a similar right to sell medical services to the United States. Thus, in any future global market for virtual reality medicine, American doctors can expect to face stiff foreign competition. The truth is that the United States has no monopoly on good medicine. Doctors and medical technologists in other countries have repeatedly shown that, given similar levels of funding, they can match their American counterparts in ingenuity and originality. In fact, many key medical developments in recent decades have been pioneered outside the United States. Examples include the development of heart pacemakers (invented by Siemens of Germany in the 1950s), the first heart transplant (performed in South Africa in the 1960s), and the first cloning of an animal (performed in Scotland in the mid-1990s).

This is not to disparage American medicine, which is rightly noted for its pioneering doctors. Certainly, if virtual reality is ever accepted as a routine medical tool, some top American doctors will carve out a lucrative niche for themselves providing "virtual" treatment to plutocratic foreign patients. But given that many lower-wage countries boast fine surgeons who charge less than equivalently skilled American surgeons, it is easy to guess which way overall U.S. trade in virtual reality medicine would run.

Gingrich's analysis overlooks the fact that American health care costs are greatly inflated by a dysfunctional American legal system. In an attempt to ward off disingenuous malpractice suits, American doctors not only must invest in exorbitantly expensive insurance but are forced to waste much precious time and resources on medically unnecessary tests and procedures. Foreign doctors who are not subject to such burdens clearly have a major competitive edge. Thus, if the American health-care market were ever opened up to foreign competition, demand would create its own supply. Encouraged by the prospect of earning huge American fees, foreign doctors in such Old World centers of medical excellence as London and Vienna could afford to invest in the best education and the most advanced equipment and still dramatically undercut their American counterparts. In the long term, even the Europeans might find themselves being undercut as, thanks to the dissemination of the latest medical techniques via cheap modern communications, poorer countries got into the act.

There are similar problems with most other proposed efforts by Americans to sell services abroad via virtual reality. The result is that, in almost every case, a global free-for-all would result in more American imports than exports.

ENTERTAINMENT:
IT'S ONLY ROCK AND ROLL

Entertainment has been one of the fastest-growing of all American industries in recent decades. In fact, it has grown so large that it is now regarded by postindustrialists as a cornerstone of the American economy.

But is the entertainment industry living up to the postindustrialists' hopes? It certainly is in the case of feature films, which we will consider separately in the next section. As for other sectors of the American entertainment industry, which in combination probably account for ten times as many workers as the feature film business, there are major concerns about the economic and—still more so—the social value of the industry's contribution.

The concerns are particularly justified with respect to television, whose growth has accounted for an utterly disproportionate share of the industry's human resources. This growth has been driven by a fivefold expansion in the number of channels available to most American viewers in the last three decades.

Are television viewers getting a better service today than they did thirty years ago? Probably. But are they getting an increase in satisfaction commensurate with the expansion in the industry's scale? Probably not. One thing is certain: the explosion in the production of television programming in recent years contrasts markedly with an extremely modest increase in the American public's television viewing. As measured by the A. C. Nielsen market research organization, the typical American increased his or her viewing by less than 5 percent between 1981 and 1997. Clearly, therefore, the major consequence of the increased supply of programming was that most broadcasters suffered a declining share of audience over the years. In fact, the decline has been so precipitous that as of 2002, as measured again by Nielsen, advertising-supported basic cable for the first time boasted a prime-time share higher than of broadcast networks.

As the president of Sony Corporation of America, Howard Stringer, pointed out a few years ago, all this audience-splitting naturally has strong negative implications for the quality of the viewer's experience. "As you go from thirty-five channels to seventy-five, you diminish the audience for everything," he says. "That makes it harder to generate the advertising revenue for quality programming."

That said, from the postindustrialists' point of view, the quality of the American entertainment industry's output is less relevant than the industry's export prowess. In the postindustrialists' view, this is a trump card. Although they rarely if ever present authoritative figures to back their case, they claim that the entertainment industry is now a huge contributor to the U.S. balance of payments. But here again, they are guilty of misleading the American public. The truth is that, in relation to the amount of labor they preempt, most sectors of the American entertainment industry are quite small exporters.

Even the recorded music industry is a much less powerful contributor to the American balance of payments than is sometimes supposed. The reason should be obvious: trade in music runs two ways. Although the United States exports a lot of recorded music, it is also imports a lot. The United States is probably close to balanced trade in music with Europe. After all, several key record companies are based in Europe, most notably the largest of them all, PolyGram. Other huge European players include London-based EMI and the Bertelsmann group's BMG subsidiary.

Elsewhere, American export opportunities are curtailed by the fact that in most of the non-Western world, recorded music is local or regional in origin. Language and taste see to that. Apart from a few mega-stars like Elvis Presley and Frank Sinatra, most American musicians have little appeal outside the Western world—and certainly they derive at best only puny revenues from non-Western nations. This helps explain why in East Asia, for instance, music by local artists accounts for about 70 percent of revenues from sales of recorded music.

The export story is hardly much more encouraging in the case of television programming. American talk shows and game shows, for instance, are generally too culture-specific to have much appeal outside the United States. But even in the case of the minority of American television programs that could generate good sales abroad, foreign trade barriers conspire to limit U.S. export revenues. Even the United Kingdom, which itself is probably the world's second-largest exporter of television programs after the United States, has dragged its feet in opening its television market to American programming. For many years foreign programming was limited to just 15 percent of the British market. After the U.S. government pressed for liberalization, the British relaxed their barriers somewhat, but even so broadcasters in the United Kingdom, in common with those in other EU countries, continued to be required under European law to ensure that at least 50 percent of their programming originated in Europe.

Nor are such trade barriers to American entertainment exports likely to disappear any time soon. On the contrary, they may well become an even greater stumbling block in the future. The governments of many key nations are becoming increasingly hostile to American entertainment exports, as was notably apparent in the summer of 1998 when officials from twenty nations gathered in Ottawa to consider measures to protect their nations' cultures. Among the nations playing important roles at the meeting were such American allies as the United Kingdom, France, Sweden, Canada, and Mexico. Although these nations generally favor global free trade in everything else, they saw no ideological embarrassment in making a special exception for cultural products. Nor was there any doubt about whose cultural exports they wanted to exclude. Their target was, of course, the United States. This was made pointedly clear in the fact that American representatives were allowed to attend the meeting merely as "observers." Anthony DePalma of *The New York Times* described the treatment of the United States as an "obvious slight"; certainly the attitude of many influential participants at the meeting bodes ill for American hopes of establishing a true global free market in entertainment products.

Trade barriers apart, U.S. entertainment exports face many other problems in foreign markets. A key one is, of course, piracy. This is often thought of as a problem mainly in the Third World, but even solvent countries such as Taiwan, South Korea, and Greece have a record of lax enforcement of Western intellectual property rights.

True, some progress has been achieved in recent years. After decades of stonewalling, Japan, for instance, agreed a few years ago to raise its period of protection for copyrighted musical recordings from twenty-five years to the Western norm of fifty. As a consequence of Tokyo's previous stance, music by such best-selling artists as the Beatles, the Beach Boys, the Rolling Stones, the Berlin Philharmonic, and the New York Philharmonic was sold in Japan mainly in unauthorized local bootleg versions. But the fact that Japan has now toed the line on copyright hardly presages a general improvement in the protection of Western intellectual property rights in export markets. Far from it. Japan's change of heart was stimulated in part at least by enlightened self-interest: Japanese corporations now have important investments in such key Western music labels as CBS Records and MCA, and thus Japan's interests now lie increasingly with the gamekeepers, not the poachers.

The West faces much tougher problems in eradicating copyright abuse in other markets. Emerging economies in particular typically feel entitled to help themselves to the talents of foreign artists for free. Their attitude has deep roots in history. Even the United States was once notorious for freeloading in this respect. Up to 1891, foreign authors and songwriters had no copyright protection under American law—a fact that famously infuriated British novelists like Charles Dickens as well as such titans of British music as W. S. Gilbert and Arthur Sullivan.

These days, China is one of the biggest offenders. Reporting in the mid-1990s, Louis Kraar of *Fortune* alleged there were already then twenty-nine factories in China turning out 75 million bootleg CDs a year for sale at prices as low as $1.70. Under pressure from the United States and other Western nations, Beijing authorities subsequently clamped down on piracy, but the net effect was merely to transfer the problem to China's so-called special administrative region, Hong Kong. According to the International Federation of the Phonographic Industry (IFPI), CD manufacturing in Hong Kong was totaled an estimated 400 million units in 1998, up from a mere 60 million in 1997. The city was producing about twenty-three times more CDs than were sold legitimately within its territory. In reality, most of the production was coming from pirates and the output was destined for sale in mainland China. Since then, piracy seems to have staged a major comeback within China itself. As of 2002, the IFPI reported that up to 90 percent of music CDs sold there were pirated.

We have already noted that there are no reliable figures for the American entertainment industry's exports. But a look at the financial statements of a few typical American entertainment conglomerates is suggestive. Take, for instance, Viacom, which, with some justification, describes itself as "one of the world's largest entertainment and publishing companies and a leading force in nearly every segment of the international media marketplace." The worldwide scale of Viacom's activities is indeed impressive. Besides Paramount Pictures, these activities include:

> **MTV:** Reaching more than 340 million homes around the
> world as of 2001, MTV has been described by *Time* as "second only to God in omnipresence." Certainly among the
> world's cable networks, it is the most widely distributed.

Nickelodeon: This is one of the world's largest producers of children's programming.

Blockbuster entertainment stores: As of 2003, the group included more than 8,500 company-operated and franchised stores in nearly thirty nations.

Clearly, Viacom's reach is indeed global. But how much does this contribute to U.S. exports? The numbers are startlingly disappointing. Even with the help of a large contribution from Paramount (whose movie library includes 2,500 titles), Viacom derived just 16 percent of its total revenues from overseas in 2002. And only a small fraction of its overseas revenues, probably little more than one-eighth, represented exports from the United States.

Viacom's disappointing export performance is less surprising when we take a closer look. Most of the business it does abroad represents added value that is created abroad and therefore does not contribute in any significant way to the American balance of payments. Virtually all that the United States receives is a thin trickle of dividends and royalties.

The story of the MTV group, for instance, is revealing. Besides English, it broadcasts in Spanish, German, French, Italian, Norwegian, Swedish, Russian, Mandarin Chinese, and Japanese. Most programming in such languages is originated abroad and therefore represents a cost to the parent company. Moreover, in several cases Viacom operates with local partners; as a result, even the dividend income from the foreign businesses in large measure stays in the nations concerned.

At other major American entertainment companies, the export story is equally disappointing. Take the Walt Disney Company. Although the company's core movie business is a muscular performer in overseas markets, the fact is that movies account for only a small part of the company's total business. And as with Viacom, Disney's non-movie entertainment businesses are generally poor exporters. A glance at these businesses reveals why: they include the ESPN sports channel as well as various cable channels, not to mention the ABC Television network. It is hardly surprising that the company's exports in the late 1990s represented just 4 percent of total sales.

Many other examples could be cited, but the point should already be indisputable. In sum, there has been an explosion in the size of the American entertainment industry in recent decades, but it has not generated a noticeable return in terms of the two economic criteria that really matter: consumer satisfaction in the home market and export success overseas.

Of course, as we have noted, there is one area of the entertainment industry that is solid gold. It is time to look at the movie industry.

HOLLYWOOD: MERCHANDISING THE AMERICAN DREAM

Making movies is a great business for the United States. In marked contrast to most other postindustrial businesses, Hollywood visibly creates a balanced mix of jobs—a relatively few jobs for directors, actors, scriptwriters, composers, and other brilliant creative types, plus thousands of jobs for more ordinary mortals such as makeup artists, electricians, carpenters, painters, and drivers. Moreover, it is a growth industry, given that in the space of just seventeen years, the number of people employed in movie production and related activities in the United States nearly tripled to total more than 240,000 as of the late 1990s.

Even better, wages in the movie industry are notably high. In fact, if a survey by the Motion Picture Association of America is to be believed, movie industry wages in the late 1990s were running about 70 percent higher than the California average—making them the highest to be found in any industry in the United States.

True, as Andrew Pollack has pointed out in *The New York Times,* some movie production has migrated abroad in recent years. But most Hollywood jobs are well protected from foreign competition. After all, Hollywood movies are typically set in the United States, and this fact naturally determines where the bulk of the production work must be done. Thus, unlike running shoes or computer software programs, American movies cannot be readily outsourced to cut-price studios in Malaysia or Belarus.

And, of course, the industry's trump card is that it is a big exporter. After growing rapidly in the 1980s and early 1990s, Hollywood's international box-office gross surpassed the domestic box-office gross for the first time in 1995. In fact, movie exports have grown so large that as of the late 1990s, Hollywood seemed poised to pass the aerospace industry as the largest U.S. export earner.

What of Hollywood's future? In the short to medium term, things look great. Certainly Hollywood will remain by far the most successful of postindustrial businesses in the United States. But in the very long term, Hollywood's prospects are more questionable. As Paul Fahri and Megan Rosenfeld have pointed out in the *International Herald Tribune,* Hollywood's leadership of the world movie industry is to a large extent a function of the present dominant position of the English language in world culture.

The postindustrialists tend to take that dominant position for granted—but they shouldn't. The English language's long-term prospects are in fact largely a function of the general performance of the overall American economy. If the United States does not succeed in reversing its pattern of long-term relative decline, the English language's prestige is bound to suffer. This would tend to undermine Hollywood's position in many key foreign markets.

Take a market like Japan, which happens to be one of Hollywood's biggest export markets. Although fewer than 5 percent of the Japanese people speak English fluently, a much larger proportion has some knowledge of the language. Thus, it is almost a foregone conclusion that when Japanese moviegoers have a choice between an American movie and, say, a Polish one, the Polish one will come off second-best. The truth is that American movies appeal to the autodidact in moviegoers in many foreign markets because, by reading the subtitles and listening to the original sound track in English, non-English speakers can hope to enjoy themselves while painlessly improving their English-language skills.

Hollywood's fortunes are tied to those of the overall American economy in another way: with its abundance and its tradition of boundless economic opportunity, the United States has long been regarded by moviegoers around the world as an idealized version of what they would like their own societies to be. At least, the affluent side of American society is so regarded. By contrast, as Sharon Waxman has pointed out in the *International Herald Tribune,* movies about the poverty of American inner-city life tend to be distinct losers in foreign markets. The side of America that foreign moviegoers want to see is the American Dream. Thus, movies featuring affluent American heroes and heroines tend to enjoy a special aura of universality in the eyes of foreign moviegoers. And even though foreign moviegoers may find many of the nuances of daily life in the United States remote or puzzling, their ability to share vicariously in the American Dream helps bridge the culture gap. It is notable that British movies also benefit from a similar ability by foreign audiences to empathize with British culture. British movie directors tap into this phenomenon most successfully when they set the action in the nineteenth or early twentieth century—a period when, by no coincidence, the United Kingdom was regarded as the world's leading society.

Thanks to the American economy's domestic wealth and overseas influence, there is a huge potential market out there that justifies Hollywood's famously extravagant production budgets. The budget for just a run-of-the-mill feature film these days typically exceeds $50 million, and many Hollywood directors work with budgets several times this. James Cameron's 1998 blockbuster *Titanic,* for instance, cost $200 million, and Kevin Costner's *Waterworld* cost $175 million. Budgets like these are vastly larger than anything available even to the best directors working in the French, German, or Japanese movie industry. Of course, Hollywood's big budgets do not always translate into box-office revenues (as the notoriously unsuccessful *Waterworld* demonstrated). But in the hands of the right director, a Hollywood budget makes possible a degree of quality in casting, props, and special effects that effortlessly outclasses foreign competitors.

Clearly, therefore, if the United States loses its central position in the world economy, Hollywood will lose the various special competitive advantages it has hitherto enjoyed by virtue of its American base. And in fact, there is some evidence that the rot may already have set in. Certainly, as Samuel P. Huntington has pointed out, the reduced role of the United States in the world economy has already led to some decline in the once-unrivaled status of the English language as the world's second language. The German language, for instance, has been making inroads in continental Europe, particularly in the former East Bloc countries of Central Europe such as Poland and the Czech Republic. Meanwhile, both Chinese and Japanese are clearly gaining ground as second languages throughout East Asia.

Moreover, as other countries catch up with the United States in incomes, American society will lose some of its charm as a setting for movies. Already for many of the world's moviegoers, there are other cities nearer home that compete in glamour and excitement with New York and Los Angeles. Take Hong Kong. Given that it already comes close to the United States in per capita income, it now boasts a patina of sophistication similar to that of the most glamorous American cities. As such, it is an exciting setting for countless Chinese-language movies turned out by the Hong Kong movie industry for distribution throughout East Asia.

For now American movies continue to do well in East Asia, not least in Hong Kong itself (where *Titanic,* for instance, was by far the biggest box-office draw in 1998). But in the long run, the Hong Kong industry seems set to match Hollywood's budgets as the Chinese movie market grows. Clearly, plots about Chinese-speaking heroes and heroines set against a Chinese cultural backdrop and presented in original Chinese sound tracks have as strong a market advantage in East Asia as English-language movies about American characters have in the United States. (It should be added that in competing in China, culture is not the only barrier to American movie exports. A variety of trade barriers imposed by the Beijing authorities has consistently marginalized Hollywood's offerings in China.)

Looking to the future, it seems likely that Hollywood is going to face stiffer competition in export markets. In addition to Hollywood's dwindling cultural and linguistic advantages, there is the simple fact that as other countries become rich, their local moviemaking industries can afford to aim for higher standards.

All in all, however, Hollywood will probably continue to dominate the world movie industry for decades to come. And in fact, the net effect of American economic decline thus far has actually been to *increase* Hollywood's export revenues. This is because the main manifestation of American decline has been a weak dollar. When foreign box-office receipts are translated into dollars, they tend to rise strongly in dollar terms over the years, even though they may show little or no increase measured in local currencies.

But for postindustrialists, any realistic look at Hollywood's position carries a somber message. Heartening though Hollywood's performance continues to be, the movie industry alone is not remotely significant enough singlehandedly to sustain America's edge as the world's leading economy. Even if, against the odds, Hollywood continues to maintain and enhance its share of world movie markets, the conclusion quite clearly is that postindustrialism is not enough. There is really no substitute for manufacturing as the main driver of prosperity. It is time, therefore, to take a closer look at the opportunities afforded by modern manufacturing.

CHAPTER 5

ostindustrialists often talk as if there were no challenging or interesting manufacturing industries left in the world today. How wrong they are. The truth is that the world's most advanced economies are full of great manufacturing industries—industries that not only pay superb wages to a broad range of workers but are also strong exporters.

Take the car industry. Although as far back as the early 1980s, the noted postindustrialist John Naisbitt predicted that carmaking would soon migrate to the Third World, the car industry remains a major engine of prosperity in the First World—most notably in Germany, where it is the veritable backbone of the country's export economy.

Even the U.S. automobile industry, much criticized though it has been by postindustrialists in recent years, is a fundamental contributor to American prosperity. In particular, though it has continued to lose international competitiveness in recent years, it is second to none as a source of high-wage blue-collar jobs, accounting as it does for about one-fifth of all American manufacturing employment.

Equally in Japan, the automobile industry remains a fundamental economic contributor. In the face of predictions for years that Japanese automakers would be hollowed out by various lower-wage nations in the East Asian region, they have for the most part more than held their own. They have suffered remarkably little even from the rise of the vaunted South Korean car industry, which ranks second only to Japan's in the East Asian region in size and sophistication. In fact, although the Korean industry has enjoyed considerable success in exporting to the developing world, it has made only modest inroads into the United States, Western Europe, and other rich markets. The result is that, even with Japanese wages running three to five times higher than Korean levels in the 1990s, Japanese carmakers continue to tower almost effortlessly over their Korean rivals in total revenues. And whereas the Koreans are mere assemblers of cars, the Japanese automobile industry increasingly is switching out of assembly to specialize in much more sophisticated activities, such as making high-tech components, advanced materials, and production machinery. In fact, one of the Japanese industry's biggest customers for both auto components and production machinery has been the Korean industry, and thus the rise of the Korean industry has, on balance, been a net plus for the Japanese. The Japanese automobile industry's success in defying predictions of decline is a striking demonstration of how the postindustrialists underestimate the contribution of capital intensity and knowledge intensity in enabling the world's highest-wage nations to continue to dominate world markets even in the face of determined competition from low-wage countries.

Many other examples could be cited of how great manufacturing industries contribute disproportionately to the wealth of First World nations. Particularly notable in this regard are aerospace, construction machinery, power-generation equipment, pharmaceuticals, household appliances, and machine tools.

And then there is electronics, which more than any other industry exemplifies the message of this book. In truth, many sectors of the electronics industry have long been unjustly slighted by post-industrialists. As we will see in this chapter, this view goes to the root of the post-industrialists' misunderstandings about how the modern world economy works.

The electronics industry is relevant for another reason as well: it is quite literally the prime mover of world prosperity. The electronics industry's most obvious contribution in this regard has been to supply a rapidly growing torrent of ever more powerful and reliable components for virtually every kind of manufactured product. Sophisticated electronic components are now crucial to the function of most home appliances, for instance. They are used not only in such obvious gadgets as videocassette recorders and television sets but in air-conditioning systems, refrigerators, vacuum cleaners, dishwashers, and stoves. In virtually every such application, electronic components have not only cut the cost of the appliance but dramatically improved its performance and reliability.

Electronic components have also clearly made a dramatic contribution to improving the performance of cars in the last thirty years. Electronic fuel injection, for instance, has cut fuel consumption by nearly half. Microchip-controlled airbags have made driving much safer. Various other electronic systems have provided everything from a smoother ride to more effective braking. So important is the electronics industry's contribution that today nearly one-fifth of the entire manufacturing cost of a typical car goes to electronic components.

The electronics industry has made a less obvious but even more important contribution to the world's overall economic progress by enabling other industries to hone their production processes. Computerized production techniques have boosted productivity in a host of manufacturing industries, from shipbuilding to telecommunications. Even in such traditional industries as steel, the effect has been dramatic. As we will see in Chapter 6, computerization has been a key factor in dramatically cutting the real cost of steel in recent decades.

In a word, electronics is the mother of modern manufacturing. In the rest of this chapter, we will take a closer look at this bountiful industry and show how it exemplifies the best of what manufacturing can do for a modern economy.

A JOURNEY TO THE SOURCE OF THE ELECTRONIC NILE

Almost everyone knows that AT&T, Intel, and Microsoft have played key roles in hastening the information age. Few, however, are aware of the important contribution made by the Japanese camera maker Nikon. Even fewer have any inkling of what goes on at Nikon's glassworks in the remote Tokyo suburb of Sagamihara.

But if we trace back the long series of highly sophisticated manufacturing steps involved in making semiconductors, all roads lead to Sagamihara. The Sagamihara glassworks is the repository of highly secret, world-beating techniques that have propelled Nikon to a leading position in the manufacture of the key production equipment used to make semiconductors. It is hardly an exaggeration to say that Sagamihara is the ultimate source of the electronic Nile.

Outwardly, Sagamihara seems ill cast for its starring role in the electronic revolution. A classic Japanese *bedotaun* ("dormitory town"—the word is a combination of the English words "bed" and "town"), Sagamihara is reached from Tokyo by taking the expressway southwest for about twenty miles. You exit into a typical Japanese suburb and quickly find yourself on a narrow road that picks its way between a jumble of vending machines, convenience stores, family restaurants, garden shops, and golf driving ranges.

Turning left, you enter an even narrower road, and there just ahead at a T-junction is the Nikon glass factory. All in all, it seems like a remarkably unprepossessing little chemical works. The central building is just two floors high, built mainly of what looks like corrugated iron; it is a classic example of Japan's utilitarian, no-nonsense school of industrial architecture. To the side is a taller, more modern building with various large pipes and flues running here and there.

Apart from a few surveillance cameras and a guardhouse manned twenty-four hours a day, there is not the slightest hint here of Promethean industrial activity. Nevertheless, this plant is a world leader in making glass with uniquely powerful optical qualities that are vital in the production of semiconductors. Thanks in large part to quality improvement at this plant, Nikon came from nowhere in less than two decades to become one of the world's dominant manufacturer of so-called steppers. Almost unknown to the general public, steppers play as important a role in world manufacturing in the late twentieth century as blast furnaces did in the nineteenth. They are lithographic machines that perform the crucial function of printing circuit patterns on silicon wafers. The printing is done by focusing an image of the circuit pattern onto a photosensitive material coated on each wafer. The image is formed by shining a light through a "mask"—a stencil-like metal replica of the circuit pattern—and is progressively reduced through a series of huge lenses. It is then reproduced on the silicon wafer. Because the resolution power of each new generation of steppers is greater than that of the last, the semiconductor industry can print ever finer lines on each new generation of chips. And of course, the finer a chip's lines, the greater its information-processing capacity.

Lithography accounts for about one-fifth of the total manufacturing cost of a typical semiconductor, and thus it is the industry's single most critical manufacturing process. Not surprisingly, therefore, steppers are the mainstays of the semiconductor equipment business—a business that in a good year generates close to $50 billion in revenues.

Much of the stepper industry's huge long-term growth in sales revenues comes from price hikes, as each succeeding generation of machines offers ever greater performance. Thus, whereas the first steppers introduced in the 1960s took up little more space than a refrigerator, the new steppers launched in 2003 were ten-ton behemoths. In a complicated intertwining of mechanical, optical, and electronic components, the innards of a modern stepper look like a cross between a jet engine and an intergalactic telescope. As of 2003, a state-of-the-art stepper cost more than $20 million. This represented a twenty-fold increase over Nikon's first steppers in the early 1980s.

When Nikon entered the business in 1980, the width of the thinnest lines its steppers could print was one micron (one millionth of a meter—or about one-eightieth the width of a human hair). By contrast, its new steppers that went into volume production in 2003 were capable of printing lines of less than 0.1 micron.

All in all, the Nikon stepper business is a particularly striking illustration of the ability of great manufacturers to make more with less. Nor could there be a much more convincing illustration of how manufacturing contributes to strengthening a nation's economy. After all, virtually all the added value entailed in making steppers is created in Japan; from a standing start in 1981, the Nikon stepper business's sales had already by 2000 grown to more than $2 billion.

For the Japanese national economy, the most striking benefit has been soaring exports. Nikon exports more than 70 percent of its steppers. Moreover, even those Nikon steppers that are installed in Japanese semiconductor plants contribute strongly, if indirectly, to Japan's exports because they are engaged mainly in making semiconductors for export.

The stepper business has also been a great job creator. As estimated by the Nikon stepper executive Hisayuki Shimizu, about 5,000 of the Nikon group's workforce of more than 14,000 as of 2002 were engaged directly or indirectly in making steppers. Moreover, the stepper division's employment profile closely matches the job creation needs of Japanese society in that it offers plenty of jobs to workers of average intelligence. Specifically, nearly 50 percent of the stepper division's production workers have had no more than a high school education—a slightly higher proportion than in the Japanese workforce as a whole.

As for pay levels, Nikon ranks well up among the best employers in Japan. As of 2003, its workers earned on average about $60,000 at the exchange rate including biannual bonuses. In other words, Nikon's pay levels were comparable to those in Japan's world-beating automobile industry.

One thing is certain: Nikon's factory-floor workers enjoy an especially solid sense of job security. Nikon's stepper division workers are backed by a unique tranche of secret technological know-how that has made Nikon one of only three companies that dominate the stepper industry world-wide. Its only rivals are Tokyo-based Canon and Netherlands-based ASM Lithography. America's SVG (now part of ASM) has a few remaining percentage points of the world market.

Nikon is unique in that it boasts full in-house control of almost all the stepper industry's main production technologies, which in addition to optics include photoelectronic sensing and precision mechanics. As Nikon chief executive Shoichiro Yoshida has pointed out, this gives the company great scope to pioneer the development of new technologies in which mechanical and optical components have to be closely coordinated.

Of these technologies, optics is clearly the most important and explains much of Nikon's meteoric rise in the industry. Even before it entered the stepper business, Nikon had become the world leader in advanced optics. By the late 1970s its prowess was notably apparent in making, for instance, the ultrahigh-performance lenses used in microfiche machines. Since then, it has continued to lead in optical innovation. As explained by Hisayuki Shimizu, by maintaining its own glass factory Nikon enjoys great flexibility in developing new types of glass with superior refraction indexes. "There are various trace elements in glass such as copper and iron, and these affect its optical quality," says Shimizu. "It may take two years to develop a new glass and a further two years to develop a lens using it. Thus, if our competitors want to copy what we are doing, they will trail us by several years."

In precision mechanics, too, Nikon boasts a long history of leadership. Here its early experience with so-called ruling engines has been crucial. These are highly sophisticated devices used by engineers and scientists for cutting and marking to ultrafine tolerances. By the 1970s, Nikon was already making ruling engines that could operate within tolerances of a mere 0.1 microns.

The stepper industry's need for highly precise mechanics stems in part from the ultrademanding level of accuracy required in positioning silicon wafers for the lithography process. If a wafer's position is off by much more than 0.05 microns—little more than 1/2000 of a hair's breadth—the resulting chips may prove fatally flawed.

To understand the full significance of positioning, it is important to remember that microchips are three-dimensional devices. Like the floors in a tall building, layers of circuits are imposed one on top of the other. If each succeeding layer is not precisely aligned over the one below, the circuit connections between the layers will not line up. The mechanical challenge is greatly compounded by the fact that steppers print the same tiny pattern repeatedly on each wafer. Thus, the wafer, which typically measures twelve inches across and will later be cut into many separate chips, must be repositioned many times in quick succession to receive each separate printing. (This process has become known as "step and repeat"—hence the name "stepper.") Given that a stepper must typically process nearly two wafers a minute, wafers have to be repositioned rapidly between printings.

To achieve the necessary speed and accuracy, the stepper's mechanical parts must be machined to tolerances of hitherto unheard-of fineness—so fine in fact that steppers are said to be the most precise machines ever built. Steppers must be assembled in so-called clean rooms in which dust particles are excluded by elaborate air-filtering systems. Moreover, steppers are so delicate that even slight fluctuations in temperature can fatally disturb their mechanical settings. Thus, Nikon must take special care in transporting steppers: for export orders, for instance, the company insists on using special cargo planes that are normally used for transporting perishable fruit because these planes boast particularly reliable temperature controls.

The story of how Nikon came to prominence in the stepper business is a classic tale of United States-Japan rivalry. Like many other advanced products that are now made mainly in Japan, the stepper was invented in the United States. The concept was pioneered by the David W. Mann division of GCA Corporation, which monopolized the industry into the early 1980s. In the time-honored pattern of American business, GCA executives at first greatly underestimated the Japanese challenge and dismissed Nikon's early steppers as cheap copies.

In reality, however, even by the standards of corporate Japan, Nikon was a dangerous competitor to underestimate. For a start, Nikon's skills in the stepper industry's fundamental technologies were already at least a match for GCA's. In particular, Nikon was, of course, a leader in optics. In fact, it was already effortlessly ahead of GCA in that department: whereas GCA depended on an outside supplier, Zeiss of Germany, for lens-making, Nikon not only made all its own lenses but made them to world-beating standards of precision.

Moreover, in addition to technological leadership, Nikon enjoyed various commercial advantages by virtue of being a Japanese company. One key advantage was that the Ministry of International Trade and Industry (now known as the Ministry of Economy, Trade and Industry) in Tokyo had already targeted semiconductors in the 1970s as an industry of the future. By dint of its linguistic edge as well as the general nature of Japan's tightly integrated industrial infrastructure, Nikon could expect more than its share of the Japanese market. In particular, Nikon could expect to benefit from the fact that it was a top member of the huge Mitsubishi family of companies. This gave it more or less affirmative action status with many notable potential stepper customers.

More generally, Nikon's base in Japan gave it a crucial edge in labor quality. This edge stemmed in large part from the Japanese employment system, which discourages job-hopping and has thereby ensured that Nikon captures the full benefit from its worker training programs. Even by Japanese standards, Nikon is a particularly heavy investor in the skills of its workforce and it retrains its workers every two years to keep them abreast of advances in production technology.

Another advantage of the Japanese labor system has been that it protects Nikon from the risk of competitors acquiring its secret production know-how by hiring away its workers. Under the lifetime employment system, Japanese workers are required to give their full loyalty to their employer, and it is unthinkable for them to use their knowledge of an employer's trade secrets to win a big pay increase from a rival employer.

A final benefit of Nikon's base in Japan was a plentiful supply of long-term capital. In particular, Nikon could count on its Mitsubishi connections to ensure that it had privileged access to the torrent of patient capital available from the Mitsubishi group's various banks and insurance companies.

Perhaps the most important lesson of the stepper story is that a flagging, old-line manufacturing company can reinvent itself. Launched in 1917 by Koyata Iwasaki, nephew of the Mitsubishi group's founder, Yataro Iwasaki, Nikon was Japan's first maker of optical glass equipment. For the next sixty years—through peace and war and then peace again—camera sales boomed. But by the late 1970s, the joy had gone out of the camera business as many markets in the developed world showed signs of saturation. Nikon—in common with other Japanese camera makers—needed to develop new products.

Nikon's main rival, Canon, had already established an important beachhead in copiers and used this advantage to achieve leadership in the emerging laser printer business. (Canon supplies the key enabling components in laser printers to companies like Hewlett-Packard.)

Nikon chose to focus tightly on the stepper business. Clearly, had it not done so, it would have faced a future of stagnation, if not decline. Nikon's stepper story is a classic example of how a growth-oriented company can leverage existing manufacturing skills to develop new growth opportunities and maintain stable long-term employment for its workers.

SILICON:
ONE THOUSAND TIMES MORE VALUABLE THAN STEEL

Probably the stepper industry's nearest rival as a fundamental enabler of the electronic revolution is the silicon industry, which is also much overlooked in public discussions of the electronic age. Although the word *silicon* is promiscuously used as a synonym for *electronics,* semiconductor-grade silicon as a material is perhaps the ultimate example of a highly advanced product that postindustrialists mistakenly assume is a mere "commodity" that can be safely taken for granted.

The truth is that only a handful of highly sophisticated companies are capable of making silicon to the standards required in the semiconductor industry. And just the top three of these companies—Tokyo-based

Shin-Etsu Chemical, St. Louis–based MEMC Electronic Materials, and Munich-based Wacker-Chemie—account for well over half the world market.

In one sense, it is perhaps not surprising that people tend to take silicon for granted. As the euphoric prophets of the New Economy point out, silicon is the second most common element after oxygen and, in one estimate, accounts for an astonishing 30.5 percent of the earth's crust.

But there is a big difference between raw silicon as found in nature and the highly refined form used in the semiconductor industry. In fact, semiconductor-grade silicon is produced in only tiny volumes, and in the epitaxial form used for high-performance computer chips, it costs more than $80 an ounce. That is the equivalent of nearly $2.9 million per metric ton—or nearly one thousand times the price of steel.

The task of converting raw silicon into silicon wafers involves more than a dozen complex processes. In the words of Barnaby J. Feder of *The New York Times*, "if digital technology is a mix of mathematics and electrical engineering, then think of wafer production as the molecular chemistry that makes the digital era possible."

The silicon production process begins with quartz sand, which is reduced and refined to produce a material known as polysilicon. This looks like irregularly shaped gray rocks but boasts an almost incredible level of purity—just one foreign atom per one billion. The polysilicon is then melted in combination with minute amounts of "dopant" elements such as boron and phosphorus and converted into cylindrical ingots of monocrystalline silicon. The dopant elements are special impurities that determine the precise electrical properties of the final silicon wafer.

Another crucial stage is the slicing of the ingots into wafers. Since these wafers can be almost as thin as a postcard, the cutting requires extremely precise machinery. Afterward, the wafers are carefully cleaned and polished. In the case of epitaxial wafers, a further key process is necessary as the polished silicon slices are coated with a special layer of ultrapure silicon of an electrically different character. Chips made from epitaxial wafers generally boast enhanced reliability and make possible more complex designs, such as those used in Intel's high-performance microprocessors.

All this complexity adds up to a great business for the world's silicon wafer producers. This is notably apparent, for instance, at Wacker-Chemie, which accounts for nearly 30 percent of all the world's polysilicon and about 15 percent of its semiconductor-grade silicon. Founded in 1914 by Alexander Wacker, a German financier and industrial pioneer, Wacker-Chemie boasts deep roots in the German tradition of chemical innovation. The company originally made calcium carbide, an intermediate material needed for producing acetylene, which in turn was used to fuel the gas lighting of the early twentieth century. Calcium carbide was made in a complex process that required large amounts of electricity, a commodity that was then far more expensive in real terms than it is today. Wacker found an abundant source of water power in southern Germany, and harnessing it to generate cheap electricity, he quickly became a major producer of calcium carbide and acetylene. Of course, gas lighting quickly went the way of the buggy whip, but the chemical works he established—near the beautiful medieval town of Burghausen— soon developed other applications for acetylene in various areas of the chemical industry. Later Wacker-Chemie was highly successful in diversifying into various silicon-based products that kept output on a consistently rising tack. The most important of these at first was silicon carbide, which is used in industrial abrasives. Then came various forms of silicone, which are organic compounds of silicon used in lubricants and varnishes. Finally, in the early 1970s, the company began making semiconductor-grade silicon. Along the way, Wacker's Burghausen workforce has consistently burgeoned to the point where today it numbers more than 10,000 people, of whom about 35 percent are engaged in making semiconductor silicon.

As with most manufacturing industries, the silicon business has been highly successful in creating excellent jobs for ordinary blue-collar workers. In fact, more than 80 percent of Wacker's silicon workers are mere high-school graduates. And given that Burghausen is located in one of Germany's most prosperous regions, Wacker necessarily pays high wages.

Of course, a glance at the structure of Wacker's business shows that the company can well afford to pay superior wages. The reason is that silicon-making, in common with most advanced manufacturing business, is highly capital-intensive. Wacker's silicon works is full of the latest equipment from such specialist chemical equipment makers as Peter Wolters, Leybold Systems, and CRP Technic. In the crystal-growing process, for instance, one worker looks after as many as ten Leybold "pullers," each of which represents a capital investment of nearly $1 million.

The silicon industry is also notably knowledge-intensive. The crystal-growing process in particular is highly complex, and by dint of trial and error over the years, the main producers have accumulated a huge stock of proprietary know-how. Much of this know-how takes the form of patents that the main producers share via extensive cross-licensing of patents. The incumbents in the industry also enjoy a huge edge in productivity over would-be entrants by dint of a large reserve of trade secrets. Even something as apparently simple as the appropriate settings for production equipment are closely guarded trade secrets known only to a few top engineers and other trusted senior executives.

The level of proprietary knowledge required is constantly rising as the industry moves rapidly to ever more sophisticated and varied products. Much of the variation comes from the "doping" process, which can produce many different grades tailored to the precise needs of individual semiconductor makers. As reported by Barnaby Feder, MEMC, an affiliate of the German conglomerate Veba, now makes more than a thousand different types of wafers, each with its own exacting specifications for silicon purity, electrical properties, thickness, surface coatings, and many other characteristics. Typically, chip makers spend months testing various types of wafers, but once they decide to go with a particular wafer, they tend to remain loyal customers for years to come.

Silicon makers have also had to build up considerable proprietary expertise as they have striven to make ever larger wafers over the years. Starting with a diameter of just four inches in the early 1970s, they have moved three times to successively larger diameters. Each move has required a major leap in technology because the larger the wafer, the greater the difficulty in delivering the sort of dimensional perfection required by semiconductor makers.

The standard diameter in the late 1990s was eight inches, but the industry in the last few years has leapt to twelve-inch wafers. Larger wafers are a boon to semiconductor makers because the processing of each wafer involves high setting-up costs that are largely independent of the wafer's size; thus, the larger a wafer is, the lower the setting-up costs per chip. Moreover, the larger wafers reduce the proportion of wasted silicon. (Waste results when the final rectangular chips are cut from the circular wafer, rendering a significant proportion of the area along the perimeter of the wafer unusable; the proportion is considerably larger with smaller wafers.)

Given the level of capital and knowledge needed, virtually all the key processes in the semiconductor-grade silicon industry are conducted by high-wage workers in First World factories. Although Malaysia, China, and other growth-hungry East Asian developing nations have been trying to establish a foothold in the industry, they remain marginal players that perform only the least sophisticated processes. As Heinz Herzer, a director of Wacker's silicon-making subsidiary, points out, moving key operations to a cheap-labor location simply does not make economic sense for a leading-edge player like Wacker. "We need to operate in an advanced economy for several reasons," he says.

> For one thing, a reliable supply of electricity is absolutely essential, and this is hard to find in cheap-labor countries. If there is an electricity blackout, our crucibles would be destroyed: the liquid silicon would solidify and expand and the crucibles' heaters would be damaged beyond repair. If we had just one blackout in a year, the costs would be a lot greater than anything we could save by locating the factory in a low-wage country.

Another key reason for locating in an advanced nation is that the silicon business requires notably high-quality labor. Wacker looks particularly for reliability in its workers, a trait that is hard to find outside advanced First World countries. Germany boasts both a superb high-school education system and a long tradition of disciplined labor. Because of the nature of the silicon business, Wacker demands that its workers be highly disciplined in following rules and procedures. Even in such an apparently lowly function as dispatch, the company holds its workers to enormously high standards—and for good reason. As Herzer points out, sending the wrong wafers to a customer could result in a major business disaster. He explains: "The mistake will probably be discovered only months later, by which time the customer will have not only to write off millions of dollars of finished chips but may have to renege on its promised delivery date to its customers."

All this helps explain why, even though by the late 1990s wages in Germany were the highest of any major country, jobs at Wacker's Burghausen silicon plant—and at an epitaxial operation in nearby Wassenburg—remained secure. Even during the wrenching recessions that have periodically afflicted the electronics industry, Wacker's semiconductor division has never had to resort to layoffs. Quite the contrary. Indeed as of 2002, with the world economy in the doldrums, Wacker's silicon business announced the building of a new plant in Freiburg that would create 600 jobs. In fact, the silicon business has consistently shown strong growth over the years, and its workforce has increased more than tenfold in the last twenty-five years. Similar job growth has been experienced by Japan's silicon makers and, by all accounts, the industry can look forward to many more years of strong growth.

After all, computer engineers have for years aspired to make machines that come close to matching the capabilities of the human brain. They still have an awfully long way to go. As of 2003, the world semiconductor industry's entire output of computer memories represented the memory capacity of fewer than one hundred human brains. Great though the electronics industry's achievements have already been, the world undoubtedly has nowhere near reached satiation in its appetite for silicon.

Let's now look at the next link in the chain of advanced manufacturing processes that have made possible the information revolution—and have created some of the best blue-collar jobs in the world. It is time to visit a state-of-the-art semiconductor factory.

SEMICONDUCTORS:
AN ADVANCE ON MUSHROOM FARMING

When American semiconductor-makers were under strong competitive pressure from fast-expanding Japanese rivals in the mid-1980s, a furious policy debate raged in Washington. For many in the Reagan administration, the appropriate response seemed clear: do nothing. Their position was famously encapsulated in a remark attributed to the top Reagan administration economic adviser Michael Boskin: "Computer chips, wood chips, potato chips. What's the difference? They're all chips." Boskin later denied making this comment, but as Clyde Prestowitz, author of *Trading Places,* pointed out, it accurately summarized the Reagan administration's true attitude on the matter. Reaganites believed that the choice of which goods the United States should or should not produce was best left to the unfettered free market. If American companies found quicker, easier profits in making potato chips or wood chips than computer chips, then this was where the nation's best prospects for prosperity supposedly lay. This attitude represented a green light to take-no-prisoners corporate leaders like Jack Welch of GE and Lou Gerstner of IBM, who in the name of maximizing short-term profits spent the 1990s gutting the United States of many of its remaining high-tech jobs.

So much for ideology. In the real world, there were several flaws in this argument, of which the most obvious was that if the American economy was to remain one of the world's strongest, the United States needed not only profitable corporations but good jobs. The strong case that could be made, from a jobs perspective, for questioning the market's wisdom was made all the stronger by the fact that the profit downturn the American semiconductor makers had suffered stemmed from no fundamental slowdown in the industry's phenomenal growth rate but rather from short-term oversupply problems created by the aggressive expansion of notably farsighted Japanese semiconductor companies. These companies had clearly seen that taking short-term losses would pay off in the long run in greater market share—and better, more productive jobs for their workers.

One thing is clear in hindsight: had the United States abandoned the semiconductor business in the mid-1980s, it would have missed out on enormous subsequent growth. In just the ten years to 1996, worldwide sales of microchips multiplied fivefold to total $132 billion. Although there are no reliable figures for jobs in the semiconductor industry, a good guess is that the industry's total workforce doubled in the period.

All in all, the semiconductor industry has been a superb economic performer in recent years. In few parts of the world is this more evident than in Higashi Hiroshima, a medium-sized Japanese town that is home to one of the world's largest advanced semiconductor fabrication plants.

Measuring four hundred meters long and about thirty meters high, the plant is located in a semirural setting on the outskirts of the town. This region has seen industrial glory before: it supplied much of feudal Japan's iron and salt. But these days the immediate vicinity is a quiet residential district. Just beyond is scenic countryside dotted with traditional tile-roofed farm cottages. From the workers' canteen, you look out on a picture-window view of woods and mountains. There is not even a hint of other industrial activity in sight. All in all, the area looks more like the setting for a pricey ski resort than for one of the world's most massively capitalized factories.

The plant is operated by NEC, which for many years has ranked as one of the world's largest maker of semiconductors. By comparison with America's leading semiconductor maker, Intel, NEC is a more interesting company to look at because it has based its success almost entirely on world-leading manufacturing skills, whereas Intel's growth has come largely from a so-called market lock-in—its virtual monopoly in making chips for Wintel-standard computers.*

When this writer visited Higashi Hiroshima in the late 1990s, NEC had just finished building a new extension full of state-of-the-art manufacturing technology. The extension, code-named A2, was expected to lead the world in mass-producing chips with lines as thin as 0.25 microns—one-quarter of one-millionth of a meter. This was an important advance on the semiconductor industry's previous mass-

---

* The Wintel standard denotes computers which use Intel microprocessors and Microsoft's Windows operating system.

production best of 0.28 microns, and it paved the way for NEC to pioneer the production of 256-megabit memories. Each of these packs enough capacity to store Shakespeare's complete works four times over. These memories, which became widely used in the first years of the new century, are four times more powerful than the state-of-the-art 64-megabit memories that were just entering the mass-production stage as of 1998.

Perhaps the most impressive thing about A2 was its price tag—a cool $630 million. It is a good example of the pattern for Japanese companies to make their largest investments at home—a pattern reflected in the fact that though NEC operates more semiconductor factories abroad than in Japan, fully two-thirds of all the investment capital it pours into its worldwide semiconductor business each year goes to domestic operations. Given that the additional workforce NEC needs to operate the A2 facility totals fewer than 500, each worker is backed by more than $1.4 million of capital—or about 140 times the investment needed to create each new job in the Indian software industry. And this takes account merely of the capital tied up in physical assets. Additionally, workers at Higashi Hiroshima are backed by billions of dollars' worth of proprietary know-how, which NEC has painstakingly accumulated over a period of two decades at the leading edge of the semiconductor industry.

Clearly the Higashi Hiroshima plant is a classic example of manufacturing's ability to create superb First World jobs. Moreover, in common with other manufacturing operations, the plant has created an excellent range of jobs: nearly 80 percent of NEC's Higashi Hiroshima workers are mere high-school graduates, a considerably higher proportion than in the Japanese workforce as a whole. Perhaps the best thing about the Higashi Hiroshima plant is the pay: For a 50-year-old worker, wages plus bonuses came to well over $60,000 a year as of the late 1990s.

The plant also illustrates the tremendous growth that is possible in a leading-edge manufacturing business. Founded in 1988, the plant has been in an almost constant state of frenzied expansion ever since—an expansion that at last count brought the total work force to 1,400, up from just 300 initially. Since nearly 60 percent of the workforce has been hired locally, the effect has been to transform prospects in the local employment market, where previously agriculture was the fundamental source of jobs. In fact, other than silicon chips, the area's most notable product is *matsutake* mushrooms, which grow under pine trees and are a characteristic flavoring ingredient in traditional Japanese cuisine. The evidence of the 1990s is that the job prospects are better in semiconductors than in mushrooms—not to mention wood chips or potato chips.

LET THERE BE LASERS:
LIGHT AS AN ALL-PURPOSE TOOL

Next to computer chips, the most important enabling components of the electronic revolution are undoubtedly lasers and other high-tech light-emitting devices. In contrast with computer chips, however, the highly advanced and important business of manufacturing laser devices gets little attention in the media. This is perhaps understandable given the laser industry's amazing diversity. There are hundreds of different types of laser devices, made from widely different materials and used in highly varied applications. Even in their physical dimensions, lasers are startlingly varied. Many are tiny, sometimes no bigger than a pinhead. Others are as big as a room—one experimental laser developed at Stanford University in the 1980s, for instance, ran to forty feet in length.

The one thing they all have in common is that they create a highly homogenized form of light. Whereas a ray of sunlight consists of a mixture of widely different wavelengths, a laser emits "coherent" light—that is, light whose wavelengths are contained within one narrow band.

Laser technology has created a host of manufacturing opportunities for high-tech companies in many advanced nations. In Germany, for instance, manufacturers are particularly strong in laser-based cutting devices, which in various forms are now widely used everywhere from shipyards to hospital operating theaters. The Germans are also leaders in laser-based welding devices, which, like the cutting devices, harness the ability of gas-based lasers to concentrate energy in a very focused way. This ability is a major advantage in dealing with metals that boast both high heat conductivity and a high melting point. Aluminum, for example, was notoriously difficult to weld effectively until lasers came along. The problem is that applying heat to any point on a sheet of aluminum is a bit like pouring water into a sieve; the heat dissipates rapidly throughout the sheet, thus making it difficult, with prelaser welding techniques, to raise the temperature of the area targeted for welding. Lasers are more effective than traditional heating methods because they apply massive amounts of heat very rapidly to the targeted area. Laser welding devices are often huge and typically use such lasing mediums as carbon dioxide or nitrogen. Among German laser companies, notable players include Lambda Physik and Trumpf.

In the United States, too, several high-tech manufacturers have developed important laser-based businesses. A key example is San Diego–based Cymer, which has pioneered the manufacture of the highly sophisticated laser-based etching devices used in state-of-the-art steppers for the semiconductor industry. Spectraphysics and Coherent have established important positions in argon-based lasers. Another notable American player in the laser business is Perceptron, which specializes in making laser-based measuring devices.

To see the potential of the laser industry to full advantage as a source of excellent jobs and strong exports, however, it is necessary to look beyond developments in the United States and Germany to Japan. The Japanese are key players in several of the most important areas of the laser business. They are strong in cutting devices, for instance. They are also leaders in laser-based precision instruments. Tokyo-based Komatsu, for instance, is now challenging Cymer in making lasers for the stepper industry. But perhaps the ultimate success story of the Japanese laser industry is Sony Corporation, whose recent experience with lasers represents a classic illustration of the economic virtues of advanced manufacturing.

Sony's specialty is laser diodes, a product category it entirely dominates worldwide. Laser diodes are tiny devices that are most familiar as the enabling components in compact disk players, CD-ROMs, and digital videodisc players. They are also crucial in laser printers. Even more important, they are key components in the telecommunications industry, where they are used to send pulses of light through optical fiber networks. As Paul Saffo, an analyst with the Institute for the Future in Menlo Park, California, has pointed out, laser diodes are in fact the ultimate driver of the telecommunications revolution.

In the circumstances, Sony's leadership of the laser diode business constitutes a classic tale of the economic virtues of advanced manufacturing. Sony got its start in the industry as recently as the early 1980s and has been on a path of breakneck growth ever since. On the strength of an estimated threefold increase in its factory workforce, it has expanded its monthly output from less than 300,000 units in 1982 to fourteen million units in 1998. This amounts to a phenomenal sixteenfold increase in labor productivity, and it has been powered in large part by Sony's success in maximizing its "yield"—the proportion of flaw-free units in its total production. In laser diodes, as in other electronic components, yield is a crucial determinant in that, in the absence of ultrastrict quality controls, as much as 90 percent of a factory's output may have to be scrapped because of defects. As we pointed out in Chapter 1, one well-known technique for improving yield is to filter the factory air to remove all but the most minute particles of dust and other contaminants. But in truth, many of the secrets of improving a factory's yield are highly elusive and can be discovered only by a careful, laborious process of trial and error.

The scale of the difficulties in this field is nicely illustrated by a story often told in the Japanese electronics industry. As the story goes, a semiconductor factory was suffering notably erratic yield levels: sometimes the yield of good products was very high, sometimes very low. The problem baffled engineers for months until a humble factory-floor worker noticed a correlation between poor yields and the local train schedule. Subsequent inquiries proved that minute vibrations from passing trains were periodically playing havoc with the production process. The story may be apocryphal (it is hard to imagine the sort of razor-sharp engineers who run Japan's semiconductor factories not checking for vibrations at an early stage in their investigations), but it illustrates in microcosm the wide diversity of factors that must be considered in identifying the causes of yield problems.

Not surprisingly, the know-how needed to maximize yields is among the most closely guarded secrets in advanced manufacturing. Not only does Sony decline to enter into any discussion of its yield-maximizing know-how, but it carefully restricts entry to its laser diode factories. We do know, however, that a team of top engineers led by the Sony general manager Osamu Kumagai has raised the company's yield to well over 90 percent in recent years. By comparison, the company achieved a yield of less than 10 percent in the early stages of production in 1982. It is probably no accident that Kumagai is one of the world's foremost experts on gallium arsenide, the advanced semiconductor material that is the key ingredient in Sony's laser diodes.

Sony's yield achievement alone accounts for a nearly fivefold boost in labor productivity. On top of this, the company has achieved other major productivity improvements thanks, for instance, to massive investments in robot-driven automation systems.

As a result, Sony has cut its prices by more than 90 percent since the early 1980s. Along the way, the company has implemented a major qualitative improvement in its products by both shrinking their size and boosting their performance. The results can be seen in consumer markets around the world. Sony's success in honing its laser diode production know-how helps explain why CD players are now everywhere—not only in the First and Second Worlds but increasingly even in the Third World. They are evidently far more numerous than the record-players they superseded. Since CD players were first sold in 1982, they have achieved total cumulative sales of a phenomenal 550 million units—one for every ten residents of the planet. Moreover, Sony's success in improving the capabilities of its laser diodes has paved the way for extensions of the product for use in CD-ROMs and digital video disk players (which work off disks that contain more than seven times as much digitized information as ordinary music CDs). The result is that as of the late 1990s, Sony had grabbed a 60 percent share of the $4 billion world market for laser diodes.

It is a market that continues to grow rapidly thanks to breakthroughs both in finding new applications for lasers and in developing better and cheaper lasers. One major breakthrough recently has been in the manufacture of blue lasers. These had hitherto been available only in huge gas-based versions that cost $50,000 each. Now Nichia Chemical Industries of Anan, Japan, has developed tiny blue laser diodes based on the semiconducting material gallium nitride that are expected eventually to be mass-produced for less than $2 a piece.

For the laser industry, this represents a major landmark because, among other things, blue light has a much shorter wavelength than red, the color of most laser diodes manufactured thus far. A shorter wavelength enables a laser diode to read smaller marks on CD platters; if blue lasers become widely available, they will enable the information industry to pack four to five times as much information onto CD platters. This is just the beginning of the possibilities for blue lasers. Engineers believe that down the road blue lasers may play a crucial role in a host of applications, in everything from color fax machines and copiers to ultrahigh-capacity optical fiber networks.

Already blue light–emitting diodes, which are simpler devices than lasers but work off the same basic chemical breakthroughs, are being made in mass-production volumes and have opened a host of opportunities for new products. A key point is that blue is one of the three primary colors. Since cheap green and red lasers are already available, the development of cheap blue light-emitting devices completes the color "palette." One immediate result is to make possible the development of vast outdoor television screens made up of millions of light-emitting diodes.

In another application, arrays of light-emitting diodes that produce white light may soon be used to replace traditional lightbulbs in many applications. As noted by Gerhard Fasol, a Tokyo-based scientist who has coauthored a book on the blue laser with the blue laser inventor Shuji Nakamura, the traditional lightbulb is based on a century-old technology. Unlike its first cousin, the radio valve, the ordinary lightbulb has not succumbed yet to the semiconductor revolution. But with the development of cheap blue lasers and light-emitting diodes, the lightbulb's days may be numbered. One application in which light-emitting diodes are already beginning to replace lightbulbs is in traffic lights. "Bulbs are very inefficient for traffic lights," says Fasol. "The reason is that much of the energy they consume is emitted as invisible infrared rays and is dissipated as heat. In the case of a yellow lamp, perhaps only one-tenth of the energy consumed creates visible light. Light-emitting diodes are more efficient in that more of the energy they use goes directly to creating light."

In Fasol's estimate, a move to light-emitting diodes would cut the energy costs of traffic lights by 75 percent. Moreover, the new traffic lights promise huge savings in maintenance costs because light-emitting diodes last at least twenty times longer than lightbulbs, and at the end of their lives they fade out gradually, rather than failing suddenly. Thus, not only would replacements be needed much less frequently, but they could be organized on a regular schedule that would make much more efficient use of maintenance workers' time.

For now, Nichia is claiming the lead in mass-producing the blue laser diode. But other companies are racing to develop rival products, most notably an affiliate of the Toyota Motor group. Either way, it seems that further extensions of the laser diode concept are likely to continue to create jobs mainly in Japan.

In fact, the laser diode business's heavy concentration in ultrahigh-wage Japan is perhaps the best illustration of this book's proposition that high wages rarely constitute a significant competitive disadvantage in advanced manufacturing industries. And, of course, other parts of the world where the laser manufacturing business is strong are also noted for high wages. Germany, for instance, is hardly a low-wage location. Neither is Santa Clara, where Coherent, one of the largest U.S. players is based. Ditto for San Diego, home to Cymer.

As for job security, the industry's evidently explosive growth prospects bode well for the future. Certainly, new applications are being found for lasers all the time, and most of these applications play to the existing, highly secret know-how of the industry's incumbents.

The last word on the prospects should come from Sergey Krayushkin, a top Russian laser expert. He draws an analogy with the history of magnets. Magnets have been around for many hundreds of years, yet people still keep inventing new applications for them. He comments, "Lasers have been around less than forty years so we are really just at the beginning."

INTIMATIONS OF THE NEXT BIG THING

So far in our look at the electronics industry we have focused on production machinery, materials, and components. In concluding our analysis, it is time to look at final consumer products. It is the pace of innovation in new consumer products that ultimately is the industry's main engine of growth.

In the last few decades alone, we have seen the introduction of an enormous spate of blockbuster electronic products—most notably videocassette recorders, camcorders, compact disk players, fax machines, and, of course, personal computers.

It is a spate that shows no signs of drying up. In recent years a wealth of recently developed products like cellular phones, digital cameras, and high-speed modems have made the explosive transition from the early-adopter stage to mass-market acceptance. Meanwhile, many fascinating new products are likely to break through by the end of the first decade of the twenty-first century. Examples include car navigation equipment and robot vacuum cleaners, which indeed are already being marketed to early adopters in Japan. Also on the horizon are intelligent kitchens complete with intelligent talking refrigerators (that will tell you, for instance, when you are running low on milk).

The growth opportunities generated for manufacturers of everything from semiconductor silicon to laser diodes are clearly huge. But in terms of manufacturing opportunities, probably none of the recently developed consumer products packs more potential than digital television. In concluding our review of the electronics industry, therefore, we will take a closer look at the enormous economic possibilities just this one new consumer product presages for the electronics industry.

In its most advanced form, digital television delivers high-definition images that provide up to six times as much detail as conventional television. The result is wonderfully sharp pictures that promise soon to do to conventional color television what color television did to black-and-white a generation ago. Certainly most experts sense that at the right price, almost everyone will want high-definition television's movie-style picture quality.

That said, the huge potential importance of high-definition television (HDTV) has so far been obscured by some unfortunate missteps in the concept's introduction. In particular, high-definition has got off to a disappointing start in Japan. A pioneering version has been operated by NHK, the Japanese national broadcasting company, since the late 1980s, but even in the first years of the new century, sales of HDTV sets in Japan were still languishing at derisory levels.

The NHK system's disappointing showing is highly misleading, however, in that it stems from special factors that do not speak to the concept's general potential. NHK moved too early and in so doing backed the wrong technological horse. It went with an old-fashioned analog version of high-definition that had been in development in Japan since the 1960s. Just as NHK launched its system, breakthroughs in video compression in the United States suddenly rendered it more or less obsolete. These breakthroughs made it feasible for broadcasters to abandon analog technology and move decisively into the digital era. Although digital HDTV does not deliver an appreciably better picture than Japan's analog standard (in fact it is generally admitted that digital pictures are somewhat inferior to analog ones), it boasts other advantages that clearly give it an enormous market edge in the long run. One key advantage is that digital television sets can readily be made compatible with other digital devices, most notably personal computers. Thus, digital HDTV has opened up many exciting opportunities to blend pin-sharp vision with superfast computing.

Once the feasibility of a digital approach became obvious around 1990, Japanese television set makers lost faith in NHK's analog standard and did little to push sales of analog HDTV sets.

As of 2003, however, their moment seemed finally to have arrived, as NHK began rolling out a highly advanced new system known as "digital terrestrial television" (DTTV). This provides a highly advanced signal system that allows broadcasters great flexibility in serving viewers. One choice is to use the available bandwidth to transmit full HDTV pictures. Alternatively, broadcasters can broadcast several different standard-definition channels where before they could broadcast only one. DTTV also allows for television channels to be viewed on personal computers. Using a split-screen format, a computer user can even surf the Web while watching television. Moreover, DTTV eliminates the need to buy new adapters and other hardware to keep up with broadcasting breakthroughs. Instead DTTV viewers can download software that will update their receivers for new services whenever needed.

In the United States, too, the story is that after many disappointments, HDTV seemed finally, as of this writing (2003), to be on the verge of general acceptance. Its progress had previously been stymied by squabbles between interested parties, notably one dating back to the 1980s about how to share the available broadcast spectrum between the telecommunications industry and the broadcasting industry.

Moreover, in common with other entertainment innovations before it, HDTV has been greatly hindered in the United States by a simple chicken-and-egg problem. On the one hand, profit-conscious broadcasters have not been prepared to put out much HDTV programming before viewers are equipped to receive it; on the other hand, because there has been so little programming, viewers have had little incentive to invest in the expensive new receivers. Nonetheless, thanks in part to regulatory imperatives, HDTV broadcasts began to become widely available in the first years of the new century. As recorded by Jon Healey of the *Los Angeles Times,* more than 80 percent of viewers in the United States were within reach of at least one digital channel by 2002. And in many cities there was already plenty of choice—as many as 10 digital channels in Los Angeles, for instance.

Even so, HDTV will probably take several years to win broad consumer acceptance. In the meantime, several things must happen. Most important, the cost of sets will have to continue to fall. Priced originally at around $10,000 in the early 1990s, typical HDTV sets had dropped to around $4,000 by the end of the 1990s. As of 2003, low-end models had broken through the $1,000 price point and thus seemed poised for an explosive growth in sales.

Further price reductions seemed to be in the pipeline. In principle, there is no reason why the industry cannot reduce prices dramatically once the American broadcasting industry achieves critical mass in the amount of high-definition programming material it puts out. From that point on, increased sales volume would enable manufacturers to spread their fixed costs over more units, thus making possible significant price reductions, which in turn would generate further increases in volume, leading to even deeper price reductions. Given that an exceptionally high proportion of the total cost of making HDTV sets consists of up-front research and development spending, manufacturers enjoy tremendous scope to cut prices once they achieve sufficiently high levels of volume.

With luck, therefore, HDTV could reach critical mass by the middle of the first decade of the twenty-first century. Who, therefore, will garner the lion's share of the spoils? Japanese manufacturers in particular seem well positioned to profit from the changeover. Take Mitsubishi Electric. It was the only manufacturer to have HDTV sets in American stores when the official U.S. move to digital television began in late 1998. Then, in the spring of 2002, Mitsubishi again led the industry by boldly announcing that it would no longer make analog sets but only digital ones.

Mitsubishi is only the most aggressive of the several Japanese manufacturers who have led the charge in HDTV. Their leadership has come as a surprise to many observers who had earlier portrayed Japan as lagging in high-definition technology. In reality, however, the Japanese lagged merely in the standard their own national broadcasting company had chosen for the home market. Japan's domestic standard is, of course, largely irrelevant to the Japanese television set industry's export prowess. In fact, Japanese set makers have long been renowned for their ability to tailor their products to meet widely varying broadcast standards in different export markets. In any case, most of the manufacturing work involved is largely the same, irrespective of whether the sets are geared to receive digital or analog signals.

One thing is certain: there will be plenty of business to go around. Already manufacturers in Europe and the United States as well as in Japan are gearing up for a bonanza. Important opportunities await not only makers of sets and components but makers of materials and manufacturing equipment.

The semiconductor industry alone is set to enjoy a field day. The new sets require not only powerful memory chips and microprocessors but many specialized chips such as digital signal processors. Speaking in the late 1990s, John Stich of Texas Instruments estimated that each HDTV set then required between $250 and $350 worth of semiconductors. Thus, as Stich pointed out, the semiconductor industry was in line to generate fully 60 percent as much revenue from a typical HDTV as from a high-end personal computer. Given that HDTV is likely eventually to achieve much broader market penetration than high-end personal computers, the outlook for the semiconductor industry is clearly encouraging.

HDTV will also create a big new market for makers of miscellaneous components, such as speakers, channel changers, and set-top cable equipment. There is even a likely bonanza here for the laser diode industry. Although laser diodes will not participate directly in the boom (because they are not required in stand-alone television sets), they will benefit indirectly as the crucial enabling components in new high-definition digital versatile disk players. These complements to HDTV sets are expected to achieve major sales.

Probably the most interesting manufacturing opportunities will be for makers of screens. As yet, no manufacturer has come up with a completely satisfactory screen technology to make the most of the new medium. For the moment, the screen technology of choice remains the venerable cathode-ray tube, the technology that has dominated the television industry since the 1940s. This plays directly to the interests of Japanese corporations, which have long dominated the cathode-ray tube industry. Sony and Toshiba in particular have fully mastered the technologies involved in making HDTV-standard cathode-ray tubes. (They have already been making similar tubes for many years for use as high-end monitors in the computer industry.)

But there is a problem here: to savor high-definition in its full glory, the screen should be as big as sixty inches. Although it is technically possible to make cathode-ray tubes that large, they are not an ideal solution because they are too bulky for most living rooms.

The television set industry is therefore working on several less bulky screen technologies. One alternative is the liquid-crystal display, which boasts the key advantage of being a flat panel that typically is only about one inch thick. But given present levels of manufacturing technology, liquid-crystal displays are disproportionately difficult to mass-produce in large sizes. Moreover, they fall well short of the cathode-ray tube in picture quality: not only are they generally less bright, but they are not as effective in keeping up with fast-action images.

In the search for a successor to the cathode-ray tube, therefore, many electronics companies are developing new types of flat-panel displays that do not suffer the disadvantages of liquid crystal. The most advanced contender so far is the so-called plasma display. Like a liquid-crystal display, this is a flat panel. In picture quality, it comes close to matching the best cathode-ray tubes. Unfortunately, however, despite its slim appearance, a plasma display is exceedingly heavy (often weighing as much as 200 pounds). Thus, it cannot safely be hung on the wall of a typical living room. Its weight is a function of the fact that the screen must be divided into thousands of separately addressed chambers, each enclosed in its own glass housing. Because a plasma display also demands a great deal of power, it emits a lot of unwelcome heat. Moreover, plasma displays, like large liquid-crystal displays, are difficult to mass-produce and thus are extremely expensive. Although manufacturers of plasma displays will undoubtedly cut prices as volumes increase, it seems unlikely that they will ever get their manufacturing costs down to the low levels that prevail in the cathode-ray tube industry.

In view of all the problems with the various existing screen technologies, there is clearly a major market opportunity for an innovative approach. The hiatus is seen by some American engineers as a chance for the United States to make a comeback in display technologies after a long fallow spell in which the Japanese have effortlessly led the field in all three proven technologies—cathode-ray tubes, liquid-crystal displays, and plasma displays.

For the foreseeable future, however, the main contender will remain the plain-vanilla cathode-ray tube. Most of the early sets are likely to feature cathode-ray tubes with screens manageably sized in the thirty- to forty-inch range. The bet is that this formula will provide an attractive enough picture to propel the early stages of the concept's market acceptance.

How big could the HDTV industry become? An educated guess is that it could be generating at least $20 billion in annual sales by 2010. Meanwhile, the market for broadcast equipment, satellite dishes, and other ancillary products could add another $15 billion to $20 billion.

Given prospects like these, it is fair to say as we conclude our look at the electronics industry that its best years are still in the future. Of course, this is not to say that all the technologies we have reviewed here are likely to enjoy boundless growth forever. But the electronics industry is nothing if not resourceful, and its incumbents have a long record of success in evolving new technologies when existing ones have run their course. Certainly electronics is a classic growth industry. And given how difficult it generally is to break into this industry (in that its more advanced areas require disproportionately high levels of both capital and know-how), it clearly constitutes a showcase of the economic advantages of manufacturing in creating jobs and highly exportable products.

But as postindustrialists are quick to point out, not all manufacturing industries offer such rosy growth prospects. In fact, many manufacturing industries are quite mature, and their growth prospects are correspondingly curtailed. But are such industries dinosaurs, as the postindustrialists suggest? In most cases, no. As we will now see, some of the oldest manufacturing industries remain pillars of some of the world's richest economies. It is time to look at some golden oldies.

CHAPTER 6

It is often assumed that just as people have life cycles, so too do industries. An industry starts as an infant, grows rapidly, becomes mature—and then it dies. Or so conventional wisdom has it.

But is death really as inevitable for industries as for people? Hardly. In fact, some of the world's oldest manufacturing industries have shown remarkable resilience over the years, and even in the twenty-first century, they continue to make important contributions to the world's prosperity.

Take the ceramics industry. With a history dating back to ancient China, it is assuredly an old industry. Yet, even in the late twentieth century it continues to set a fast pace in product innovation—a pace so fast in fact that several leading ceramics companies have carved out vital positions for themselves in high-tech industries. Kyoto-based Kyocera, for instance, has increased its sales more than 170 percent in the last ten years, largely on the strength of a dominant position in supplying high-tech ceramic packaging to the world semiconductor industry. Other ceramics makers have developed new heat-resistant materials that are essential in everything from jet engines to power-station turbines. Ceramics makers are also playing a vital role in the growing pollution-control industry, most notably in making the key materials in the catalytic converters that minimize noxious emissions in automobile exhaust gases.

Similarly, with a history almost as old as that of ceramics, the glass industry maintains a steady pace of innovation that has kept it at the fore-front of technological progress in the late twentieth century. For example, the special forms of glass used in making steppers, as described in Chapter 5, are vital for the semiconductor industry. Elsewhere in the glass industry, the venerable Corning company, among others, has played a key enabling role in the telecommunications revolution with its devel-opment of the highly sophisticated forms of glass used in fiber optics.

Another notably mature industry that continues to thrive even in the late twentieth century is printing equipment. Admittedly, this fact has been somewhat obscured by the disappearance of several once world-beating U.S. printing-equipment makers. But far from reflecting a gen-eral decline in demand for printing equipment, their fate stems entirely from a failure to keep up with changing technology.

Their Japanese rivals, by contrast, have been adept at riding the techno-logical tiger and as a result have gone from strength to strength. A notable example is Japan's Mitsubishi Heavy Industries, which is now a world leader in the huge high-speed presses used in the newspaper industry. In fact, these days even the *Washington Post* is printed on Mitsubishi machines.

Perhaps the ultimate proof of the printing equipment industry's enduring strength is in Germany. The Germans, after all, have been lead-ers in printing technology since Gutenberg's time more than five cen-turies ago. They still are. Such German companies as Roland and König & Bauer-Albert are major suppliers of presses to the world's newspaper companies. As the dominant maker of printing presses for magazines, Heidelberger Druckmaschinen ranks as the world's largest maker of printing equipment. Employing 21,000 people, most of them in Germany, it derives more than 80 percent of its sales from foreign markets—and thus is a classic illustration of how strongly manufacturing can bolster a nation's balance of payments. And even in these days of such vaunted "paperless" media as CD-ROM encyclopedias and Internet databases, the chairman of Heidelberger Druckmaschinen, Hartmut Mehdorn, is facing the future with confidence. "The world needs printed goods," he says. "No electronic media will kick printing out. Advertising will go on, packaging will go on, newspapers will go on." Mehdorn believes the industry will continue to show decent growth for many years to come—and will certainly outpace most service industries.

Admittedly, a common characteristic of even the most economically significant of the world's mature manufacturing industries is a pattern of declining employment. But this hardly justifies the postindustrialists' portrayal of such industries as "deadbeats," let alone "dinosaurs." Far from being a drag on the overall economy, these industries are actually, on balance, major contributors to economic growth. And it is precisely because they have reduced their labor requirements in recent years that they have done so much to spur growth. Remember that the key to economic growth is to make more with less; in this respect, reducing the labor input per unit of output is even more important than reducing material inputs. These industries' job cuts are simply the flip side of their success in boosting labor productivity.

Of course, this does not gainsay the fact that the dislocation caused by job cuts can be painful. But in a well-managed economy, the effects of such dislocation can be minimized by, for instance, ensuring that most if not all job losses result from attrition rather than layoffs. And as the Japanese experience has repeatedly demonstrated, attrition is a feasible remedy provided that an industry plans sufficiently far ahead. But even when layoffs are unavoidable, these are generally preferable to the wholesale abandonment of mature industries advocated by the postindustrialists.

The postindustrialists view their slash-and-burn approach to old industries as "creative destruction," but in fact, it is far more destructive than creative. Sacrificing a whole industry because it has become a little overstaffed makes no more sense than chopping down a fine apple tree because it has become a little overgrown.

In the rest of this chapter, we will take a detailed look at the hidden virtues of three mature manufacturing industries that are particularly scorned by the postindustrialists—shipbuilding, textiles, and steel. Let's be clear. These industries have their problems, and they are, therefore, hardly our strongest examples of the merits of manufacturing. Nonetheless, as we will see, the postindustrialists are utterly wrong in advocating the indiscriminate shutdown of such industries.

SINK OR SWIM?:
WISE SHIPBUILDERS MAKE THEIR OWN LUCK

Probably no important manufacturing industry has been written off so often as shipbuilding. Predictions of the wholesale demise of the First World shipbuilding industry have been a commonplace of Western economic discussions since at least as far back as the mid-1970s. Yet, nearly a generation later, the First World continues to account for nearly 70 percent of all new tonnage launched each year—and for close to 100 percent of the world market in many of the industry's most sophisticated subsectors.

Although business was notably slow in many areas of shipbuilding as of 2003, the industry's merits should not be judged on its performance during a bad patch. Certainly, those who in previous downturns chose to write off the industry's future have been repeatedly confounded. Take the long shipbuilding slump in the latter half of the 1970s and the early 1980s. While this slump was painful, it hardly signaled the industry's demise. The problem was merely a huge hangover of excess shipping capacity built up during the hectic boom that preceded the oil crisis of the mid-1970s. It took several years for the resulting shipping capacity glut to clear. But clear it finally did.

In fact, shipbuilders have enjoyed generally rising demand since the 1980s. And for good reason: the world needs ships. Shipping capacity grows in line with world trade, which in turn grows in line with rising living standards, especially in the developing world. Reflecting quickly rising living standards in developing countries, demand has grown particularly in recent decades for bulk carriers to ship key commodities around the world. Measured in terms of the industry's standard tonne/mile yardstick, coal shipments, for instance, have nearly quadrupled since 1970, iron ore shipments have nearly doubled, and grain shipments have increased by about one-half. The result is that, according to figures compiled by *Fearnleys Review,* an Oslo-based shipping publication, the world's shipping fleet has more than doubled since 1970.

Another factor that has encouraged postindustrial commentators to take an overly cautious view of the First World shipbuilding industry has been the rise of low-wage competition. In particular, South Korean shipyards have been remarkably successful in boosting their market share in the last three decades. To the postindustrialists, this is an indication of how far the shipbuilding industry has "fallen" in terms of industrial sophistication in recent years. But the real message is quite different. In reality, South Korea's rise reflects how far that nation has advanced. Thus, the postindustrialists are profoundly wrong in imagining that South Korea's rise presages a general migration of the shipbuilding industry to the Third World. The fact is that South Korea is the only developing country that has had any success in becoming a significant force in shipbuilding in recent decades. That more developing countries have not broken into the industry is hardly surprising given the formidable barriers that would-be entrants face. Just the most obvious barrier is capital. South Korea raised the enormous amounts of capital needed to get established in the industry by enforcing tough economic policies that few other developing nations would dare to impose on their citizens. Another barrier is that the industry requires large amounts of special production know-how. South Korea was lucky in this regard: thanks to various mutually advantageous partnerships with Japanese shipbuilders, it received important transfers of midlevel Japanese production technology.

In any case, the South Koreans' success is actually much exaggerated. They continue to lag in labor productivity, particularly in comparison with the Japanese, who for years have been investing heavily in highly automated production processes. At the big Kure yard near Hiroshima, for instance, no less than sixteen huge robots work tirelessly handling such major assembly operations as fitting and welding. Thanks to investments like this, Japanese shipyard workers are about twice as productive in welding and four times as productive in cutting and painting as their Korean counterparts. Thus, as recounted by the Tokyo-based shipbuilding expert Seiji Nagatsuka, Japanese shipbuilders require only about half as much manpower to build a typical oil tanker as the Koreans. Given that shipbuilding is a capital-intensive industry in which wages account for only one-quarter to one-third of total costs, the Japanese remain highly competitive despite paying wage rates about three times Korean levels.

Aside from superior productivity, another way in which more advanced nations have met the Korean challenge has been by specializing in the more sophisticated subsectors of the industry, where the South Koreans lack the expertise to compete effectively. Several major Japanese shipbuilders, for instance, lead the world in making ships' engines and components for such engines. This is a great business given that the engine can account for as much as 10 percent of the total cost of a ship. The Japanese are also the world's leading source for ship navigation equipment, marine electricity generators, and the superpowerful pumping equipment used in oil tankers.

Meanwhile, various European shipbuilders have withstood the Korean challenge by concentrating on especially sophisticated vessels. Finland has been a standout in this regard as a leading maker of both luxury liners and ice-breakers. European shipbuilders have also become big suppliers of offshore oil-drilling equipment. This has proven to be a godsend in particular for Belfast-based Harland and Wolff. After suffering a near-death experience in oil tankers in the 1970s, Harland and Wolff has now exited the shipbuilding industry to concentrate on oil rigs and related equipment. Although the company is a mere shadow of its former self (in its glory days as the world's most advanced shipyard, it built the *Titanic*), it boasts important expertise in various technologies that have enabled the oil industry to drill in ever deeper water. As recently as the 1970s, offshore oil producers were rarely capable of operating in water more than six hundred fifty-six feet deep, but these days can operate in fifteen times that depth.

In Japan too, product innovation has been a key strategy in responding successfully to the Korean challenge. Japanese shipyards have led the industry, for instance, in developing liquid natural gas carriers. These are highly sophisticated vessels that require, among other things, advanced refrigeration equipment and super-reliable safety systems. The Japanese have also pioneered the introduction of double-hulled oil tankers, which are designed to minimize the risk of disastrous leaks of oil following collisions and other mishaps.

In common with other Japanese manufacturing industries, the Japanese shipbuilding industry is constantly scanning the horizon for opportunities to create innovative products. Here are some key areas where Japanese shipbuilders have recently been concentrating their research and development spending:

Wave power electricity-generating plants: Under the guidance of the Japanese government, Japanese shipbuilders are developing special vessels that will harness wave power as a new environmentally friendly source of energy. They have already built a working prototype, the *Mighty Whale*, which has demonstrated the idea's viability in certain specialized uses such as powering coastal fish farms and water purification facilities.

Faster ships: Japanese shipbuilding engineers are developing dramatically faster ships that not only offer greater speed for passengers but enable operators to get more work out of their fleets. An early example of Japan's new generation of fast ships is a high-speed car ferry launched by Mitsubishi Heavy Industries in 1997. Built according to a relatively conventional steel-based design, it achieves a top speed of nearly fifty miles an hour and cruises at forty miles an hour. It can thus cut journey times by as much as one-half compared to earlier car ferries. Now Japan's naval architects are leveraging aerodynamic techniques learned from the airplane industry to develop new catamaran-style and hydrofoil vessels that will achieve even greater speeds. A team led by Kawasaki Heavy Industries, for instance, is developing high-speed cargo ships that will cruise at nearly sixty miles an hour—three times as fast as the most modern conventional cargo vessels. Perhaps the ultimate dream in the high-speed genre is superconductivity-driven ships, which are now being developed as part of a national research project. The aim is to build ships with cruising speeds of 100 miles an hour or more.

Floating airports: These are being mooted by Japanese ship-builders as an elegant way to relieve chronic congestion at many of the world's airports. The idea is to create new airports that float in the sea near major coastal cities. These airports would rest on thousands of huge, shallow-bottomed pontoons made from a special new corrosion-resistant type of steel. The pontoons would be locked together to create so-called mega-floats. One key advantage of floating airports is that they can minimize noise pollution by ensuring that takeoffs and landings are routed over water. These airports could be towed to other locations if necessary, and they would save, of course, on land acquisition costs—a crucial consideration for many major East Asian cities that are chronically short of space. They would be invulnerable to earthquakes and, so long as they were not sited in shallow inshore water, to tsunamis. Moreover, variants on the mega-float idea are being promoted as environmentally desirable solutions for siting many other infrastructural facilities such as container berths, oil storage facilities, power-generation plants, and waste disposal facilities.

The message of all this innovation is clear. For all the postindustrialists' gloom, the shipbuilding industry is not only alive and well but likely to remain a significant provider of high-wage manufacturing jobs for many years to come. Certainly, its record so far has been impressive. Moreover, not only has the shipbuilding industry survived as a First World activity, but it remains particularly strong in precisely those First World nations where wages are highest. Take Denmark. With a per capita income in 2003 about equal to that of the United States, Denmark boasts one of Europe's largest shipbuilding industries.

Or take Singapore, where per capita incomes at market exchange rates are about two-thirds American levels. Singapore's shipbuilding output in some recent years has been more than seven times that of the United States. In many ways, Singapore's performance is even more striking compared with that of the United Kingdom, a nation that for historical and geographic reasons has always been a bigger player in shipbuilding than the United States. By the late 1990s, Singapore's shipbuilding output had surpassed that of Britain. Rubbing salt in the wounds for the British is the fact that wages in Singapore in 2000 were as high as in the United Kingdom. What a turnaround compared to the early 1950s, when the United Kingdom, then a notably high-wage economy, dominated the world shipbuilding industry and Singapore, then a low-wage British colony, was known mainly for doing repair work for the Royal Navy.

Of course, the real eye-opener for those who maintain that shipbuilding can no longer support First World jobs is Japan. As should be abundantly apparent by now, Japan has doggedly maintained its lead as the world's largest and most successful shipbuilding nation despite paying some of the world's highest wages. The result is that as of the late 1990s Japanese shipbuilders and their suppliers employed more than 100,000 workers, many of them in such affluent places as Yokohama, Kobe, and Nagasaki.

Few postindustrialists can be more surprised by all this than the noted postindustrialist John Naisbitt, who in his book *Megatrends* predicted that Japan would soon be toppled as the world's dominant shipbuilder by Brazil. That was in 1982. As of 2003, Naisbitt has been confounded twice over. First, of course, by the Japanese, who boosted their output by fully 20 percent in the interim. Meanwhile, Brazil has remained a negligible player in the industry.

Evidently, the idea that shipbuilding was destined to become a Third World activity was less a megatrend than a megablooper.

A STITCH IN TIME:
THE WORLD'S OLDEST INDUSTRY INVESTS FOR TOMORROW

The textile industry is probably the world's oldest manufacturing industry. Certainly, it can claim to be one of the first industries in which full-scale machines, as opposed to simple tools such as axes and knives, were put to use in boosting human productivity. Both the spinning wheel and the cotton gin, for instance, go back to ancient India. Silk was produced on an industrial scale in China five thousand years ago. And weaving machines were used by the Egyptians even earlier.

As of the beginning of the twenty-first century, therefore, the textile industry is undeniably mature. But does this mean that the postindustrialists are right to suggest that its glory days as a mainstay of First World employment are over? Hardly. In truth, the postindustrialists' dim view of the textile industry is based on an entirely superficial view of what the industry does. When they think of the textile industry, they consider mainly just one sector—apparel making. Apparel making is, of course, a highly labor-intensive activity that requires little or no proprietary production know-how. Thus, it is now, for understandable reasons, migrating rapidly to lower-wage nations.

What the postindustrialists forget is that apparel making is only the final stage in a series of production processes and as such accounts for a relatively small proportion of the textile industry's total value added. Many of the industry's earlier stages, such as spinning and weaving, are much more economically sophisticated. And before these stages, there is an even more sophisticated stage—the production of the many advanced machines used these days to make the world's fabrics and apparel. Thus, when we take a broader view of the textile industry, we find plenty of activities that require large amounts of both capital and proprietary know-how and as such provide numerous secure and well-paid First World jobs.

Of course, it has to be admitted that the textile industry is not a fast-growing one. But even in this respect, it has more to offer than the postindustrialists give it credit for. As the top Japanese textile executive Hidetane Iijima has pointed out, viewed in global terms, textile making remains a growth industry. After all, most people wear clothes most of the time, and with rising populations, there are more people to clothe each year. This helps explain, for instance, why many subsectors of the industry have shown strong growth in recent years. In the synthetics industry, for instance, output has more than tripled since 1970. Nor is the synthetics story merely one of rising volumes: many of the world's textile makers have boosted their revenues by moving into the production of higher-quality fibers and fabrics as consumers become more affluent. The industry's growth has been further spurred by constant product innovation, which has taken textile makers way beyond clothes and even household furnishings into highly innovative new product categories.

All this helps explain why the big players in the world synthetics industry are such advanced companies as Hoechst of Germany and Toray of Japan, not to mention Milliken & Company and Du Pont of the United States. Admittedly, some developing nations have also entered the business lately. Taiwan in particular has done so successfully, but that is hardly an indication that the entire synthetics business is migrating to the Third World. Quite the reverse: as with the rise of South Korea in shipbuilding, the real significance of Taiwan's emergence in synthetics is that Taiwan is rapidly converging on First World standards of industrial sophistication. Certainly Taiwan can no longer be considered a low-wage economy. Thanks to three decades of breakneck growth in which its per capita income increased thirty-three-fold, its wage levels have now drawn level with those of several member nations of the European Union.

One thing is clear: the synthetics business generally requires First World levels of investment. Billions of dollars of capital have been invested in polyester alone in recent years, and the result is that manufacturers have reaped an abundant harvest in booming sales of advanced new forms of polyester fiber. Using the latest production technologies, leading manufacturers can now make polyester in weights as low as 0.7 dpf (deniers per foot—the standard measure of fineness in the textile business), which is finer than silk. By contrast, as recently as the 1970s even the best manufacturers failed to achieve a fineness much better than 5 dpf, which resulted in a thick, unsupple fiber that became notorious for its uncomfortable texture and dowdy appearance.

According to Martha M. Hamilton, writing in *The Washington Post* in the late 1990s, textile mills and yarn spinners in the United States alone were investing more than $2 billion a year in upgrading equipment as demand for polyester increased. But the really big capital spending programs have been in Japan, where major textile companies like Toray now derive as much as one-fifth of their sales revenues from new forms of polyester. The Japanese have been highly successful in developing *shingosen* versions of polyester endowed with special properties that have suddenly made them favorites with the world's fashion designers. The result is a proliferation of amazing new fabrics. As reported by Gale Eisenstodt of *Forbes,* some *shingosen* fabrics have a feel similar to wool gabardine, others have a surface like peach skin, and still others resemble a blend of silk and linen.

Moreover, polyester boasts practical advantages for the textile industry in that its enormous strength has paved the way for the use of advanced production equipment such as new, ultrafast looms of the sort pioneered in the United States by Milliken & Company. And though polyester's ability to keep its shape is not to everyone's taste, it is a boon for many consumers. Polyester is, for instance, the key ingredient in many of the most modern versions of no-iron shirts.

The higher grades of polyester are increasingly seen not as a substitute for, or supplement to, natural fibers, but as fibers that can stand on their own merits and are in many ways superior to natural fibers. In fact, some of the new fibers are so stylish that women's jackets made from 100 percent polyester can be sold for more than $1,000.

As the Du Pont marketing executive Jeff McGuire points out, polyester's great advantage is the same feature for which it has been reviled in the past: it is plastic. "With a man-made fiber, you can custom-make the fiber to get a different aesthetic," he says. "You can't reengineer cotton or wool."

If the synthetics industry's success were confined to apparel, it would be significant enough. But the industry has also been developing many markets far removed from apparel. Take, for instance, the rapidly growing use of new types of high-strength nylon in car airbags and tires. This market has been successfully targeted by, among others, Solutia Corporation, a new company formed in 1997 as a spin-off of Monsanto Corporation's textile interests. Using the latest production technology licensed from Japan, Solutia operates an advanced nylon facility in South Carolina serving the automobile industry.

In their search for new markets, some textile companies have ventured even further afield. The Dutch giant Akzo Nobel, for instance, has developed a lucrative business making membranes for such high-tech medical applications as blood oxygenation and hemodialysis. Interestingly, Akzo Nobel makes its membranes at Wuppertal, in Germany's high-wage Ruhr Valley. Moreover, its factory there is the successor to a textile-dyeing business founded in the eighteenth century. There could hardly be a more persuasive illustration of the fact that an old industry *can* keep reinventing itself—and in the process continue to support a wide range of well-paid First World jobs.

Nor is Akzo Nobel alone in choosing to locate its membrane business in an advanced First World nation. Its Paris-based rival, Rhône-Poulenc, makes membranes in Switzerland. Given that Rhône-Poulenc operates in more than 160 countries, it could easily have located its membrane operation somewhere with lower wages. So why Switzerland? Part of the answer undoubtedly is that because membrane-making is a high-tech business requiring both large amounts of know-how and capital, factory wages represent only a small proportion of total costs. By locating its production in Switzerland, Rhône-Poulenc suffers only a relatively small disadvantage in higher wage costs—a disadvantage that is more than offset by such key Swiss advantages as high-quality labor and a generally superb industrial infrastructure.

Among the many advanced products into which the textile industry has diversified in recent years, probably none has been more technologically challenging than carbon fiber. The manufacturing process starts with polyacrylonitrile fibers, which are similar to the synthetic fibers widely used in the knitwear industry. These are first carbonized and then wound into filaments. Simple though this series of steps may seem, high-quality carbon fiber has proven extremely difficult to produce in volume—so much so that, as the industry has moved to ever higher levels of production technology in recent decades, many weaker players have fallen by the wayside. The manufacture of this key material has thus become more and more concentrated in the hands of a few ultra-advanced Japanese textile manufacturers that have invested billions of dollars in constantly improving their production technologies. With vital applications in everything from sports goods to aircraft components, carbon fiber is one of the world's fastest-growing high-tech materials. Even Boeing must buy its carbon fiber from high-wage Japan because no other nation can make the material to the appropriate specifications.

So much for fibers. Now let's look at the machinery side of the textiles business, which, as already mentioned, is particularly sophisticated and therefore a superb source of First World jobs in countries like Japan, Germany, and Switzerland.

The story of the rise of the Swiss textile equipment industry is particularly instructive. Boasting a reputed global market share of more than 30 percent in the late 1990s, the Swiss claim to be the world's leading suppliers of textile equipment. Admittedly, much of their expansion has come not through internal growth but rather through takeovers of foreign rivals. But far from undermining jobs at home, this expansion has probably strengthened them. For one thing, the newly acquired foreign operations provide the home factories in Switzerland with new markets for advanced components and subassemblies. And in any case, the Swiss have little incentive to move domestic jobs to foreign subsidiaries because most of these subsidiaries are located in other notably high-wage countries. Take the big Swiss weaving equipment-maker Sulzer Ruti. Besides Switzerland, it manufactures in only two other countries—Japan and Germany. Meanwhile, the leading Swiss-based maker of spinning machinery, Rieter, does most of its foreign production in places like the United States and Germany.

Why has the Swiss industry been so successful? For a start, it boasts a long tradition of technical expertise. Rieter, for instance, has been making spinning equipment since the early 1800s. Admittedly, as the precipitate decline of both the British and American textile equipment industries has demonstrated, long experience alone is hardly sufficient in an industry as sophisticated as this one. Thus, we have to look elsewhere for the decisive factors in Switzerland's success.

Investment has clearly been one such factor. Where investment is concerned, the Swiss tend to reserve the lion's share for the home factories. At Rieter, for instance, although only 35 percent of the workers are employed in Switzerland, its home textile equipment operations consume nearly half of all its capital spending.

High levels of spending on research and development have also been a crucial factor in Switzerland's success. Take Saurer Gruppe, a Swiss-based maker of spinning and twisting equipment. It routinely invests more than 5 percent of its sales in R&D. Spending on this scale helps explain why Saurer is constantly launching new products—to the point where, as of 1999, about 80 percent of its sales revenues were coming from machines launched in the previous two years. One key objective has been to redesign its machines to minimize the number of parts. In some of its ring-spinning machines, for instance, it has reduced the part count by as much as 45 percent. This has not only helped streamline Saurer's manufacturing processes but rendered its machines both more reliable and easier to maintain. Thus, Saurer's Germany-based Zinser division is now the market leader in ring-spinning equipment, ahead of Swiss rival Rieter and Japan's Toyoda. Meanwhile, in winding machines, the company's Schlafhorst division boasts a market share of 30 percent, putting it second only to Japan's Murata, with 40 percent of the market. Perhaps the sweetest news of all is that Schlafhorst's open-end spinning machines boast a world market share of 60 percent. At Sulzer Ruti, too, research and development has been a major factor in the company's success. Particularly owing to the introduction of air-jet technology in the 1970s, Sulzer Ruti claims to have boosted the operational efficiency of its machines by 300 percent.

The bottom line, for our purposes, is that the Swiss textile equipment industry employed about 10,000 workers as of the late 1990s in Switzerland alone, not to mention another 15,000 overseas. In view of the fact that not only are Swiss wages among the world's highest but virtually all of Switzerland's textile equipment is exported, there could hardly be a clearer demonstration of the enduring strengths of manufacturing.

Moreover, for its customers in the wider textile industry, Switzerland's success in building ever more reliable and more productive textile equipment has been a key reason why many of the world's most advanced spinning and weaving companies continue to employ thousands of well-paid workers throughout the First World.

Clearly, the textile industry has come a long way in the last several thousand years. But one thing has not changed: it is still a business in which the leading nations of the day can compete to win.

STEEL:
A "SUNSET" INDUSTRY ON WHICH THE SUN NEVER SETS

Steel, our third golden oldie, is the classic of the genre. Almost universally scorned by the postindustrialists, steel is widely considered to represent the very antithesis of all the promise of the information economy. In particular, steel is regarded as facing notably poor growth prospects in the developed world. On the face of it, this view seems to be well grounded in the facts. After all, steel output has been stagnant in most developed nations since the 1980s.

But there is less to the steel industry's stagnation than meets the eye—much less. For a start, the global output figures have been distorted by the collapse of the old Soviet Union, which has resulted in widespread industrial disruption in many Eastern European countries. Even in the First World, the picture of apparent stagnation is far less serious than it appears. For one thing, much of the sluggishness has resulted from a unique factor that now seems to have largely run its course—a regulation-driven effort to reduce car weights. This spurred a secular move by carmakers to use plastics and aluminum instead of steel in many applications, but the steel industry is now fighting back vigorously by investing in new ways to improve steel's strength-to-weight ratio. In particular, more than thirty of the world's top steelmakers are cooperating in the ULSAB (ultra light steel auto body) research program, which is being undertaken jointly with the world automobile industry. The program's aim is to come up with ways of increasing steel's strength-to-weight ratio to improve its competitiveness vis-à-vis plastics and aluminum.

The effort to develop better steel for the car industry is an example of a general trend among the world's most advanced steelmakers to compensate for stagnant *volume* by raising the *quality* of their output—a strategy that has helped keep unit prices rising buoyantly. Thus, even in the most developed nations the picture of stagnating volume conceals a much less disturbing underlying trend in sales revenues.

At the end of the day, therefore, we find that the steel industry supports thousands of notably well-paid jobs in some of the world's richest nations. Take the United States. Even after years of closing outdated steel mills, the United States remains one of the world's biggest steel producers and produces more steel per capita than, for instance, lower-wage Britain. As of 2003, more than 120,000 workers were employed in the industry in the United States and their annual wages averaged more than $44,000. Admittedly, employment levels in the industry are sharply down from the 1970s but, thanks in part to long overdue trade measures by the Bush administration, the pace of attrition of steel jobs had slowed as of 2003.

Nowhere is the correlation between steel and well-paid jobs exemplified more spectacularly than in tiny Luxembourg, where the Arcelor steel company recently produced more steel than USX-U.S. Steel. In fact, steel accounts for nearly one-quarter of the principality's total exports. Given that Luxembourg recently boasted the world's highest per capita income, this would certainly seem to give the lie to the idea that steel is a low-wage industry.

If further proof is needed that the steel industry has a future in the developed world, it lies in the high levels of investment apparent at many of the world's leading steelmakers. Japanese steelmakers consistently invested at about three times the rate of their American counterparts in the 1990s, a fact that helps explain why, even though steel wages are now higher in Japan than in the United States, the United States has continued to import huge amounts of steel from Japan. (Japanese dumping, of course, helps explain some of the U.S. imports—but this is significant only in the case of a few kinds of steel.)

All this is not to suggest that everything in the garden is rosy. Certainly, steel is hardly the most persuasive example of the strengths of manufacturing. It is, of course, notorious for cutting jobs. In the United States alone, the industry has cut its work force by two-thirds since 1980. And similarly severe cuts have been made in the United Kingdom and France. Given the industry's job-cutting record, it would be natural to conclude that the industry is a loser. Natural—but wrong.

The truth is that the industry's tendency to cut jobs is the flip side of its greatest success—the enormous progress it has made in raising labor productivity in the last fifty years. The key to this progress has been heavy investment in new production technologies. As the economic commentator Robert Kuttner has pointed out, steel is a classic example of a supposed "sunset" industry that in reality boasts some highly advanced technologies.

The industry's progress has been driven in large part by innovations in the blast-furnace method of producing steel, which is used almost universally in the world's largest steel mills. Blast-furnace productivity has been dramatically boosted in the last fifty years by the adoption of the basic-oxygen process. This process, invented by a state-owned Austrian steel mill, involves pumping vast amounts of oxygen at supersonic speed into the furnace to boost heat levels, thereby drastically speeding production. The basic-oxygen process in turn was made possible by earlier breakthroughs in the chemical industry that dramatically reduced the price of industrial oxygen.

Steel industry productivity has also received a strong boost from the introduction of continuous casting, an energy-saving process in which steel billets are produced in a single step. This replaced a wasteful two-step process in which the metal had to be heated twice over.

The Japanese have been among the earliest to exploit both basic-oxygen furnaces and continuous casting, and as a result they have not only cut their unit labor costs by 90 percent in the last five decades but achieved reductions of up to 50 percent in their energy consumption. All this helps explain why Japan has multiplied its steel output twentyfold in the last five decades—and in the process has gone from an obscure also-ran to the world's largest steel exporter.

A very different production process figures in another part of the steel industry's spectacular story of rising productivity—the electric-arc process. In contrast to the blast-furnace method, scrap iron rather than iron ore is generally the major input in this process. One key benefit of the electric-arc process is that it uses much less energy. It also provides a convenient way to recycle vast amounts of scrap metal that would otherwise represent a major environmental problem. Moreover, since it uses electricity rather than coke as the heating agent, it cuts down on the notorious levels of noxious emissions entailed in steelmaking.

Beyond these advantages, electric-arc furnaces offer a chance to achieve ultra-high levels of labor productivity, as the rise of the North Carolina–based Nucor Corporation has spectacularly demonstrated. Nucor's proudest boast is that it pays some of the world's highest blue-collar wages while achieving unit labor costs that are among the world's lowest. Powered by leading-edge electric-arc furnace production technology, it has multiplied sales revenues 180 times in thirty years. Long famous for its no-layoff policy, it boosted its total work force by more than 60 percent in the eight years to 2003.

Since scrap is expensive to transport, electric-arc furnaces are at their best operating on a small scale and using whatever scrap can be sourced locally. Their small scale is an advantage in that they can be operated more flexibly than blast furnaces and in particular their output can be fine-tuned to take advantage of short-term changes in demand for different kinds of steel.

All in all, the electric-arc method has been tremendously successful. As of the 1990s, the electricity required to produce a ton of steel by this method had been cut to just 400 kilowatt-hours—down from as much as 635 kilowatt-hours in 1965.

So successful has the electric-arc method been that by the mid-1990s demand from mini-mills had pushed scrap prices to record levels in many nations. In fact, a growing shortage of scrap is now powering a leap to a new variant on the technology using specially preprocessed iron ore known as DRI (direct reduced iron).

Even with the blast-furnace method under pressure from environmentalists and the mini-mill business increasingly constrained by scrap shortages, the industry expects to continue to increase output quite substantially in the years ahead with the help of DRI-fed electric-arc furnaces and other innovations. According to Roskill, a British consulting firm, the global industry's output in 2005 is expected to total 883 million tons—an increase of 17 percent over 1996's 750 million tons.

Besides improving productivity, steelmakers in the world's most advanced nations have also been making dramatic improvements in the quality of their products in recent years. In particular, they have been developing stronger steels for a variety of applications from car engine parts and radial tires to machine tools and precision equipment. They have also developed new varieties of steel with special properties that, for instance, improve the efficiency of electric motors, generators, and other electrical devices. Other new steels are designed to damp down vibration and, by extension, noise. They have important applications in everything from motorcycles and washing machines to fan heaters and photocopiers.

Beyond improving their products, some of the world's most aggressive steelmakers are also developing new markets for steel. The Japanese, for instance, have been leading the development of lightweight forms of galvanized steel to replace traditional two-by-four lumber in house-building. Steel's advantages include not only low cost but resistance to fires and earthquakes. And given that a typical wood-framed house consumes nearly forty trees, steel-frame housing is also being promoted as an environmentally friendly alternative that saves the world's forests. Japanese steelmakers are also finding new markets for especially strong, weldable steel for skyscrapers. Nippon Steel has suggested that such steel may soon enable the construction industry to build buildings as high as three hundred floors—or nearly three times the height of Chicago's Sears Tower.

Another key growth strategy for many of the world's top steel companies has been to supply steelmaking equipment to other steelmakers around the world. Austria's Voest-Alpine, for instance, is a big maker of continuous casting equipment. The Demag subsidiary of the big German steelmaker Mannesmann makes both rolling mills and continuous casting equipment. In Japan, Kobe Steel leads in DRI equipment, Nippon Steel makes mini-mill equipment, and NKK makes both mini-mill equipment and advanced, environmentally friendly coke-making equipment.

One thing is clear: the equipment business is one of the steel industry's brightest areas of growth. All postindustrial talk to the contrary, the world desperately needs more steelmaking capacity if residents of the developing world are ever to approach Western-style living standards. China alone represents a huge market for equipment—a point that is obvious when we remember that China will need to boost its steel output to a colossal 800 million tons a year if it is ever to match Japanese output levels on a per capita basis. At that point, China's output alone would be more than that of the entire global industry as of 2003.

All this growth is driven by a fundamental factor too often overlooked by the postindustrialists: steel is a great material. It is notably easy to work and shape. And in its various forms, its hardness and tensile strength are highly useful to the human race. It also boasts valuable electrical and thermal properties. Best of all, it is extremely inexpensive thanks to the abundance of iron ore in many parts of the world. (Iron is the fourth most abundant element after oxygen, silicon, and aluminum.)

No wonder the president of Nippon Steel, Akira Chihaya, commented: "Steel has been and will remain a basic material in our lives. The steel industry is not only alive and well in the information society but can be expected to continue expanding."

Let's now take a look at a specific example of a leading-edge First World steel mill and see how it illustrates this chapter's main message—

that an old and apparently terminally troubled industry still has plenty of potential to create superb First World jobs.

SUMITOMO:
PIPE MAKER TO THE WORLD

For visitors to Sumitomo Metal Industries' pipe-making works three hundred miles west of Tokyo, the first impression is of a typical rust-belt operation. The pipe works is one unit buried deep within a huge fifty-year-old steelmaking complex that positively fills the landscape on the outskirts of Wakayama City.

From the main gate, you are taken by chauffeur-driven limousine on a meandering one-and-a-half-mile journey through a maze of machine-age towers, vents, and cranes. On arrival at the new pipe works, you are suddenly fast-forwarded into the robot age. Viewing the production process from a gangway high above the works floor, you immediately notice that the plant is fully automated. So much so, in fact, that the works floor is normally completely devoid of labor. And what a works floor it is: measuring 850 yards long, 110 yards wide, and 30 yards high, it is equal to the area of about ten soccer fields.

The day this writer visited happened to be exceptional in that a single tiny human figure was just visible amid the plant's vast sea of clattering and hissing machines—a maintenance engineer who, clipboard in hand, was checking on one of the vast machines.

The only other humans to be seen anywhere were five blue-collar workers watching computer monitors in a quiet, glass-enclosed aerie perched well above the works floor. The glass shields these workers from one of the noisiest environments imaginable. The main production process involves taking solid cylinders of orange-red steel and then hollowing them out in a single swift and deafening ramming action. The cylinders, measuring about one foot in diameter and as much as ten feet in length, are tossed around like so many drum majorettes' batons as they are prepared and positioned for the ramming process. Even on a cold

November day, the glow from each cylinder as it passed at a distance of fifty feet away recalled the reflected heat from a city sidewalk in August.

The only disappointment is that the end-products of all this twenty-first-century industrial magic seem pretty unremarkable. To the nontechnical eye, after all, pipes are merely pipes. But in the eyes of pipe users, Sumitomo pipes are to other pipes what Rolls-Royces are to other cars—the best. Measuring as much as sixteen inches in diameter in finished form, they are destined to be used in applications where extreme strength and reliability are critically important. A key market is in the world oil industry, where their unrivaled ability to withstand high pressures and corrosive chemicals is now enabling oil producers to develop wells in ever more hostile and remote environments.

One key to the reliability of Sumitomo's pipes is their extreme smoothness. They are almost entirely free of the surface blemishes that can greatly weaken other pipes after prolonged exposure to hostile conditions. Sumitomo's pipes, moreover, are made in lengths of up to forty-four feet, about 20 percent longer than those of most of its rivals. Again, to a nontechnical observer this feature seems unremarkable, but as the Sumitomo general manager, Takeshi Kirimoto, points out, pipelines made from longer pipes require less welding—a key saving given how expensive it can be to deploy expert welders in remotely situated oil fields.

It is not surprising, therefore, that Sumitomo's pipes fetch notably high prices—typically, at least 50 percent more than ordinary steel pipes. Moreover, demand has been so strong that the plant has been working around the clock since it opened.

All this adds up to a superb business that makes a strong contribution to the health of the Japanese economy. For a start, the plant exports about half of its total output. Surprisingly perhaps, given its high degree of automation, the plant has also created a plethora of excellent jobs. In addition to the five men in the control room, about 1,500 employees work four shifts a day behind the scenes in maintenance, inventory management, and other support functions. Best of all, with about 60 percent of its workers being high school graduates, the plant has clearly created a well-balanced range of jobs.

Moreover, these jobs look highly secure for as far ahead as anyone can see. The point is that the plant cost $700 million; thus, each job is backed by nearly $470,000 of capital on average. The plant is also very knowledge-intensive. Its production is based on a new process that has been in development since the 1960s. Sumitomo reckons that the new process achieves about 30 percent more output per worker than the well-known Mannesmann process, which hitherto has been the world steel industry's standard method of making high-quality pipes.

The bottom line on Wakayama is this: with bonuses, an ordinary forty-five-year-old blue-collar worker earns about $65,000 a year. This is three times what some of India's most brilliant minds earn writing world-class software in Bangalore.

Having satisfied ourselves that even old and troubled industries can play a surprisingly strong role in the world economy as we enter the twenty-first century, let's now move to the other end of the manufacturing industry spectrum and look at the exciting prospects that await us in new manufacturing industries now just about to take off.

THE FUTURE: CHAPTER 7
AN EXPANDING UNIVERSE

What of the future of manufacturing? Almost without exception, economic commentators are gloomy about the prospects. Somehow, it has become conventional wisdom that most of the world's manufacturing industries are fated at best to grow only slowly in coming decades. To the commentators, it seems that the world's manufacturing industries are so glutted with overcapacity that there is simply not enough purchasing power to buy all the goods that could be made. One such commentator is William Greider, whose gloomy articulation of this view in his book *One World, Ready or Not* was widely discussed in the American media in 1997.

But the truth is that the gloomsters could hardly be more wrong. As we will see in this chapter, it is absurd to suggest that the world's manufacturing industries are suffering from a general glut of capacity. In the twenty-first century, as in the past, the world's consumers will be more than happy to increase their consumption as fast as their budgets allow, and thus they will provide a ready market for all the merchandisable goods that can be made. Moreover, they will increasingly insist that these goods be made in the most environmentally friendly ways possible. All of this adds up to an historic challenge for the world's leading manufacturers—and an historic opportunity.

UNLIMITED HORIZONS:
THE CHALLENGE OF THE DEVELOPING WORLD

One key growth opportunity for great manufacturers lies in the developing world. This point was memorably made by the late Japanese industrialist Akio Morita in *Made in Japan,* a book he wrote with Edwin M. Reingold and Mitsuko Shimomura. Morita believed that as manufacturers continue to boost their production efficiency, they could hope to bring prosperity to more and more of the world's poorer regions. This view had been a factor in his thinking ever since the early 1960s, when his Sony Corporation first broke through in a big way in world markets.

> It seemed to me at the time that with two-thirds of the world's population living at a very low economic level, the developed world had a responsibility and opportunity to help them into a higher economic sphere, which would be a benefit to everyone. . . . I am reminded of the story of two shoe salesmen who visited an underdeveloped country. One cabled his office, "no prospect of sales because nobody here wears shoes." The other salesman cabled, "send stock immediately—inhabitants barefooted—desperately need shoes."

Morita's point was that developing economies can be viewed two ways— optimistically or pessimistically. And Morita himself was a convinced optimist. His ebullient message was that manufacturers will never lack for exciting new challenges while so many of the developing world's people have yet to attain the basics of a Western consumer lifestyle.

This message should not come as a surprise to us. In fact, the whole history of the world's progress toward ever increasing prosperity bears out Morita's optimistic view. Remember that every market started with bare-footed customers. Little more than two centuries ago, even today's most advanced nations were probably no richer than most of the present-day Third World. The fact that these nations have in the interim achieved steadily increasing incomes is a tribute to the enormous progress manufacturers have made over the years in boosting their efficiency and thereby both increasing their output and making their products afford-able to an ever expanding range of consumers.

Even in recent decades, the speed with which manufacturers have spread prosperity further into previously poor parts of the world has been spectacular. According to Care International, the proportion of the world's people who live in absolute poverty has fallen from 70 percent to 30 percent in just the last three decades.

Of course, Morita's story was intended as a parable, and as such it some-what oversimplified the process by which the First World can benefit from growth in the developing world. In reality, the First World sells few shoes to emerging nations. Instead, it sells such nations *the means to make shoes for themselves.* Specifically, it sells them shoe manufacturing equipment. And the First World's increasing efficiency in making shoe manufacturing equipment has enabled local shoe manufacturers in the developing world to achieve big increases in output, thus making their products affordable to more and more people. Hence, people in formerly barefoot nations such as South Korea and Taiwan are now as well shod as people in the West.

The point is that the key way that the First World can help foster pros-perity in poorer nations is to provide the producers' goods that these nations can use to make consumer goods for themselves. The First World also enjoys many lucrative opportunities to sell the emerging economies all sorts of sophisticated infrastructural equipment, such as power-generation plant, telecommunications systems, earth-moving equipment, oil refiner-ies, railroad locomotives, ships, and aircraft.

Clearly, for the First World suppliers of such goods, the potential for future sales growth is almost limitless. That being so, why do so many

Western commentators imagine that the future world economy will be dogged by an increasingly severe glut of manufacturing capacity? These commentators fail to realize that an economy is a highly dynamic instrument that adjusts constantly to the changing balance between supply and demand. This dynamism is apparent in the way that demand increases rapidly in newly industrializing nations. The gloomsters forget that when a developing nation approaches First World standards in manufacturing efficiency, its workers almost automatically acquire the purchasing power to make a commensurate increase in their consumption. This increased purchasing power enables them either to buy the products they make or to buy imported goods paid for by exporting such products. Either way, for the world's consumption to increase in step with rising production capacity, all that is needed is for governments to maintain reasonably intelligent demand-management policies.

One factor that powerfully contributes to the false impression that the future global economy will be permanently paralyzed by a dearth of purchasing power is that many emerging economies save much of their income. Thus, in the short run, consumer demand in these nations consistently seems to Westerners to be lower than it "should" be. But the gloomsters overlook the fact that to forgo consumption today is not necessarily to forgo it forever. To the extent that these nations save more today, they can assuredly consume more later—because their high savings rates will accelerate the speed at which they become rich. In any case—and this is the crucial point—the high savings rates of these nations today in no way diminishes the First World's immediate export prospects. Quite the reverse: because these nations are saving so much, they represent major markets for *investment goods* such as factory machinery, construction equipment, electricity-generating plant, telecommunications equipment, and a host of other sophisticated machinery—precisely the sort of manufactured products that do the most to sustain the prosperity of the world's most sophisticated economies.

One thing is certain: many emerging nations will become rich much sooner than almost anyone in the West anticipates. Even more important than capital, education is a key driver of growth in such nations. With literacy now spreading rapidly in many parts of the Second and Third Worlds, previously poor nations have suddenly acquired an unprecedented capacity to absorb efficient new production technologies from richer nations. As the Hong Kong–based investment manager J. Mark Mobius has pointed out, Indonesia is a prime example. Sixty years ago, only one in ten Indonesians could read; now well over 60 percent can do so. Moreover, better communications are accelerating the speed with which emerging economies absorb new production technologies.

In common with most other seasoned observers in the East Asian region, Mobius discounted suggestions in the West that the East Asian financial crisis of 1997–98 would permanently hamper the region. In reality, as became abundantly clear in subsequent years, the crisis was no more than an isolated air pocket with negligible consequences for the region's long-term prosperity. In that sense, the crisis closely resembled the financial panics that periodically afflicted the United States in the latter half of the nineteenth century. This was a period when fast-expanding industries like steel often suffered devastating bouts of overcapacity as entrepreneurs like Andrew Carnegie got ahead of themselves in their soaring optimism about the future. Yet, this optimism was vindicated by later recoveries that carried the United States to successively higher levels of prosperity.

The key point here is that the process of industrialization is becoming easier all the time as the technologies available to each successive emerging economy become more efficient and easier to use. Hence, each newly industrializing nation achieves developed-country status faster than its predecessors. As the first nation to industrialize, the United Kingdom took fully fifty-eight years to double its output; the United States took forty-seven years, and Japan just thirty-four years. These days, as China's recent growth has demonstrated, this feat can be performed in as little as ten years. And, on Mobius's predictions, other emerging nations may soon beat even China's record.

All in all, the developing world is clearly set to grow at a fast pace in the years ahead—and for the First World's manufacturers of production machinery and other advanced producers' goods, this growth will bring an embarrassment of export opportunities.

OPPORTUNITIES NEARER HOME

Even in the world's richest nations, the idea that there is any general glut of manufacturing capacity is clearly absurd. The reality is that most citizens of the advanced world still have plenty of obvious unsatisfied needs—needs that they would be delighted to satisfy if only they could afford to. Thus, the only thing that stands in the way of even greater consumption in the advanced world is the ability of manufacturers to achieve further reductions in their production costs—reductions that would make their products affordable to a wider range of First World consumers.

The potential for further increases in consumption in the First World is particularly obvious in the case of the 10 to 20 percent of the First World's population who live below the poverty line. But few even among the First World's better-off residents feel as affluent as they would like. Certainly, in an era of keeping up with the Joneses, they can think of a long list of material goods that are still beyond their means— a better car, a new living room suite, a second home, a remodeled kitchen, a sailboat. . . . The list is almost endless, and it will keep the world's manufacturers busy for many years to come.

As if this were not enough, the world's manufacturers will also be called on to manufacture many new kinds of goods that have not yet even been invented. Leadership in such innovative products has long represented one of the main sources of high-quality manufacturing jobs for advanced economies, and there is no reason to expect this to change in the twenty-first century. That said, innovation is constantly underestimated as a source of economic growth and employment. By definition, it is difficult to predict the nature of future inventions. But the point, for our purposes, is that history is on our side in suggesting that the future contributions of new inventions will prove of far greater economic importance than almost anyone currently expects. Certainly, all past evidence indicates that the market potential for revolutionary new products and technologies has consistently been underestimated even by the supposedly best-informed experts.

Take the telephone. It seems amazing now, but when Alexander Graham Bell first publicized this epoch-making invention, few even in the telecommunications industry understood its enormous market potential. Executives of Western Union, for instance, were so unimpressed that they turned down Bell's offer to sell his patents for a mere $100,000—an amount that within a few years seemed like a pittance in comparison to the device's explosive growth. Western Union's attitude reflected a general view in the American telegraph industry that the new talking device was merely a "toy." In the British telegraph industry, too, the experts were notably skeptical. Speaking in the British House of Commons in 1879, Sir William Preece, a top British telegraph executive, said of the telephone: "I fancy the descriptions we get of its use in America are a little exaggerated, though there are conditions in America which necessitate the use of such instruments more than here. Here we have a superabundance of messengers."

Below are examples of other inventions whose epochal economic significance at first went unrecognized:

> **Computers:** When computers were first used in World War II, most experts viewed computing as a military technology that would have few peacetime uses. Even top executives of IBM were reputedly highly skeptical about the prospects for computers.

> **Transistors:** Experts initially believed that applications for transistors would be confined largely to a narrow range of special devices, such as hearing aids, where the advantages of miniaturization were particularly obvious. The general lack of excitement was reflected in the *New York Times'* decision to give the first report of the invention just four column-inches at the bottom of page 46 (below an item about *Waltz*

Time, an NBC radio show that enjoyed some modest prominence at the time).

Copiers: After a tiny company called Haloid invented a plain-
paper copier in 1959, it invited several major manufacturing
corporations to help it develop the idea—but met with a wall
of yawning ennui. Studying the idea on behalf of a major corporate client, the consulting firm Arthur D. Little dismissed
plain-paper copying as a narrow niche unworthy of the attention of a large corporation. In the end, after running out of
other options, tiny Haloid went it alone and quickly proved
the skeptics wrong. So much so that, under its new name of
the Xerox Corporation, Haloid went on to become one of the
fastest-growing manufacturers of the mid-twentieth century.

Lasers: The laser was originally so underappreciated that
lawyers at Bell Laboratories, where the device was invented in
the 1950s, wondered whether it was worth patenting. In truth,
of course, lasers were soon to become one of the key enabling
technologies in a host of advanced industries, not least in Ma
Bell's own heartland of telecommunications.

Microprocessors: When the microprocessor was invented in
1970, its potential to revolutionize the computer industry was
widely overlooked. Industry experts imagined that the computer industry would buy no more than 2,000 microprocessors annually. Even Intel, which invented the device and went
on to make huge profits from it, was slow to recognize the
potential and initially concentrated on selling microprocessors
to makers of such minor products as pocket calculators, vending machines, and cash registers.

Countless other similar instances could be cited of great new manufacturing opportunities that were unrecognized at first—but the point is

already clear. Even industry experts rarely have the vision to see more than a few years ahead in anticipating the often huge economic consequences of new products and manufacturing technologies. We should not be too hard on them: caution is generally prudent at the outset because there are usually enormous production engineering challenges to be overcome before an invention can be turned into a low-cost mass-market product. Of course, time and again, engineers subsequently succeed in achieving huge reductions in production costs, but these reductions are by no means guaranteed and cannot be taken for granted at the outset.

Moreover, it is precisely the most innovative products—in particular those that cater to hitherto unmet human needs—that are the most difficult for early observers to evaluate accurately. As the science writer Robert Pool has pointed out in his book *Beyond Engineering*, it takes more imagination than most people possess to recognize an unmet human need and to realize that a particular invention will satisfy it.

How far ahead into the future can we assume that innovation will continue to deliver exciting new manufacturing opportunities? Actually, the potential for innovation to power future growth in manufacturing is almost unlimited. In the future, as in the past, the font of manufacturing progress will be science, a font that humans are only beginning to exploit. As the iconoclastic young Stanford University economist Paul Romer has pointed out, the world has as yet hardly even scratched the surface in exploring science's secrets. Writing in *Time* magazine in 1998, he pointed out that only a tiny fraction of all the materials that will play an important economic role in the future had so far been discovered.

He posed the question: "Suppose you gave a child a chemistry set containing sixty different chemicals from the Periodic Table. How many distinct mixtures could she make?"

The amazing answer: 100 billion billion mixtures.

As Romer acknowledges, many of these mixtures would prove to be "boring." But others would be highly exciting. He adds:

> Humans are adept at converting low-value raw materials into high-value mixtures. This is in fact the essence of economic growth. First

we find new recipes for mixtures that are more valuable than their ingredients. Then once we have a good recipe, we do a lot of cooking. . . . Counting the number of random mixtures possible with different elements from the Periodic Table only begins to suggest the scope for future discovery. The realm of possible things is incomprehensibly larger than the realm of existing things. We will never run out of things to discover—a reassuring fact since the process of discovery is the mainspring of economic growth. . . . The opportunities symbolized by the child's chemistry set mean that growth in income per person can persist into the indefinite future.

In short, the future of manufacturing is an expanding universe, and any advanced nation that wants to continue to play a prominent role in world affairs in the twenty-first century should bear this uppermost in mind.

PROSPECTS FOR INNOVATIVE PRODUCTS: AN ENDLESS LIST

Having satisfied ourselves that in principle the future for innovative new manufactured products is almost limitless, let's now attempt to sketch out a few specific examples of how technology may soon create important new opportunities for First World manufacturers.

Robots and automation

Heralded for generations, robots are taking a long time coming—but they *are* coming. In fact, unseen by consumers, they are already an increasingly important factor in industrial production. In particular, as we noted in Chapter 5, they have helped both shipbuilders and steelmakers achieve dramatic gains in labor productivity in recent years. Robots also play a key role in the electronics industry. They are invaluable, for instance, in assembling devices like laptop computers whose components are too small for human hands to manipulate accurately. That said, the world has nowhere near exploited the full potential of automation to reduce labor costs in both manufacturing and service industries. In the future we are going to see many radical new uses for automation. One idea: automated door-to-door distribution systems that would deliver goods to urban stores and homes by robots operating in vast new underground transportation networks. The Japanese are already considering building such a system under Tokyo; it would dramatically reduce the number of goods vehicles on the city's crowded roads, leading to a general speeding up of traffic.

Voice recognition systems

Scientists have been working for years to develop electronic devices that can understand the human voice. Although such devices have hardly been developed beyond the primitive stage, they are expected by about 2020 to reach a level of sophistication at which they will enable humans to operate a broad range of electronic equipment entirely by voice command. Although voice recognition seems at first sight to be mainly an opportunity for software makers (Bill Gates in particular is reportedly eyeing it excitedly), its implications for hardware manufacturers are probably even larger than for software makers. Certainly, the world's semiconductor manufacturers have long viewed voice recognition as a potentially prodigious user of semiconductors. In addition, the rise of voice recognition will greatly expand the usefulness of—and market for—various types of established electronic gadgets, such as the personal computer. Now confined mainly to offices and homes, the personal computer could soon acquire a new lease on life as standard equipment in cars. With voice recognition cutting out the need for a keyboard, drivers would for the first time be able to operate a personal computer safely while they commute.

Environmental protection

If rising world consumption is not to lead to environmental disaster, manufacturers right across the board will have to develop more environmentally friendly products. Perhaps even more importantly, manufacturers will have to develop more environmentally friendly *methods of production*. As the environmentalist Ross Gelbspan has pointed out, the widely held view that environmental protection laws hurt a nation's economy is simply false. The truth is the opposite: good environmental policies create rather than destroy jobs.

The most urgent priority is to install so-called end-of-pipe pollution mitigation devices in every factory and power plant that currently pollutes the environment. The classic example of such a device is the "scrubber"—a machine that cleans the emissions from industrial smokestacks. Scrubbers have been in general use in the West's major economies for many years, and it is now urgent that they also be deployed in the nations of the former East Bloc and in the developing world. These devices must also be made more effective and less expensive. Longer term, entirely new and cleaner methods of production will have to be developed to minimize environmental damage.

Another key goal will be to develop ways to conserve energy and materials. As the environmentalists Amory and Hunter Lovins have documented, many household gadgets, such as refrigerators and air-conditioning systems, could be made much more energy-efficient at little cost if only manufacturers focused on energy efficiency as a key goal. Spurred partly by greater consumer awareness and partly by international regulation, advanced manufacturing nations will focus on making the world a cleaner place—and will reap great economic advantages from that endeavor.

Health care

The population of people aged sixty-five and over is set to double in many of the world's most advanced nations in the next thirty years. Besides generating rapidly rising sales for manufacturers of everything from hair restorers to heart pacemakers, this boom in the number of seniors will require innovative solutions to the problem of long-term nursing care. As we have seen, household robots are coming, and they undoubtedly will provide part of the solution. More generally, mechanized devices like stairlifts will become much more prevalent. Other new technologies, such as superconductivity and biotechnology, will open up opportunities for advanced manufacturers to develop lucrative new approaches to health care.

Hydrology

The world's water resources are signally failing to keep up with expanding populations. The result is that, according to World Bank figures, per capita water supplies have fallen by one-third in the last twenty-five years. The water shortage in many nations not only is a drastic problem in itself but is beginning to constrain the growth in world food supplies. Yet, if the World Bank's forecasts are to be believed, demand for water will increase by 650 percent by 2025. Clearly, the world is facing a major crisis. It is one that advanced manufacturers can play a key role in overcoming.

Manufacturers can, for instance, help the world use existing water supplies more intensively. To take just one example, large amounts of water could be saved in agriculture alone if new drip systems were widely adopted to channel water directly to where it is needed—at the crops' roots. Already, drip systems are being manufactured on a limited scale; as reported by Sandra Postel in *Technology Review,* they have in some cases cut farm water usage by as much as 60 percent. So far, however, drip systems have been too expensive to be widely adopted by the world's farmers. The race is on to find ways of manufacturing them more economically.

Another approach to the looming crisis is to build more efficient and effective systems for recycling waste water. Already, this challenge is providing useful opportunities for various manufacturers in the First World, notably in Germany and Japan. Moreover, in the longer term, breakthroughs in desalination may come to the rescue. President John F. Kennedy once suggested that inventing an inexpensive way to produce freshwater from the sea would dwarf all other scientific achievements. He may have overstated the case, but desalination has already grown to be a significant industry. Its growth prospects, however, are constrained by the fact that existing desalination technologies require enormous amounts of energy; hence the fact that desalination so far has been little used outside a few oil-rich nations. (As of the mid-1990s, just three such nations—Saudi Arabia, the United Arab Emirates, and Kuwait—accounted for 46 percent of the world's entire desalination capacity.) Now engineers are racing to develop more energy-efficient approaches. One promising system, announced by Desalinadoras AVF of Spain, would use the natural pressure of gravity in a 700-meter shaft to force seawater through a fine membrane that filters out the salt. As reported by David White of the *Financial Times* of London, this system promises to cut energy costs by 72 percent and would also be considerably less expensive in capital expenditures.

Nanotechnology

The nanometer—one-billionth of a meter—has given its name to a promising new industry devoted to hyper-miniaturized manufacturing techniques that aim to manipulate matter on an atom-by-atom basis. The most famous example so far of nanotechnology in action has been a successful effort by researchers at IBM to arrange thirty-five atoms of xenon to form their employer's name. While this feat may in itself seem to be of only trivial significance, it represents a spectacular demonstration of the principle that atoms can indeed be manipulated individually. It therefore presages the possibility of producing a vast array of consumer goods by new atom-by-atom production methods. In an example cited by *The Economist,* we may one day be able literally to assemble beefsteaks in a highly efficient, entirely artificial process that dispenses with the clumsy and land-intensive business of raising cattle—a business that has, of course, changed little since the Stone Age. In *The Economist*'s vision, billions of tiny assembly-robots housed in a new kind of kitchen gadget would start with a supply of atoms of carbon, nitrogen, hydrogen, and oxygen. By pushing these atoms around in appropriate ways, the robots would in a matter of minutes create a confection of proteins and carbohydrates that in all respects would not only look and taste like steak but contain the same nutritional elements. After their meal, consumers could disassemble the leftovers back into the original atoms, thus obviating the need for any cleaning up. All this is still, of course, little more than science fiction. But in the fullness of time, nanotechnology promises huge increases in efficiency over traditional production methods.

Let's now take an extended look at a few areas in which future manufacturing opportunities appear to be particularly obvious. We will begin by looking at the prospects in various energy-related fields and then move on to transportation.

A NOBLE QUEST:
ENERGY FOR ALL

All recent conventional wisdom to the contrary, the world is *not* awash in surplus energy. True, measured in real terms, energy prices have dropped to levels not seen since the halcyon days of the early 1970s. But to imagine, as many Western commentators do, that energy today is "ultracheap" is a classic example of the Western tendency to view the world too narrowly. The fact is that, for most of the world's population, energy remains almost as scarce today as ever. So scarce in fact that, on a per capita basis, energy consumption levels in many Third World nations run less than one-fiftieth that of the United States.

Even many better-off citizens in such nations still use kerosene for heat and light; poorer people make do with burning cow dung and other agricultural wastes. Either way, such energy sources are a serious health hazard. Breathing kerosene fumes, for instance, can do as much damage as smoking two packs of cigarettes a day. Moreover, kerosene is a notorious cause of household fires. Meanwhile, in addition to being a health hazard, the burning of agricultural wastes deprives the land of important soil nutrients, thereby contributing to a general cycle of increasing rural destitution.

Clearly, therefore, even in the midst of the energy "glut" of the late twentieth and early twenty-first centuries, many—perhaps a majority—of the world's people remains pitifully short of energy for such basic needs as light and heat. Moreover, their output of all sorts of basic consumer products remains cruelly stunted because of a lack of energy. Remember that energy is the largest single cost in the production of many crucial industrial materials and components. It accounts for about one-fifth of the cost of steel, for instance, and nearly one-third of the cost of aluminum. And of course, large amounts of energy are needed to run factory machines and to power the trucks that distribute the factories' output to consumers.

Plentiful supplies of energy are needed even in the efficient production of food, which is, of course, the most basic consumer product of all. If the world only had more energy, it could dramatically increase its output of many key farm products. Just a few kilowatt-hours of electricity expended on stirring the water in Third World fish ponds, for instance, could boost production of shrimps by 100 percent. Similarly modest amounts of electricity could be used to power Third World chicken coops, thereby greatly increasing the output of eggs. If the Third World had enough energy to operate advanced mechanized agricultural methods, it could multiply its output of such important crops as wheat and rice severalfold.

All in all, therefore, if the rest of the world is ever to match First World living standards, the pressure on world energy supplies is inevitably going to increase. In fact, the enrichment of China alone makes this almost a foregone conclusion. If China's growth continues at a fast pace, the Chinese by 2020 may need as much energy as the entire world consumed in 1990. Of course, in the meantime rigorous conservation measures may reduce the West's energy consumption somewhat. Even given great success in conservation, however, world energy supplies will probably have to increase by more than 70 percent simply to accommodate China's rise.

Where is all this energy going to come from? This is a crucial question for the security of the world in the twenty-first century. And it is one that must be urgently addressed if we are not to return to the periodic energy crises that twice sent the world economy into a tailspin in the 1970s.

Unfortunately, the supposed energy "glut" of recent years has bred a dangerous sense of complacency among the world's policymakers and opinion leaders. Nowhere has this complacency been less justified than in the case of oil. The truth is that in believing that the world enjoys a permanent glut of oil, the energy optimists are living in a fool's paradise. As Franco Bernabé, chief executive of Italy's national oil company, ENI, has pointed out, recent optimism has been driven by inflated estimates of the world's reserves of oil. In particular, the officially stated estimates of proven oil reserves for many member nations of both the OPEC oil cartel and the former Soviet bloc have, for various reasons, been greatly exaggerated.

Thus, although the official figures seem to suggest that the world has been finding more oil than it consumes, in reality the reverse is the case. Speaking to *Forbes* magazine's Howard Banks in the late 1990s, Bernabé pointed out that a mere half a dozen major new oil fields had been discovered in the previous thirty years. The rate of discovery of new oil had fallen by more than 85 percent since the early 1960s.

In any case, even in the unlikely event that the world's pace of oil discovery speeds up in the years ahead, concerns about global warming clearly place an upper limit on the extent to which the world can rely on oil for its future energy needs. After all, the consensus among the world's scientists is that consumption of oil and other fossil fuels must be sharply reduced if we are to avoid a disastrous warming of the earth's atmosphere in the next century. Meanwhile, the other major established source of energy, nuclear power, seems unlikely to fill the gap, given growing concerns about the possibility of such negative side effects as Chernobyl-style meltdowns.

In the circumstances, therefore, it is reasonable to expect that renewable energy will play an increasingly important part in boosting the world's energy supplies in the years ahead. The problem so far has been the high cost of the equipment needed to turn renewable energy into electricity. But several of the world's leading manufacturers are now making rapid progress in developing more efficient production technologies that will greatly expand the prospects for renewable energy in the new century. Certainly, developing such technologies will prove to be one of the most important manufacturing challenges in coming decades. To this exciting challenge we now turn.

NATURE'S INEXHAUSTIBLE BOUNTY: WATER, WIND, AND SUNSHINE

Of the main sources of renewable energy, only water power has been widely exploited. Wind power is still greatly underexploited, and solar power has hardly even begun to make a contribution.

Clearly, the potential for renewable energy is huge. Even water power, which in some estimates already generates fully one-fifth of the world's total electricity supplies, has tremendous potential for further growth.

Particularly in the Second and Third Worlds, there remain numerous opportunities for further development of water power. The point is illustrated by China's development of the spectacular Three Gorges Dam. This will raise the water level of the Yangtze River by as much as 590 feet and promises to supply an astounding one-tenth of all China's expected electricity needs by the time of completion in 2009. This will represent about twice the electricity output of Egypt's Aswan Dam, the famously large hydroelectric project of the mid-twentieth century.

Its displacement of 1.3 million people is just one of the reasons the Three Gorges project is highly controversial, but the important point for our purposes is that, with a budgeted cost of $24 billion, it has offered huge opportunities to top First World manufacturers to supply everything from pile drivers to bulldozers. The pickings are proving particularly rich for a few key Japanese, German, and Swiss electrical companies that are supplying a total of twenty-six sets of power-generation equipment.

Making such equipment is a classic example of the sort of advanced manufacturing business that postindustrialists overlook in belittling manufacturing's contribution to the prosperity of the world's richest nations. Virtually invisible to the public, this industry nonetheless already boasts annual revenues of nearly $80 billion. For generations, it has been dominated by a cozy club of top engineering companies like Westinghouse and General Electric of the United States, Hitachi and Toshiba of Japan, Brown Boveri of Switzerland, and Siemens of Germany. Given that would-be challengers face huge entry barriers, the industry's incumbents are likely to remain safely protected from competition from low-wage nations for many years to come. It is a formula not only for large profits and high wages but for strong exports.

Another traditional form of renewable energy that has been creating many new manufacturing jobs in the First World is wind power. Wind power's prospects have been transformed in recent years by technical breakthroughs that have dramatically increased its electrical efficiency. One major improvement has been better design for wind turbines. Wind turbine blades used to be based inappropriately on aircraft propeller designs. Manufacturers have now redesigned the blades to capture wind energy efficiently over a broader range of wind speeds and directions. In addition, certain undesirable side effects of the earlier turbines, particularly noise emission and interference with television reception, have been eliminated or suppressed.

Already wind power has become fully economical in many parts of the Third World, particularly in remote villages far from national electricity grids. Such villages have typically had to rely on diesel generators, but wind power is now a more competitive option. Diesel generators are being replaced by wind turbines in nations like Indonesia, South Africa, Chile, and Argentina, and the electricity needs of one million households in India and nearly one hundred thousand in Mongolia are now powered by wind.

All this helps explain why, with an annual growth rate of 25 percent, wind power has been the fastest-growing energy source in recent years. As of the late 1990s, its contribution to the world's electricity supply was running about eight times higher than in 1985.

Yet the growth in wind energy has nowhere near run its course. According to the leading environmentalist Christopher Flavin, China alone boasts enough untapped wind power to double its existing electricity supplies. The United States boasts even more spectacular wind power opportunities. The untapped wind power in just its three windiest states—North Dakota, South Dakota, and Texas—is enough to supply all U.S. electricity needs.

Of course, there are major technical problems in making full use of available wind power. For a start, the world's windiest places are typically so remote that the power they might generate would be largely lost in transmission before it reached significant population centers. Nonetheless, as the technology improves, even moderately windy sites that are much nearer to big cities may soon become fully competitive sources of power. Certainly the pace of progress in the technology has been impressive: the cost of wind-generated electricity has declined steadily by about 10 percent a year since the early 1980s. No wonder that Roger Taylor of the Colorado-based U.S. National Renewable Energy Laboratory has predicted that wind may soon be a more economical source of power than coal. If optimists such as Joseph J. Romm and

Charles B. Curtis are to believed, by 2020 annual sales of wind-generated electricity could reach as high as $50 billion—a scale that would presage immense opportunities for many First World manufacturers.

Who will reap the richest prizes? Judging by the early running, German manufacturers seem particularly well placed. Germany's wind turbine makers have benefited from state subsidies that have dramatically increased wind power use in recent years—so much so that Germany has now passed the United States to become the world's largest producer of wind-generated electricity. Among German suppliers, the Thyssen steel group seems particularly strong, given its edge in corrosion-resistant steels that promise to transform the wind turbine industry's lackluster reliability record. Denmark, like Germany, boasts an extensive subsidy program and now derives 6 percent of its electricity from wind; the result is that it, too, is strong in the manufacture of wind turbines. Meanwhile, Japan seems to have targeted wind turbines as a key export business of the future. The Osaka-based trading company Tomen, for instance, has already launched a $1.2 billion program to install one thousand wind turbines in various parts of Europe.

Another traditional source of renewable energy that promises many exciting opportunities for the world's advanced manufacturers is so-called biomass. The term refers to a host of biological materials that can be burned to create heat, the most familiar form of which is firewood. Until recently biomass was little used in generating electricity because much of the heat created from burning it went to waste. Biomass was thus a viable source of electricity only in a few areas where it could be harvested particularly cheaply. Now, however, technological breakthroughs in gas turbines have dramatically increased biomass's yield of electricity. This development, of course, opens the way for power stations to pay much higher prices for biomass—a possibility that could powerfully stimulate supply by making it economical for farmers to produce biomass as a main crop rather than an incidental one. That would be good news for the world's environmental future given that biomass boasts a low sulfur content that contrasts particularly with that of coal. Biomass also emits much less carbon dioxide.

Of course, for true believers in renewable energy, even biomass is a secondary player compared to solar energy. The challenge of harnessing the sun's power has been a cause célèbre for visionaries and utopians since 1839, when the French scientist Edmond Becquerel discovered that sunshine can generate electricity in photovoltaic materials. And there is good reason to pursue this challenge: as calculated by the Deutsches Museum in Munich, the amount of solar energy hitting the earth totals about 1.4 billion kilowatt-hours a year—equal to about 15,000 times the earth's entire energy consumption in the 1990s. It will never be possible to harness more than a tiny fraction of this energy, but even so, the potential is huge.

Unfortunately, solar energy has an image problem because of a long record of failing to live up to the promises of its most ardent supporters. "Solar power is one of those things that's always just around the corner," commented Jonathan Weber, writing in the *Los Angeles Times*. "Just a few more technical advances over here, and a little government help over there, and we'll have solved all our energy and pollution problems once and for all—it seems like we've been hearing that for thirty years now."

Nonetheless, as Weber went on to point out, the public's waning interest in solar energy is unwarranted. The truth is that in the last two decades, solar has made great strides toward establishing its right to be taken seriously. In particular, the solar energy industry has greatly improved its production efficiency, to the point where its costs as of the late 1990s had fallen by more than 90 percent compared to those of 1975.

And this is evidently just the beginning. The solar energy industry has high hopes of making further cost cuts thanks to, for instance, lower prices for photovoltaic silicon, the key enabling material used in most solar panels. Like semiconductor-grade silicon, which it closely resembles, photovoltaic silicon is an extremely expensive material in itself, and it is also expensive to process. Several solar panel makers, most notably Munich-based Siemens Solar, a subsidiary of Germany's giant Siemens Electrical Corporation, are now racing to develop thin-film photovoltaic materials. These are typically less than one-fiftieth the thickness of the 300- to 400-micron layers of photovoltaic silicon used in conventional solar panels. Of course, such thin-film versions of silicon are generally less efficient in converting sunshine into power. On balance, however, because they are so much less expensive, they offer clear advantages in many applications. These advantages seem to be increasing all the time as ways are found to boost thin-film's energy conversion ratio.

The early leader in the race to develop thin-film seems to be Siemens Solar, which is already the world's largest maker of solar panels with a world market share of almost one-fifth. Siemens is betting on a variety of thin-film known as copper indium diselenide (CIS). In combination with a subsidiary in California, Siemens in 1997 achieved a world record with CIS-based panels: an energy conversion ratio of 11.1 percent. This was a significant improvement on the previous world record, also set by Siemens, of 10.1 percent. It was even more impressive compared with the rates of around 5 percent that thin-film materials were typically achieving as recently as the early 1990s.

Experts like Princeton's Robert Williams have predicted that both CIS and another version of thin-film known as cadmium-telluride could achieve energy conversion rates as high as 15 percent by 2010. Thus, assuming the industry simultaneously reduces production costs, solar panels could come close to matching the competitiveness of ordinary coal-generated grid electricity within a decade.

The industry's prospects of achieving further cuts in its manufacturing costs look good. As John Driver, head of manufacturing at London-based BP Solar, points out, experience in other manufacturing industries suggests that with every doubling of cumulative volume, unit costs fall by around 20 percent. He adds: "We see no reason why our experience with solar panels should be any different."

Even in the absence of dramatic improvements in production efficiency, it is clear that solar energy is here to stay. Solar is already a fully competitive source of energy in remote areas that do not have grid electricity. Such areas are mainly in the Third World but are by no means confined to it—even some remote parts of the United States do not have grid electricity. To the extent that such areas have had any electricity at all, they have generally drawn it from diesel generators. So how does solar energy compare with diesel? In the first few years, not very well. Even given the recent significant reductions in the cost of solar panels, solar energy systems are typically at least twice as expensive to install as diesel generators. But as the years go by, their low running costs—just one-tenth those of diesel—add up to a huge advantage: thus, measured over a period of ten years, a solar energy system is only about half as expensive as a diesel generator.

Solar's edge is not only that it requires no fuel but that, with no moving parts, it requires virtually no maintenance. Thus, it is particularly competitive in remote regions where deliveries of fuel and parts are often hampered by bad roads. Moreover, solar enjoys an important additional advantage: it is much more environmentally friendly than diesel. It does not emit noxious gases into the atmosphere, and it is silent—a big bonus for anyone who has ever had to put up with the constant din of a diesel generator. Moreover, solar dispenses with the risk of fuel spillages, which are a serious problem with diesel generators. Such spillages are particularly unfortunate when they occur in remote mountainous areas because they can pollute the drinking water of thousands of residents lower down.

With all these advantages, solar is already fully viable in a rapidly growing number of special applications. A good example is remote communications facilities. Everywhere from Sulfur Mountain in California to Antikythira in Greece, repeater stations, which relay telephone and broadcast signals, are now powered by the sun. Radio listeners in Cyprus can thank twenty-eight solar-powered stations installed in 1989 for their radio reception. The world's intercontinental aircraft now rely on signals from solar-powered terrestrial beacons on certain routes. Solar energy also comes into its own in powering remote lighthouses.

Of course, applications of this sort are extremely specialized, and in the aggregate they do not add up to very much. But they provide good profits that go a long way toward funding the industry's heavy ongoing program of research and development. The hope is, of course, that in the long run research and development will bring costs down to the point where the industry can develop a potentially vast market in the Third World. Just how vast the prospects are is apparent from the fact that fully

40 percent of the world's entire population still does not have grid electricity. Solar promises to be particularly efficacious in certain regions of India, China, South America, and Africa, where the proportion of residents without grid electricity rises to as much as 90 percent. Moreover, most such people are unlikely to be connected to the grid anytime soon given that the cost of building transmission lines—at as much as $10,000 per mile—is vast in relation to local income levels.

Already, the solar energy industry has made a start on tapping the potential of the Third World. These are some showcase examples of how dramatically just a little solar energy can transform the lives of thousands of Third World residents:

> **Water supply:** Solar-powered pumps are providing 300 tons of drinking water daily in the arid Sahel region of Senegal. The water is sufficient for the needs of 6,000 villagers and their livestock.

> **Health care:** Vaccines stored in more than 250 solar-powered refrigerators in Kenya have enabled the World Health Organization to vaccinate 70 percent of the nation's children against polio.

> **Communications:** Ten remote islands off Fiji now have a modern telephone service thanks to solar panels supplied by BP Solar. Meanwhile, Siemens has supplied solar-powered equipment that has connected 8,500 new telephone users in rural Mexico to the country's central telephone system.

Contemplating the opportunities in the Third World, Siemens Solar chief executive Gernot J. Oswald waxes ecstatic. "It is very exciting," he says. "A typical Third World domestic system may generate enough power for only three 50-watt lamps and a black-and-white television, but for consumers who would otherwise have no electricity, this is very high-quality power."

According to Siemens's calculations, if the total installed capacity of solar energy panels were to grow by just 15 percent a year, enough electricity would be created by around 2020 to meet the household needs of 1.2 billion Third World citizens and to power water-pumping and medical facilities.

Unfortunately, however, residents of the Third World are generally too poor to finance even the modest $300–500 up-front investment required from each household for a basic solar energy system. Most of the Third World installations showcased in the industry's brochures have been funded by First World aid organizations. Still, there is hope. As John Driver of BP Solar points out, in most parts of the Third World there is *some* disposable income, as is evidenced by, for instance, the number of scooters on the roads. Moreover, solar is cheaper in the long run than the candles, kerosene, diesel fuel, and batteries that currently provide energy to two billion Third World residents.

Oswald suggests that the solution is the development of so-called microbanking services to collect payments of as little as a few dollars from householders, who thus purchase their energy systems in regular installments. The idea has been pioneered by Bangladesh's Grameen Bank, with famously successful results, and Oswald is hopeful that it can be widely adopted elsewhere in the poorer parts of Asia. He is less hopeful, however, about some parts of Africa, where, he declares gloomily, "there is no money."

Assuming that solar costs continue to come down and that microbanking systems are successfully developed in Third World markets, Oswald foresees that solar energy will prove a powerful catalyst for change. Solar's role merely in lighting homes at night will transform millions of lives, particularly in equatorial regions where the sun sets early all through the year. Children can continue their education into the evening and adults will watch television, a pastime that Oswald suggests will do much to curb Third World birth rates.

We have already cited solar's role in pumping water in Senegal. Pumping water is in fact regarded as one of the most productive and cost-effective early applications for solar. Without energy to power pumps,

Third World villagers often have to draw their water by hand. Typically this task falls to women, who in some parts of the Third World must walk as many as three miles a day fetching water for their families. Thus, just a little energy could transform the lives of millions of women, who would then be free to apply their time to such potentially enriching pursuits as intensive gardening.

Solar can also contribute directly to boosting the output of Third World craft workers, who often work in places too dimly lit for efficient production. Oswald cites a project in India in which textile workers doubled their production and achieved a tenfold increase in quality after electric lights were installed.

In the long term, cheap solar-powered telecommunications could help Third World residents participate in the global economy. It is not inconceivable, for instance, that within a few decades educated young citizens of previously remote parts of the Third World could start producing computer software under contract for the wealthy corporations of the developed world. This would boost the local income structure, enabling more residents to finance their own solar energy installations without the need for First World subsidies. In fact, solar could improve lifestyles in remote areas so much that the flight of young people to the Third World's already grossly overcrowded mega-cities could be significantly reduced.

Thus, as solar helps many parts of the Third World bootstrap themselves out of abject poverty, it will simultaneously become a major First World manufacturing industry. A virtuous circle of effects will appear as rising sales volumes help the industry cut its prices, lower prices stimulate demand, and sales are thereby further increased. At some point, solar's costs could become widely competitive with fossil fuels, presaging explosive growth even in advanced nations.

Not surprisingly, despite much professional caution among photovoltaic engineers, several well-informed optimists continue to talk up the industry's prospects. Take the British oil executive John Browne. In a highly optimistic speech in 1997 in his then capacity as chairman of BP solar's parent company, British Petroleum, he predicted that the entire renewable energy industry could account for more than 5 percent of the world's total energy by 2020, and perhaps as much as 50 percent by 2047. Although he did not specify what solar's share in the total would be, it was clear that he believed it would play a leading role.

Browne's expectations are modest, however, compared to the analysis of the Boulder-based energy expert William Hoagland. Writing in *Scientific American,* Hoagland has predicted that solar energy alone could provide as much as 60 percent of the world's electricity by 2025. The full significance of this prediction is apparent only when you realize that Hoagland's figures project a 265 percent increase in global demand for electricity by then.

One thing is undeniable: from an admittedly tiny base, the manufacturing opportunities in solar energy are now growing very rapidly. In conservative estimates, sales revenues are growing by between 15 and 20 percent a year. And some key players seem to be quietly doing considerably better than the average. Take Siemens Solar. Notwithstanding its public concern about the difficulties that lie ahead, Siemens Solar sold five times more photovoltaic capacity in the five years to 2001 than it had sold in its entire previous thirty-year history. Meanwhile, BP Solar is planning by 2007 to have boosted its output tenfold over 1997.

Perhaps the most encouraging news from the solar energy industry is that it has made considerable progress on a crucial—if little known—measure of fundamental efficiency: the industry's energy input-output ratio. This ratio compares the total amount of energy produced by solar panels with the amount expended in manufacturing them. Whereas in the early days the input of energy required was typically three times the eventual total output, the position has now been exactly reversed. As of the late 1990s, solar panels generated at least three times as much energy as the energy required to make them. In other words, in energy terms, if not in terms of total costs, solar is already showing a large net "profit" for planet earth.

If solar fulfills its promise, it will be a massive source not only of excellent jobs but of lucrative export opportunities for many First World nations. Already a host of First World companies are participating in the industry. The most visible players are, of course, the solar panel makers, a category that includes not only British Petroleum (which since 1999 has merged its solar operations with Solarex) and Siemens but Tokyo-based Showa Shell Sekiyu and Kyoto-based Kyocera. These players depend in turn on a host of suppliers for key inputs such as photovoltaic materials. The making of such materials is a highly sophisticated First World business that has so far been dominated by German and Japanese chemical companies.

How much will the solar energy business add to the world's manufacturing job base? For optimists, the prospects are almost limitless. According to Hermann Scheer, a member of the German parliament who is also president of an association called Eurosolar, the solar energy industry could eventually employ an astonishing two million workers worldwide. Meanwhile, Romm and Curtis contend that, taken in aggregate, the entire range of renewables may prove to be a larger source of new jobs than the much-vaunted information industry. Their conclusion:

> The world is on the verge of a revolution in energy and environmental technologies. . . . This revolution can be expected to create a number of industries that collectively will provide one of the largest international markets and one of the largest sources of new high-wage jobs in the next century, with annual sales in excess of $800 billion.

So much for energy. Now let's look at future manufacturing opportunities in one of the industries that stands to gain the most from more abundant energy—transportation.

GOING PLACES:
NEW FRONTIERS IN TRANSPORTATION

The American transportation expert Martin Wachs has perhaps put it best: "Mobility is an underrated human right. You can never have enough of it."

Certainly, experience in the United States suggests that a nation's desire to travel grows with each passing year. As of the early 1990s, the total distance traveled annually by a typical American—including commuting, business travel, and pleasure trips—was about 15,000 miles. This represented a rise of about 100 percent in 30 years—a period in which real incomes in the United States rose by about the same proportion. According to the American transportation experts Andreas Schafer and David Victor, this correlation is not a coincidence. Writing in *Scientific American*, they have posited a fundamental relationship: for each increase of one percentage point in living standards, Americans tend to increase their travel mileage by one percentage point as well. In the developing world, the propensity for people to travel more as they get richer is even more pronounced: in the thirty years to 1990, the Chinese, for instance, increased their travel mileage by three percentage points for every one-percentage-point increase in living standards.

Schafer and Victor predicted that people everywhere would continue to increase their mileage in the twenty-first century. And because people tend to allocate a relatively fixed amount of time to travel, they will use ever faster vehicles.

All this presages vast business opportunities for manufacturers of everything from bicycles and buses to helicopters and supersonic jets. Adding spice to the challenge is the likelihood that makers of the transportation equipment of the future will have to contend with increasingly tough environmental regulation and considerably higher fossil-fuel costs. These considerations demand manufacturing creativity, and it is already apparent that many of the world's great manufacturers are enlisting their best production engineers and designers in the effort to meet the challenge.

One key area of opportunity is cars. All conventional wisdom to the contrary, the global car industry is suffering no permanent glut of capacity. As Alex Taylor III of *Fortune* has argued, demand for cars in emerging economies is likely to soar in the years ahead. The reason is that for every person who owns a car in the developing world today there are probably at least twenty others who aspire to own a car one day. With rising productivity, the car industry will successfully cater to more and more of this potential market as the years go by.

The real challenge for the global car industry is not to find markets to absorb its ever increasing production capacity but rather to meet progressively tighter environmental regulations. Thus, there is little doubt that those carmakers that lead in developing more environmentally friendly products will be well placed to dominate the industry in the next century.

In the long term, perhaps the most exciting source of environmentally friendly power for cars is so-called fuel cells. But for the immediate future, many leading companies are focusing on electric cars. These cars generate virtually no noxious gases, provided, of course, they are run on a nonpolluting source of electricity such as hydropower; they are nearly silent and, in part because they dissipate little energy when braking, highly energy-efficient. When the driver needs to slow down, excess momentum is removed by using the motor as a dynamo: the slowing effect created simultaneously generates electricity that recharges the battery. Electric cars also enjoy the advantage that, in contrast to gasoline-driven cars, they consume no energy while idling.

Unfortunately, however, until battery capacity can be dramatically increased, it looks like electric cars will play only a minor role on the world's roads in the twenty-first century. In the meantime, leading automakers are well advanced in developing a compromise solution, so-called hybrid cars, which use an electric motor in tandem with a conventional gasoline engine. The concept relies heavily on highly sophisticated electronic controls that enable the car to switch smoothly from one power source to the other as speed and road conditions dictate. In common with electric cars, hybrids achieve excellent energy efficiency because their electric motors function as generators that recharge the battery while braking. Hybrids also offer a considerable reduction in noise levels and in emissions of noxious gases.

Another exciting challenge for advanced manufacturing nations is to develop so-called intelligent cars that will eventually drive themselves. A stepping-stone toward this goal will be to build electronic safety systems into both cars and roads to reduce the risk of accidents. One noted prophet of such systems is Masakazu Iguchi, director of the Japan Automobile Research Center. Pointing out that human error is responsible for nearly 90 percent of car accidents, he has called on the car industry to develop safety precautions that would prevent drivers from falling asleep, delaying necessary maneuvers, or failing to watch the road. He suggests that sensors be installed in roads to measure driving conditions and set limits on each car's speed. At the approach to a bend in the road, for instance, a device in the road might alert the car's on-board control system to apply the brakes automatically. Similarly, an optical system might detect a pedestrian in a car's path and take appropriate avoiding action.

As for the goal of driverless cars, European engineers have already built an experimental car equipped with eighteen video cameras that has driven itself at speeds of up to nearly one hundred miles an hour on German highways. Of course, manufacturers will have to overcome many problems before a vehicle like this is feasible for ordinary driving conditions, but Iguchi expects automated driving to become a reality on expressways by the mid-twenty-first century. In the meantime, the first driverless vehicles are likely to be used in routine service in limited environments such as large factories and airports. But in the fullness of time, automatic control systems may become so effective that the elderly, the sick, and even the very young may eventually be able to venture out unaccompanied in driverless cars and be assured that they will arrive safely.

Of course, no matter how much progress the world's leading manufacturers make in developing intelligent road systems and better, more economical cars, such breakthroughs alone will be far from sufficient to provide all the mobility the world will need in the twenty-first century. If experts like Schafer and Victor are right, the share of world traffic volume accounted for by high-speed transport—a category to which they assign both planes and ultra-fast trains—will soar from just 9 percent in 1990 to 25 percent by 2020. Given that the whole transportation pie will also increase dramatically, this means that, in absolute numbers, passenger miles traveled by high-speed transport will multiply more than six times.

Not surprisingly, therefore, the world's passenger jet makers foresee a bonanza in the twenty-first century. China's growth alone could presage an "astounding" increase in demand, according to Boeing's chief executive, Philip Condit.

Already various plans are being floated for faster passenger jets. The

Japanese, for instance, have mooted the possibility of building a supersonic passenger jet that would fly twice as fast as today's conventional jets and would enjoy a range 70 percent longer than Concorde's. Although suggestions emerged that the project might be cancelled after the failure of a test model in Australia in 2002, the Japanese have rarely proved to be quitters in the past: one way or another they can be expected to be leading players in any broad commercialization of supersonic travel.

Other leading manufacturers see the key opportunity in aircraft design as making larger rather than faster planes. The European Airbus consortium, for instance, is planning to build a giant new plane with as many as 656 seats—an increase of 25 percent on the maximum capacity version of the Boeing 747. Airbus has committed nearly $10 billion to the project, making it the largest single investment in the history of aviation. By making extensive use of carbon fiber and other advanced materials, the company expects the new plane to weight 10 to 15 tons less than an equivalent sized Boeing 747. This will generate huge savings in running costs, most notably a 13 percent reduction in fuel consumption. As a result, the fuel consumption per passenger will be about the same as for a midsize car.

Of course, given the limits on the world's energy and other resources, even larger cost reductions than this will be necessary if long-distance travel is ever to become a routine prerogative of residents of today's Third World. As it happens, such cost reductions are already in sight in the form of high-speed trains. As the economist Wallace C. Peterson has pointed out, these trains can be as much as ten times more fuel-efficient than planes. And unlike planes, they do virtually no damage to the earth's threatened ozone layer.

Of course, even the fastest trains are not as fast as planes. Running at up to 190 miles an hour, both Japan's famous bullet train and France's TGV are less than half as fast as a typical passenger jet. But this is less of a disadvantage than it appears given that train stations are usually more accessible than airports. In reality, total door-to-door journey times for fast trains often compare well with air travel time.

Not surprisingly, the fast-train business is a highly promising one for many leading manufacturers. In China alone, the opportunities are immense. Officials are investing $12 billion in a new 800-mile high-speed track between Beijing and Shanghai. The investment is the centerpiece of a major overhaul of the country's decrepit rail network, and it will enable trains to achieve speeds of more than 150 miles an hour—a dramatic improvement in a country where until the mid-1990s train speeds of less than 40 miles an hour were the norm. Meanwhile, South Korea and Taiwan are also developing ultrafast train networks. In Europe, too, major rail investments are planned that will link Eastern Europe with the fast-train networks of France and Germany.

In the worldwide race to develop faster train systems, one nation is conspicuously on the sidelines—the United States. In truth, passenger rail service has advanced little in the United States since the 1930s (when, as Glenn Miller's "Chattanooga Choo Choo" reminds us, American trains set the pace for the rest of the world). The United States was passed in rail technology by leading Japanese and French rolling stock manufacturers in the 1960s, and it has continued to fall further behind ever since. In fact, even in the late 1990s few American trains ran faster than about eighty miles an hour—little more than half the speed that the Chinese are now aiming for. Yet, there is no inherent lack of potentially profitable routes for fast trains in the United States. In fact, given that American cities are dispersed widely over a huge land mass, the United States could probably make better use of fast trains than almost any other nation. Certainly, there is no fundamental economic and technical barrier to the United States aspiring to lead in high-speed trains. The key barrier is dysfunctional politics: the development of rail systems in the United States has repeatedly in recent decades been opposed by powerful industrial lobbies, most notably that of the automobile and airline industries.

The result is that American manufacturers of rail equipment have fallen more and more behind their counterparts in Europe and Japan. In fast trains, much of the exciting work in recent decades has been done in France. The French claim, for instance, a considerable edge in various technologies designed to reduce the weight of trains. Lower weight is, of course, a key objective in that the damage caused to tracks by fast-moving trains is otherwise prohibitively expensive to repair. The French have, for instance, designed cars with just one bogie instead of two. (Bogies, the sets of wheels on which the train is carried, account for a considerable proportion of a train's total weight.) The French have also taken large amounts of weight out of the trains' enormous electrical transformers as well as the car bodies. These innovations have encouraged the French to talk about manufacturing a new generation of trains that will cruise at up to 225 miles an hour and could eventually achieve speeds as high as 250 miles an hour.

As if this were not enough, German and Japanese manufacturers are now close to success in developing a completely new type of train propulsion system that could eventually achieve still higher speeds. In this new system, known as magnetic levitation (or "maglev" for short), the train is supported not by wheels but by high-strength magnets, which enable it to hover about an inch or so above the track. With mechanical friction thus greatly reduced, the train can deliver a notably smooth ride even at extremely high speeds.

One problem for the maglev concept, however, is that it requires a vast investment not only in new trains but in the construction of a completely new type of track. Moreover, the success with which engineers have been able to speed up conventional trains in recent decades has dramatically narrowed the once commanding lead in speed and comfort that maglev promised when research began on the concept more than three decades ago.

Nonetheless, the prospects are good that maglev will generate major manufacturing opportunities in the end. Certainly, the huge up-front costs entailed in laying down maglev tracks are not necessarily a barrier for capital-rich nations like Japan and Germany. Such nations can afford to take an ultra-long-term view, given that the maglev concept's heavy up-front costs can be readily recovered over literally centuries of subsequent service. In fact, maglev promises to be an excellent long-term investment in that its plane-style advantages in speed and comfort will allow maglev operators to price their seats at close to airline levels. Operators' outlays on energy and other ongoing costs will be only a fraction of airlines' costs.

Beyond maglev, the transportation industry bristles with a host of other opportunities for innovative manufacturers. Private planes and helicopters, for instance, are likely to enjoy enormous growth in the twenty-first century as their cost falls rapidly thanks to more efficient manufacturing methods. Opportunities will also abound in road freight transportation. Trainlike trucks may be developed to pull several trailers, each equipped with automatic guidance equipment and independent brakes to ensure that it remains safely on the road. The result would be large savings not only in drivers' wages but in general overheads.

Clearly, therefore, the manufacturing opportunities in transportation are, if anything, even larger than in the energy industry. Already, the contenders in the field read like a *Who's Who* of the world's great manufacturing companies.

CHAPTER 8

I f America's drift into postindustrialism continues unchecked, we can safely predict a drastic deterioration in the American economy's performance in the decades ahead. In particular, the outlook is for continuing subpar growth in personal incomes. And the worst affected are likely to be poorer Americans. Given that, on the author John E. Schwarz's figures, the proportion of Americans who are poor increased by nearly 50 percent in the last three decades of the twentieth century, postindustrialism clearly presages a further worsening of the single most conspicuous economic problem the United States has suffered in recent decades. Even for middle-class Americans the income outlook is for, at best, lack-luster growth—certainly much lower growth than what middle-class Americans had become used to up to the mid-1970s.

Postindustrialism also bodes ill for America's foreign trade position and, by extension, for its continued ability to project economic power abroad. Although many feel-good commentators try to gloss over the significance of trade (America's imports, they say, don't matter very much because they account for "just" 14.5 percent of gross domestic product), trade is actually crucially important. Trade, after all, is a nation's fundamental economic connection with the outside world, and among other things, this means that in the long run it is the most important determinant of a nation's ranking in the world income league. Thus, nations that fail to produce enough of the right sort of exports inexorably sink down the league table.

Anyone who is unconvinced on this point need merely look at other nations that in the past have failed to rectify persistent trade deficits. The fate of Argentina is perhaps the ultimate warning of what could be in store. Like the United States today, Argentina in the early part of this century ranked among the world's richest nations in per capita income. But thanks in large part to persistent neglect of its chronic trade deficits, it dropped steadily in the world income league table over the years to the point where it recently ranked lower than such developing countries as Thailand, Syria, and Lithuania.

If the United States continues to neglect its trade problems, the moment of truth is likely to come in the form of a major dollar crisis. In the event of another dollar crisis similar in scale to the crisis it suffered in the early 1990s, the American economy could be displaced almost overnight by Japan as the world's largest economy. As of this writing (in spring of 2003), the dollar had weakened somewhat vis-à-vis the euro but it was still remarkably overvalued by comparison with most East Asian currencies (particularly the Japanese yen, the Taiwanese dollar, and the Chinese renminbi). It was clear that the dollar was being kept on a life support machine by the central banks of the principal capital-exporting nations, most notably Japan and China.

The best way to grasp the scale of the gathering dollar crisis is to ask a question: how much would the dollar need to be devalued before the United States could hope to balance its trade? Bearing in mind the fact that the American manufacturing sector has become progressively more hollowed out in the last quarter century, the size of the necessary devaluation is now almost too large to contemplate. The shocking truth is that even if the dollar were to be devalued by more than 50 percent vis-à-vis the major East Asian currencies, the bet is that America's trade would still be in deficit.

For as long as America's main foreign trade partners continue to support the dollar (by, for instance, investing their surpluses in U.S. Treasury bonds and other American investments), a full-blown dollar crash can be forestalled. But the longer the dollar remains artificially high, the more devastating the ultimate adjustment will be.

Clearly, therefore, the need for drastic policy changes is now urgent. But before the United States can implement realistic measures to recover its lost manufacturing leadership, it must first understand the full extent of its problems. Unfortunately, a whole host of factors have hitherto hidden from Americans the full seriousness of their predicament. We have mentioned one of these factors already—free-market ideology, which, as we noted in Chapter 1, powerfully but spuriously supports the postindustrialists' confidence in the information economy as a superior source of future wealth. Many other factors are also at work, and we will consider them in this chapter.

"A FRENZY OF RELIGIOUS INTENSITY": THE PRESS AND POSTINDUSTRIALISM

One of the key reasons the American people have been so complacent about America's drift into deindustrialization is that they have been badly blindsided by the American press. Although the American press can generally claim a proud record of objectivity and reliability in its coverage of most types of news, it is far from a neutral observer in the postindustrial debate. Not only have press commentators been among the most extreme enthusiasts of postindustrialism but, to the extent that they canvass other opinions and insights on how the world economy works, they tend to gravitate to like-minded sources in think tanks and academic life. Admittedly in the wake of the dot-com crash of 2000 and 2001, the press has become somewhat more guarded in its enthusiasm for postindustrialism than it had been in the late 1990s. Even so, most press commentators remain knee-jerk postindustrialists who are remarkably unconcerned about the virtual demise of American manufacturing in recent years.

Perhaps we shouldn't be too surprised by the press's partisanship. After all, given that the press is a founding member of the information society, its own vested interests are clearly at stake in the postindustrial debate. Even though reporters rarely if ever consciously take this into account in their coverage, the fact remains that they display a marked unconscious bias in favor of postindustrialism.

In any case, at a personal level, press reporters have their own reasons to feel good about the information revolution. They have, for instance, benefited disproportionately from the emergence of ubiquitous and user-friendly word-processing in recent years. Certainly, few reporters who remember the multiple retypings and messy handwritten changes of predigital journalism would want to turn the clock back.

Another factor that favorably influences journalists' attitudes to the information economy is the Internet. Although, as we have seen, the Internet is generally still too shallow to be of much value for serious business research, it is a godsend for reporters and editors in, for instance, checking routine facts. At the click of a mouse, a reporter can turn up anything from a government official's middle initial to a screen actor's marital record. For reporters who remember the old days when they had to pore over faded clippings in a dusty news library, conjuring up such information effortlessly out of the ether seems like magic. We need hardly be surprised, therefore, that, as the syndicated columnist Richard Harwood noted, the press's hyping of the Internet was indefatigable in the late 1990s.

Essentially, as Kurt Andersen pointed out at the height of the dot-com stock bubble, journalists, in common with financial professionals, have become computer-dependent. He added: "What journalists and financial professionals haven't understood . . . is that almost no one else finds computers and the Internet quite so essential. As a result of this improbable accident of history, . . . [information] technology now sits at the center of a speculative frenzy of religious intensity."

Even some of the world's most influential media organizations have clearly succumbed to this frenzy. The *Wall Street Journal* and *The Economist* magazine are notable cases in point. Each betrays a consistently uncritical enthusiasm for postindustrialism that clearly owes much to a doctrinally driven tendency to endorse almost any new trend that emerges in America's free-market economy. Unfortunately, where doctrinal issues are at stake, neither *The Economist* nor the *Wall Street Journal* (at least in its editorial pages) can be relied on to report contrary evidence accurately, let alone fairly. *The Economist*'s attempts to understand the issues are further distorted by the disadvantage of its British base. Although the British economy has been in relative decline since the mid-nineteenth century, this does not stop *The Economist* from presenting the United Kingdom as still the world economy's ultimate trendsetter. Thus, just as the United Kingdom long ago began exiting manufacturing for such postindustrial services as finance, *The Economist* argues that the United States should be following the Mother Country's "lead."

If the postindustrial mania were limited to doctrinally driven publications like *The Economist* and the *Wall Street Journal,* it would be bad enough. But unfortunately, the mania has now also gripped other publications less noted for their doctrinal biases. Take *Fortune* magazine. Here is an institution that up to 1993 was so convinced of the pivotal importance of manufacturing that it refused to include anything but manufacturing companies in its famous Fortune 500 roll call of America's ultimate corporate greats. In subsequent years, however, *Fortune* swung so violently to the opposite extreme that it often in the late 1990s seemed to be an uncritical booster of all things postindustrial. *Fortune*'s enthusiasm for postindustrialism is apparent, for instance, in a portentous list of "cool companies" it has been publishing annually since 1993. "Cool" in this case is intended to mean technologically exciting, and the unmistakable subtext of *Fortune*'s cool company list is that manufacturing is no longer cool. The 1997 list notably exemplified the point that not a single manufacturer was considered worthy of inclusion. All fifteen companies that did make the list not only were postindustrial operations but were almost laughably insignificant. One of them, a sort of electronic clippings service called ideaMarket, employed just eighteen people, and most of the others were not much larger. In aggregate, all fifteen companies employed a total of a mere 2,781—in other words, little more than the number of people IBM hired in a good month in its days of manufacturing leadership (when its contribution to America's job base made it a truly cool company).

If the press's role had been limited merely to lionizing obscure, untried cyberspace start-ups, things would have been bad enough. But the press did its readers' understanding of the issues an even greater disservice in its constant hyping of the American economy's performance in the deindustrializing 1990s. By the latter half of the decade, many press commentators had become so convinced that the United States had undergone a full-scale economic renaissance that they were talking as if American corporations had "the world at their feet."

Admittedly the press had a good excuse in that everything *seemed* to be going so well for the American economy in the late 1990s. Corporate America was showing healthy and generally rising profits and on Wall Street stock prices were, of course, soaring. But even in the euphoria of the late 1990s, evidence abounded that the United States was living in a fool's paradise. The point is, of course, that the U.S. current account deficits were more or less spiraling out of control. And to the extent that America's manufactured imports were coming largely from such ultrahigh-wage nations as Germany and Japan, it was hard to see how "healthy and competitive" the American economy truly was. After all, the sense of American economic decline that had been so much discussed in previous decades was driven more than anything by the perennially deteriorating trade position. But to press commentators, the trade problems were merely a "quibble." Some quibble. In the decade of the 1990s, America's current account deficits totaled $1,423 billion. This was an increase of more than 78 percent on the total for the 1980s (the 1980s performance was, of course, considered disastrous by commentators at the time). Moreover, the increase in the 1990s came despite a major de facto devaluation in the latter half of the 1980s that was supposed soon to dispose of the deficits for good.

To the extent that commentators focused at all on the U.S. trade problem in the late 1990s, they tended to see it somehow as evidence of America's fundamental economic superiority: a "booming" United States was sucking in imports from the "stagnant" economies of Europe and East Asia.

Just one of the many obvious problems with this argument, however, was that more than one-quarter of America's imports were coming from nations where wages were actually higher than those of the United States. This begs an historic question: Why wasn't the United States capable of making such goods for itself? Few press commentators asked the question. Even fewer answered it. The sad reality is that after the rundown of so many once-great American manufacturing industries in the previous two decades, the United States simply did not have the capacity anymore to meet its consumers' needs from its own manufacturing resources.

The press's role in obscuring the extent to which American manufacturers are failing to hack it in world markets has been compounded by its portrayal of manufacturing as a consistently dull career suitable only for self-evident second-raters. This explains why, as noted in *Made in America,* a study published by the Massachusetts Institute of Technology in 1989, manufacturing departments in corporate America have come to be regarded as dead ends—places "where you go and stay until you die." This contrasts sharply with the position of manufacturing in Japan, where, as the MIT study reported, "production has far greater stature [than in the United States] and attracts some of the most qualified and competent technical and management professionals."

The American press's tendency to belittle manufacturing naturally colors its attitude to the world's great manufacturing economies. This is notably apparent in the case of Germany, whose economic arrangements are constantly being slighted by ill-informed American press commentators. An article in *Fortune* in 1997 illustrated the pattern. The magazine reported that manufacturing accounts for 30 percent of jobs in Germany versus just 16 percent in the United States. *Fortune* commented that this was "a sure sign" that German manufacturers were "seriously overstaffed."

But were they? For anyone who had eyes to see, the real reason for Germany's large manufacturing workforce was obvious: Germany is a highly successful exporter. Given that German manufacturers typically export nearly two-thirds of their total output, they clearly have a good excuse for employing a large manufacturing labor force.

Moreover, trade also helps explain why the United States has such a small manufacturing labor force—because, of course, the United States these days relies on imports for nearly one-third of all its consumption of manufactured goods. One thing is certain: with German wages running well above American levels, Germany's manufacturers have not become dominant players in export markets by being "overstaffed."

Press commentators also tend to be absurdly disparaging about the manufacturing economies of East Asia. In particular, they tend to be patronizing about Japan's key high-tech industries. A notable case in point is computers, a field in which Japan is consistently portrayed as an also-ran. The only evidence adduced for this assertion is that the Japanese do little exporting of desktop computers (they long since vacated this space because it is a low-tech assembly business). The fact is that the Japanese are absolutely dominant in other areas of the computer industry that are vastly more sophisticated than the desktop business.

Take supercomputers. Although in the early 1990s it was widely predicted that new so-called "massively parallel" technology would soon put the United States securely in the lead in supercomputers, the reports proved to be little more than wishful thinking. By the beginning of the new century, Japan was further ahead than ever. As of 2003, Japan's fastest computer, the so-called Earth Simulator, was nearly five times faster than the fastest American supercomputers, two equally fast Hewlett-Packard machines installed in Los Alamos. The Japanese machine is used to predict weather and earthquakes. The American machines are used to design nuclear weapons.

Of more economic importance, the Japanese are way ahead in the manufacture of key components. A classic example of such components is the tiny laser diodes that, as we pointed out in Chapter 5, play such an important enabling role in the Information Age. Japan's leadership in miniaturization is easy to overlook, but the point is that, since the industry's earliest days, the key technological challenge in computers has always been to get ever greater performance out of ever smaller components. This is by no means an insignificant challenge. To make things smaller requires not only ever higher standards of purity in materials and accuracy in machining but constant innovation in addressing problems like overheating (which is a key concern in, for instance, tiny friction-bearing parts of the sort used in CD-ROMs). In essence, the superpowerful notebook computers made by such Japanese giants as Toshiba, Fujitsu, and Hitachi are the pinnacle of the computer industry's fifty-year quest to pack ever more performance into ever smaller packages.

The press's uncomprehending attitude toward Japan's extraordinary success in computer miniaturization is part of a fashion for the business press to dismiss many highly sophisticated manufactured products as "commodities." The term is much used in reference to, for instance, advanced electronic components that are made to industry-standard designs. Typical of such components are liquid-crystal displays. The key to success in such a product is supreme manufacturing efficiency and consistently high quality. Companies that fail to meet these tests have nowhere to hide. The result is that the field of contenders in such undifferentiated "commodity" products has thinned rapidly to a highly exclusive group of massively capitalized, relentlessly driven Japanese companies like Toshiba, Hitachi, NEC, Sony, and Sharp. These are the Wimbledon finalists of manufacturing—companies whose production technology is so far advanced that, even though they pay higher wages than their American counterparts, they are little troubled by American competition. In other words, they are a charmed circle. Yet, when the press refers to such companies' products as "commodities," the implication is the diametric opposite—that the fields concerned are wide open to competition from low-wage countries. Thus, *commodities* is a weasel word that hides from the American reading public how far ahead Japanese manufacturing companies truly are.

Of course, if Japanese manufacturers are doing so much better than their American counterparts, this prompts an obvious question: why has the Japanese economy been doing so badly in recent years? Why indeed. It is time to find out what really happened to the Japanese economy in the 1990s.

THE ENIGMA OF JAPANESE ECONOMICS: IT'S THE SURPLUSES, STUPID!

One of the biggest factors encouraging Americans to view postindustrialism complacently in recent years has been the conviction that, even after the collapse of the dot-com bubble, the United States stands gloriously unchallenged as the world's sole economic superpower. It is all such a contrast with the 1980s, when the United States was widely perceived as losing ground inexorably to an ever-burgeoning Japan. To the postindustrialists, therefore, the logic would appear to be watertight: because a postindustrial United States has "turned the tables" on Japan's "machine age" economy, there could hardly be a clearer demonstration of the superiority of postindustrialism.

There is only one problem with this: the United States has not turned the tables on Japan. Far from it. In the ways that matter to policymakers on both sides of the Pacific, Japan has continued to gain on the United States over the last decade and has done so precisely because it has stayed the course in manufacturing.

But how can all this be reconciled with the American press's picture of Japan as the worst-performing major economy of the 1990s? It cannot, of course. In reality, Western observers suffer major comprehension problems in covering Japan's highly counterintuitive economy—problems that in recent years have consistently concealed Japan's enormous underlying economic strengths.

We'll look at these comprehension problems in a moment, but first let's be clear: any summary of the case against the "lost decade" myth must start by acknowledging that Japan has, of course, suffered serious financial strains in the last decade. This present writer would be the last person to deny these strains. After all, he was virtually alone among Tokyo-based observers in predicting them: in a series of articles he began in September 1987 in a London-based financial magazine, he identified the fundamental weaknesses in Japan's bubble economy and outspokenly predicted Japan's real estate, banking, and stock implosions of the 1990s. All that said, the effects of these troubles have been massively exaggerated in the Western press. The truth is that the wider Japanese economy has quietly thrived—so much so that, in many of the ways that matter to Japanese policymakers, Japan has actually now surpassed the United States.

As recounted by conventional commentators, Japan's story in the last twenty years is a morality tale of the perils of overarching ambition. It begins in the early to mid-1980s when Japan suddenly seemed to be sweeping all before it. But just as this new Sparta was on the verge of vanquishing the freedom-loving West, fate—in the form of the Tokyo stock market crash of 1990—intervened. The wheels came off the Japanese economic pantechnicon. Ever since, Japanese leaders have been engaged in increasingly comic efforts to get them back on.

This story has enormous appeal in the West, not least for the free-marketeers who edit the business pages on both sides of the Atlantic. But the main reason why this story has been so widely accepted is because a key interested party on the other side of the world wants it to be believed—to wit, the Japanese economic establishment. For Japanese economic planners, the basket case story yields many benefits, of which only the most obvious has been its powerful effect in cooling the West's once dangerous anger over Japanese trade policies. Japanese planners also see a second crucial benefit, in that by appearing to discredit those American intellectuals and policymakers who in the late 1980s raised the alarm about East Asian economic competition, the myth of Japan's "lost decade" has long ago snuffed out several embryonic efforts begun then to stage a government–led American industrial renaissance.

The truth is that dozens of facts contradict the gloomy consensus on the Japanese economy. Here are just a few:

- Living standards increased markedly in Japan during the "lost decade" of the 1990s—so much so that the Japanese people are now amongst the world's richest consumers. This is apparent in everything from their stylish and well-cut clothes to their world-beating life expectancy rates. Their homes are filled with the most advanced versions of electronic gadgetry. Japanese drivers drive the world's newest and best-equipped cars. Following major improvements in the 1990s, the Tokyo system is now one of the world's most sophisticated. Japanese mobile phones are the world's smallest and most sophisticated. Even on vacation, the Japanese people have never had it so good. Although vacation travel dropped off markedly after the atrocities of September 11, 2001, up to that time, travel out of Japan had been growing by leaps and bounds. In 2000, for instance, the number of Japanese citizens holidaying abroad totaled 14,582,000—an increase of 80 percent on 1989.

• Japan's trade position has continued to strengthen rapidly. Its current account surpluses totalled $987 billion in the "disastrous" 1990s. This was nearly 2.4 times the total recorded in the 1980s (when Japan was already seen as the "unstoppable juggernaut" of world trade).

• Although you might have expected the Japanese yen to have declined sharply against the U.S. dollar in recent years, the reverse has been the case: as of the summer of 2003, it stood 23 percent higher against the U.S. dollar than it had at the end of 1989.

• At last count, the all-important Japanese savings rate, which has been the main driver of the country's success, was 8.7 per cent of GDP. By comparison, the rate for the United States was 5.7 per cent and for Britain only 4.5 per cent. In the 1990s, Japan routinely accounted for nearly 30 percent of all new savings in the OECD group of rich nations. It is sometimes suggested that Japan's high savings rate is a problem. If so, it is a problem that most of the world's nations would be delighted to have. (To the extent that there are excess savings in Japan, these can be easily and—in national power terms—usefully deployed in buying foreign assets.)

- In flat contradiction of suggestions that Japan's banking troubles have starved industry of capital, investment per job in Japanese manufacturing has consistently run at about twice the rate of the United States over the last decade.

- Although the eagerness with which Japanese investors snapped up foreign assets in the 1980s was a major reason why Japanese expansionism came to be eyed so suspiciously in the West, Japan's net foreign assets have continued to mushroom. As measured by the IMF, they nearly quadrupled in the eleven years ended in 2000. How do we reconcile this with reports that the Japanese banks' problems have been forcing a wholesale retreat by Japanese finance from foreign markets? The reports are nonsense. A nation's ability to export capital is a function not of its banks' financial health but rather of its trade performance. Each dollar of current account surplus creates a dollar of capital exports. So long as Japan runs huge current account surpluses, it will remain a huge capital exporter.

- As a glance at Tokyo's crane-filled skyline confirms, even in the hard-hit real estate sector the pace of investment has continued at an astonishing rate. An all-time record of more than 2.2 million square meters of new office space was due to be completed in Tokyo in 2003. On the site of a disused railyard near the Ginza shopping area, no less than twelve major buildings and many smaller ones are being erected in one huge development which will create more space than was contained in the towers of the World Trade Center.

Western analysts somehow manage to overlook the above achievements and focus instead on various alleged crises for Japan that, in reality, are no such thing.

As we have already noted, the widely aired suggestion that Japan's manufacturing industries are being driven to the wall by China is obviously bogus.

Another much publicized "crisis" is the deflationary "spiral" that Japan has experienced in recent years. The implication of the word *spiral* is that it is a development that is both uncontrollable and highly destructive. It is nothing of the sort. What Japan has been experiencing is similar to the persistent deflation the United States experienced in the late nineteenth century. This was when the United States went from a rural backwater to the world's most powerful economy.

In Japan today, as in the United States then, monetary policy has been so effective in maintaining the currency's domestic purchasing power that the economy's rapid productivity improvements translate into a steadily falling price level. This is hardly a recipe for large profit margins. The result is a feel-bad feeling in corporate Japan. Similarly, as described by the historian Walter LaFeber, the productivity-induced deflation experienced in the United States in the twenty-five-year period to 1897 was "economic hell." But it was thanks to American industry's market-glutting productivity improvements in this period that the United States succeeded Britain as the world's greatest economy.

One of the most remarkable aspects of the "basket case" story is how it keeps mutating. As in a Harrison Ford movie, no sooner does Japan dispatch one problem than a more daunting one emerges from the deep. At first, the problem was supposed to be the stock market collapse. Then, it was the banks' real estate lending. Then, other problems swiftly followed: the banks' accounting for their loan losses, a consumer spending funk, and a corporate investment strike.

In the early years of the new century, the "disaster" was Japan's allegedly out-of-control government spending. But Japan's budget problems are grossly exaggerated. OECD figures show that in the first eight years of the 1990s, Japan actually ran large budget surpluses. Since then, the government's position has deteriorated somewhat but it is still no worse than in many other nations.

It is often pointed out that Japanese government debt represented 120 percent of GNP in 2000. This does seem shockingly high—but, unbeknownst to most Western observers, it is a gross figure that should properly be netted for the Japanese government's huge and continually increasing financial assets. These include not only the world's largest foreign exchange reserves but extensive holdings of its own bonds. On a net basis, Japan's national debt represents just 51 percent of annual GDP—higher than the United States' 43 percent but lower than that of most other developed countries.

As Adam Posen of the Institute for International Economics in Washington has pointed out, the Japanese debt scare is a storm in a teacup. "Savings, public and private in Japan, is a vast multiple of the government debt, so there is no solvency problem." Moreover, when the Japanese government borrows, it borrows almost entirely from its own citizens—crucially a mere 6 percent of Japanese government debt is owed to foreigners (and most of this is believed to be owed to Japanese-owned overseas entities such as London-based Mitsubishi Finance). By contrast, as we have already noted, the United States depends heavily on foreigners, particularly the Japanese and the Chinese, to fund its national debt.

As the story of Japan's alleged public spending profligacy indicates, much of the responsibility for the West's misunderstandings must be put down to the Western press. In perpetuation of a long tradition, the press has been remarkably naïve in its choice of sources in Japan. In general, it has been heavily influenced by a few supergloomy foreign stock analysts in Tokyo. These analysts happen in many cases to be the same people who in the 1980s did so much to persuade Western investment houses to invest billions of dollars in subsequently worthless Japanese securities. Press correspondents are also blinded by Western ideas that do not apply in Japan. They assume, for instance, that the stock market plays as prominent a role in Japanese finance as it does in British or American finance. Thus, when the Tokyo stock market crashed, this was seen as comparable to the Wall Street crash. In reality, the stock market is regarded by the Japanese establishment as a rather dirty sideshow that can be neglected with impunity for years on end.

Whatever the Western media's responsibility, the lion's share of the blame for the misunderstandings rests with the Japanese establishment. The impression of dysfunctional economic management in Tokyo is no more than grand kabuki—a thespian exercise in mock distress acted out by a Japanese elite that has always believed in cloaking its agenda. Such theatrics are fundamental to Japan's administrative culture—a culture whose authoritarian ethos imposes no obligation on leaders to speak frankly to their own people, let alone to outsiders.

Officialdom has played a key role in misleading the press. Take, for example, official press packs distributed to visiting journalists that routinely describe the economy as being in a "slump". This is a word that even a country as perennially beset by economic disasters as Argentina would shrink from using about itself. Among other things, the word connotes very high levels of unemployment—several times anything in Japan, where indeed the unemployment rate has consistently remained low by international standards. In the face of unprecedented financial turmoil, unemployment averaged less than 3.1 percent in the decade of the 1990s. That compares with an average of more than 5.7 percent for the United States (in a decade in which the American economy was portrayed as the wonder of the world). It is a myth, incidentally, that Japan understates its unemployment rate; in reality, Japan uses the same OECD-approved methodology as the United States.

Admittedly, the Japanese unemployment rate did rise considerably in the last years of the 1990s, and it hit 5.5 percent in 2001. This was certainly very high by previous Japanese standards. But it largely reflected demographic rather than economic factors—specifically the rapid aging of the Japanese population. In any case, it was actually low by the standards of most other advanced economies in recent years.

Yet despite all this, even Japan's most prominent industrial chieftains joined the campaign to suggest that Japan's sky was falling. In April 1998, for instance, Sony Corporation chairman Norio Ohga went on record saying, "The Japanese economy is on the verge of collapsing." A few months later, Toyota president Hiroshi Okuda added that Japan's problems could trigger a "worldwide financial crash."

When corporate chiefs talk like this, we can be forgiven for assuming that their comments reflect their own corporations' experience. But actually nothing in the experience of either corporation remotely justified such outbursts. Quite the reverse. In fact, as these corporate chieftains were pressing the panic button in 1998, their corporations were doing notably well. In Sony's case, its profits in 1998 represented growth on 1989 of a stunning 131 percent.

True, in Toyota's case the profits growth was more modest—relative to 1989, its profits in 1998 were up a mere 56 percent. But compared to other companies in the auto industry, that was actually a standout performance. In particular, it compared favorably with the performance of Ford and General Motors in the same period. The full incongruity of Okuda's remarks became apparent in the early years of the new century as Toyota's stock market value soared. The result was that by 2003, Toyota Motor's stock market value was greater than the *combined value* of General Motors, Ford, and DaimlerChrysler. The fact is that much of the stupendous value that the world's investors recognized in Toyota Motor in 2003 had been built up in the late 1990s and a large part of that had come from Toyota's pole position in a strong—and highly protected—Japanese home market. Just how strong that home market had been can be gauged from the fact that nearly eight million more Japanese households owned a car in 1999 than in 1989. Moreover, in the case of those who already owned a car in 1989, most owned a much more powerful and comfortable model by 1999. Japan's executive class, for instance, has migrated en masse to such tony limousines as the Toyota Celsior (or Lexus, as it is known in the West) that are a world away from the antiquated Toyota Century that was standard issue for the corporate elite in the 1980s. Perhaps even more startling is the extent to which Japan now leads the world in the latest car accessories. Take car navigation devices: as of 2002, two-thirds of the entire world population of these devices, which guide drivers to their destinations, are installed in cars on Japanese roads.

Helping the boom in car ownership was the very government policies that the Toyota president seemed to be complaining about. After all, a key part of the Japanese government's economic management in the 1990s was to invest heavily in the country's road system. Japanese drivers benefited from countless major road construction projects that have considerably improved driving conditions throughout Japan. Examples include such latter-day civil engineering miracles as the Tokyo Bay undersea road tunnel and the Akashi suspension bridge, both of which have set new world records for length.

This is not the first time that Japanese leaders have been successful in understating their country's strengths. In the late 1930s, for instance, the Japanese military let it be known that Japanese soldiers couldn't shoot straight and that Japanese planes were made of paper. In the event, Japan's opening gambit in World War II, the Pearl Harbor offensive, proved a military masterpiece; and Japan's Mitsubishi Zeroes were, of course, revealed as the most sophisticated fighter planes yet built.

Corporate Japan has often used similar tactics to lull competitors into a false sense of security. Take the car industry. When I arrived in Tokyo in 1985, its mantra was that the Japanese were somehow incapable of making large luxury models. The implication, of course, was that a beleaguered Detroit could at least hope to retain a sanctuary at the top of the market. Then suddenly, in the late 1980s, Japanese carmakers launched the Lexus, the Infiniti, and other superbly built top-of-the-line limousines.

One of the few commentators who saw through the absurdity of Japan's fake slump of the 1990s was the author and former China watcher William Holstein. He commented, "Here is the world's second largest economy, which commands $12 trillion or so in wealth, and the media have created the impression that the country is on the edge of breakdown."

So how strong is the Japanese economy really? I have addressed this question before in a book in 1995 entitled *Blindside: Why Japan Is Still on*

Track to Overtake the United States by the Year 2000. From my vantage point in Tokyo as of the summer of 2003, I have seen remarkably little in the interim to undermine the *Blindside* analysis. True, on the conventional measure of an economy's size, the Japanese economy as of 2003 was only about half the size of the American one. But on many more important measures—specifically the ability to project economic power abroad—things looked quite different. Japan had long since passed the United States as the world's largest aid donor, for instance. It was by far the world's largest direct investor and as such was courted by national and regional governments around the world. Moreover, without Japan's constant injections of capital in the U.S. Treasury bond market, the American economy would literally have ground to a halt.

The book's fundamental point was that in the early 1990s Japanese leaders began a deliberate and massive campaign to exaggerate Japan's financial problems. The validity of that allegation is now acknowledged by many leading independent Western experts on Japan. It is, however, a symptom of the nature of the West's perennial problems in understanding the Japanese econo-political system that such experts are prepared to say this only in private. As one of them has acknowledged, to question publicly the conventional story that the Japanese economy suffered a "lost decade" in the 1990s would be career suicide for any Western professional who wants to continue to do business with the Japanese establishment.

What is unarguable is that *Blindside* has been vindicated in its analysis of trade trends. In essence, the book predicted Japan would continue to win hands down in its undeclared trade war with the United States. The truth is that as of 2003, Japan had established export leadership or even worldwide dominance in precisely the advanced manufacturing industries that had up to the 1980s been the cornerstone of American power.

It is important to realize that *Blindside*'s analysis of trade flew directly in the face of conventional wisdom of the late 1980s and early 1990s. The conventional wisdom, shaped assiduously by the Japanese economic system through its control of the English-language press in Tokyo, was that Japan's export industries were being increasingly seriously hollowed out by South Korea, Taiwan, Malaysia, and other low-wage East Asian nations. An early version of this canard formed the central theme of a book published by Bill Emmott in 1989. Emmott, who later became editor-in-chief of *The Economist* magazine, predicted in particular that Japan's current account surpluses would disappear by the mid-1990s. This prediction echoed the analysis of the Japanese bureaucracy at that time and was intended—by the Japanese bureaucracy at least, if not by Emmott—to calm Americans' then incandescent anger at Japan's one-way trade policies. In reality, as we have already noted, Japan's current account surpluses in the 1990s ran 2.37 times their total in the 1980s.

It was these surpluses that propelled Japan to a position of total dominance in capital exports. In the long run, this changing balance of financial power will be just about the only thing that historians will remember about U.S.–Japan economic rivalry in the 1990s—but it was the one thing that most Western observers utterly overlooked at the time.

AMERICA'S MANUFACTURING COMEBACK: A MYTH IS BORN

Policymakers who might otherwise have been concerned about America's general industrial decline in the 1990s were reassured by talk that certain important industries had staged an impressive comeback. Admittedly, in the wake of the Wall Street crash of 2000-2002 (and in the face of a concurrent massive shakeout in employment in American manufacturing), this argument was not made as trenchantly in 2003 as it had been a few years earlier. Nonetheless, the myth that American manufacturing staged a comeback in the late 1990s dies hard.

One of the most elaborate versions of the comeback myth has been propagated by Jerry Jasinowski, president of the National Association of Manufacturers. As he is clearly someone who should know what he is talking about, his views are worth examining in detail.

In his book *Making It in America*, written with the consultant Robert Hamrin, Jasinowski talked about an "historic" new dynamism in American industry and asserted:

American industry has not just caught up to the competition; it has gone beyond the competition. American manufacturing is again becoming the industrial powerhouse of the world, making enormous contributions to the quality of American life. . . . In the mid-1990s there are unmistakable signs that America's manufacturers have made a comeback—a comeback so strong that it has once again firmly put them in a global leadership position. . . . Major industries in the U.S. have come back smartly to achieve world preeminence, led by autos, steel, and semiconductors. The overall result is a highly competitive economy. . . . It is fascinating that American manufacturing has led the American economy's competitive resurgence in recent years. This should finally put to rest all the talk about a postindustrial society and "deindustrialization."

Stirring words—and words that a lot of Americans evidently wanted to believe. Certainly, Jasinowski's book collected impressive endorsements from, among others, former Chrysler chairman Lee Iacocca and the management guru Tom Peters. But where were the facts to back up Jasinowski's sweeping assertions? Actually, most of his "facts" turned out to be merely more assertions. He argued, for instance, that manufacturing's share of America's total economic output increased in the 1980s, and he produced an assertion by a Washington economic analyst to this effect. He omitted to mention that this analyst was an outlier whose estimate of a one-and-a-half percentage point increase in manufacturing's share was contradicted by many other sources, not least the United States government. In fact, official U.S. figures suggested that manufacturing's share of GDP fell by about three and a half percentage points in the period. Not only did Jasinowski fail to tell us why the numbers he cited should be trusted over the government's numbers, but he failed even to mention the contradictory evidence of the government's numbers. Quite clearly, if Jasinowski were confident of his case, he would have met the government's contradictory evidence head on. That he did not do so spoke volumes.

Elsewhere, Jasinowski reported that there has been "a tremendous resurgence of American exports" since 1985. This was true—but it was hardly the clincher he would have us believe. In reality, much of the increase in American exports was driven by an entirely predictable adjustment to currency movements: for the fact is that the dollar lost more than half its value against major foreign currencies between 1985 and 1987. With the help of a dollar devaluation, it was not necessary for exporters to achieve any volume growth to show a strong rise in the dollar value of export revenues. The point is that merely by maintaining their prices unchanged in foreign currencies, American exporters' dollar revenues soared even without any volume growth. While the currency benefit was obviously a welcome one for many erstwhile hard-pressed American manufacturers, the larger issue here was that it had been achieved at the expense of one of the most precipitate depreciations of a major currency in economic history. A country whose currency shows such weakness can hardly be said to be going from strength to strength.

While making much of America's export growth, Jasinowski had nothing to say about a less convenient fact: American imports also rose. In fact, the import rise went a long way to explain the export rise. There was a clear causal relationship here, because the final products American manufacturers have been exporting in recent years are assembled with the use of an ever rising proportion of imported components and materials. In large part, therefore, in boosting their exports American manufacturers have merely been piggybacking on the tremendous productivity increases that *other nations* have achieved in advanced manufacturing industries in recent years. The result is that, as we have noted earlier, America's current account deficits have consistently soared in recent years.

In view of the dollar's depreciation since the mid-1980s, the huge rise in imports is an especially telling indication of America's waning manufacturing prowess. Remember that the dollar's fall created an historic opportunity for American companies to win back market share they had lost to foreign suppliers in the American home market in earlier years. And in fact, hopes that American manufacturers would do just that were a major reason why then Treasury Secretary James Baker agreed in 1985 to lower the dollar's value. Certainly, by any normal logic, America's imports should have fallen after the dollar crashed. In the event, as measured from 1984, the last full year before the dollar's depreciation began, America's imports have risen at a compound rate of more than 7 percent—which, after allowing for inflation, represents a real growth of a disturbing 4 percent a year. Clearly, this trend is the ultimate rebuke to Jasinowski's contention that "American manufacturing is again becoming the industrial powerhouse of the world."

Perhaps the most surprising thing about Jasinowski's analysis was the claims he made for individual American industries. He maintained in particular that the American automobile industry had reestablished "world preeminence." But as with so many of his assertions, he offered no substantiation. But it is easy to test the validity or otherwise of this assertion. Clearly, the state of the international competitiveness of the American auto industry can be readily checked by reference to international trade figures. These were conspicuously absent from Jasinowski's analysis—perhaps understandably because they flatly contradicted him. The truth was that all through the 1990s and into the new century the American auto industry continued its pattern of doing virtually no exporting outside Canada and Mexico. Moreover, succumbing to periodic downsizings, the Detroit Big Three continued to lose share even in the American domestic market—not least to Japanese competitors. Admittedly, this latter point was somewhat obscured by a change in the composition of Japan's automotive exports. Whereas in earlier years Japanese exports consisted mainly of fully built cars, in recent years the Japanese automobile industry has been moving more and more to exporting components and materials—and big increases in exports of such products are a key reason America's trade deficits with Japan have soared in the 1990s. Given that the business of making components and materials is generally a much more economically sophisticated one than assembling cars, the Japanese have benefited twice over—and the American automotive industry has suffered a double whammy.

Steel is another industry in which, on Jasinowski's analysis, the United States won back "preeminence" in the 1990s. He based this assessment on various productivity surveys that purportedly showed that the United States was the world's most efficient steel producer. What he did not mention was that such surveys are not only notoriously unreliable but, by dint of a judicious choice of assumptions, can be made to "prove" almost anything. Certainly, the surveys he cited did not stand up to even cursory reality-checking. The point that, if the United States were truly the world's most efficient producer, we would have expected it to be a major exporter. Instead, thanks to a doubling in the volume of its steel imports since 1983, the United States remains by far the world's largest importer! Of course, none of this is to disparage the efforts of many capable people who have tried to turn the American steel industry's fortunes around in the last two decades. The truth is that their efforts have been stymied by events beyond their control, specifically dumping by many foreign steel producers in the American market. This dumping has continued so long at such a high level that it has constantly deprived the American industry of the level of retained profits necessary to pursue vitally needed investments in efficient new production technologies. At the end of the day, the fact remains that the American steel industry is now so weak that it cannot compete with foreign producers even in third-country markets (that is, markets where there are no significant local producers and where typically, therefore, all the world's producers can compete against one another on a relatively level playing field). Worse, in the years since Jasinowski wrote his euphoric assessment, most of the traditional American steel industry has gone into bankruptcy. The casualties include even such once proud names as Bethlehem, Armco, and LTV. As in the case of autos, therefore, the story of an American comeback in steel was entirely a figment of Jasinowski's imagination.

So much for America's position in traditional manufacturing industries. But what of more glamorous industries? It is time to look at how America's high-tech manufacturers are doing.

AMERICAN HIGH-TECH:
BACK AT THE LEADING EDGE?

For many Washington policymakers, disappointments in steel and autos ultimately don't matter very much so long as the United States retains a decisive lead in more advanced manufacturing industries. So how is the United States doing in such industries? On the face of it, these industries strongly improved their position in the 1990s and have ridden out the subsequent world recession as well as could be expected. This impression has been crucial in quelling concerns about the precipitate decline in the overall size of America's manufacturing workforce in the last two decades. Unfortunately, however, this impression is largely illusory. The reality is that, though American high-tech brand names are more visible than ever in the world's stores, the companies that stand behind these brand names are, in manufacturing terms, a mere shadow of their former selves. As America's high-tech manufacturers have "restructured" in recent years, they have come to depend more and more on outsourcing from East Asian rivals for their most sophisticated manufacturing processes.

A particularly significant point about corporate America's outsourcing is that much of it is done in ultrahigh-wage Japan. Other things equal, when a lower-wage nation imports a product from a higher-wage one, we can reasonably assume that the manufacturing technology concerned is one in which the importing country is lacking.

Americans got used to the idea of such outsourcing in the 1970s and early 1980s when Japanese wages were still low by American standards. Thus, American corporations could justify outsourcing from Japan on the basis that they were relying on the Japanese merely for low-level, labor-intensive workmanship, thereby, in theory at least, freeing American workers to specialize in higher-level work. These days, however, with Japanese wages generally higher than American levels, American corporations that import from Japan are effectively admitting they lag behind in the technology race.

The outsourcing trend has become something of an embarrassment at many major American manufacturing companies these days. So much so that journalists who ask questions about such issues either are unceremoniously rebuffed or at best are fed a diet of highly misleading half-truths.

Of course, when a company outsources its production, this does not necessarily imply that it is outsourcing from abroad. But as a practical matter, when American manufacturers outsource, they do so largely from East Asia. Such supposedly strong American manufacturers as Hewlett-Packard and Compaq depend on East Asian rivals not only for crucial components but for entire manufacturing functions.

For a more complete view of the extent to which major American high-tech corporations have become dependent on outsourcing in recent years, it is useful to check American corporate disclosure documents filed with the Securities and Exchange Commission (SEC). In making these filings, corporations are under some pressure to acknowledge their dependence on foreign suppliers. Among other things, failure to do so may later expose them to expensive class-action lawsuits from disgruntled shareholders complaining of being blindsided by, for instance, currency-driven cost increases.

These SEC filings often contain surprising admissions of dependence on foreign suppliers—albeit admissions that have consistently been overlooked by American media commentators toasting corporate America's high-tech "supremacy." Take, for instance, this disclosure from Hewlett-Packard in 1997: "Portions of the company's manufacturing operations are dependent on the ability of significant suppliers to deliver completed products, integral subassemblies, and components in time to meet critical distribution and manufacturing schedules. The failure of suppliers to deliver these products, subassemblies, and components in a timely manner may adversely affect the company's operating results until alternate sourcing could be developed." Elsewhere Hewlett-Packard disclosed: "For many of its products, the company has existing alternate sources of supply, or such sources are readily available." This statement sounds reassuring, but in fact, it is a lawyer's way of putting shareholders on notice that in the case of many other products, the company does *not* have any alternate sources of supply—and thus,

Hewlett-Packard is effectively dependent on single suppliers for what are crucial enabling components without which it would be out of business.

Another major American high-tech manufacturer that is surprisingly dependent on foreign suppliers is the leading maker of semiconductor manufacturing equipment, Applied Materials. In SEC filings in 1996, Applied Materials disclosed:

> The company's manufacturing activities consist primarily of assembling various commercial and proprietary components into finished systems, principally in the United States, with additional operations in England, Japan, Korea, and Taiwan. Production requires some raw materials and a wide variety of mechanical and electrical components, which are manufactured to the company's specifications. Multiple commercial sources are available for most components. . . . There have been no significant delays in receiving components from sole source suppliers; however, the unavailability of any of these components could disrupt scheduled deliveries to customers.

Many other examples could be cited of how other key American high-tech manufacturers depend on foreign suppliers for their most sophisticated components.

But surely the United States has scored some real successes in high-tech manufacturing in recent years? Yes—but far fewer than even most experts realize. Perhaps the strongest remaining American high-tech manufacturer is Boeing. But even Boeing is doing less well than it used to. Quite apart from facing increasing competition from the European Airbus consortium, Boeing has been under considerable pressure from foreign governments to transfer jobs abroad, and it has duly done so. As William Greider has pointed out in his book *One World, Ready or Not,* 30 percent of the components used in Boeing's 777 jet are made abroad. By comparison, in the 1960s, Boeing imported only 2 percent of its components. Thus, Boeing, like other erstwhile world-beating American manufacturers, is rapidly becoming a "virtual corporation" ever more dependent on suppliers in Japan and elsewhere abroad for its most advanced manufacturing needs.

Meanwhile, despite all the talk of a renaissance in the American semiconductor industry, there is actually only one truly strong American semiconductor manufacturer left: Intel. Moreover, Intel's success says little if anything about its manufacturing prowess. In fact, the company's growth in the 1980s was driven not by any fundamental efficiency edge in production engineering but rather by the company's near-monopolistic franchise in producing microprocessors for the dominant "Wintel" standard in personal computers.

In any case, Intel is just one company—and judged by the all-important criterion of jobs, not a particularly large one. At last count, it employed 79,000 people worldwide—just one-fifth of IBM's peak work force in the mid-1980s before its domination of the computer industry collapsed under pressure from the rising Wintel standard. Moreover, Intel is not as advanced as it appears. In fact, its Wintel chips are based on an aging technology known as CISC (complex instruction set computing). In the last decade, CISC has been superseded by a technology called RISC (reduced instruction set computing). RISC chips, which are noted for their use in such high-performance computers as Sun Microsystems' network servers, are made mainly in Japan.

Intel apart, there are few other semiconductor manufacturers left in the United States. This may seem surprising in view of the fact that, according to such prophets of America's purported industrial renaissance as Jerry Jasinowski, the United States has now recovered strong leadership in semiconductors. He reported that American semiconductor makers boosted their global market share from 40 percent in 1988 to 44 percent in 1993, and this supposedly put the United States back in the "top spot" in the industry. After the big decline in America's share in the first half of the 1980s, all this seemed like convincing evidence of a comeback. But the truth is that his 44 percent figure was bogus. It was based on highly misleading statistical procedures that categorize most chips outsourced by American companies from factories in East Asia and elsewhere as "American"! The only justification for this bizarre statistical treatment is that most such chips are *designed* in the United States and bear American brand names. But this hardly means they are made in America. Even Dataquest, an information-industry consulting firm that is the ultimate source of data on world semiconductor production, compiles its statistics on this basis.

Given the prevalence of such misleading statistics, how do we gauge the true state of American competitiveness? Again, there is no substitute for international trade figures. These indicate that the United States was running deficits of more than $3 billion a year with Japan alone in semiconductors in the late 1990s. Given Japan's higher wage levels, therefore, it is clear that the idea that the United States had recovered world leadership in semiconductors in the early 1990s was just another myth.

It has to be noted that many American executives think that it no longer matters that the United States imports most of its semiconductors so long as American companies do their chip-design work in the United States. From the point of view of corporations intent on boosting their short-term profits, this argument no doubt makes sense. But from the point of view of the overall American national interest, things look quite different. The basic problem is this: product development as practiced in the United States these days has become a postindustrial function. As such, it is burdened with all the usual drawbacks of postindustrialism.

For a start, it comes up short on jobs: product development creates jobs mainly for a narrow elite of university-educated workers—the same sort of workers who are favored by most other postindustrial businesses.

Moreover, in the long run, outsourcing works to the disadvantage even of American semiconductor companies' shareholders. The point is that by abandoning its manufacturing activities the American semiconductor industry loses all hope of establishing a lasting lead over foreign competitors. After all, American designs can be easily reverse-engineered, and as a matter of fact, America's best chip designs are often imitated in East Asia within weeks of their launch. Certainly they prove a far less enduring asset for a nation than proprietary manufacturing know-how. Thus, companies that lead in product development must keep on innovating merely to stay in the game, and unlike great manufacturing companies, they never get a chance to build up a reservoir of deep proprietary production knowledge that can see them through bad times.

At the end of the day, when American high-tech companies are lauded in the press as world leaders, what is being extolled is not solid manufacturing know-how but rather much less enduring postindustrial strengths.

THE LAST ILLUSION:
UNIQUELY INVENTIVE AMERICAN MANUFACTURING

We have already had much to say about the myth of superior American creativity. One further point needs to be added. Even among those few American policymakers who understand how hollowed out American manufacturing has already become, the creativity myth has had a powerful tranquilizing effect. Such policymakers reassure themselves that a relative lack of creativity will ensure that other nations' manufacturers, and particularly those of Japan, cannot independently race far ahead of their American counterparts. Such policymakers therefore take it for granted that by dint of superior American creativity, the United States can easily get back into advanced manufacturing anytime it chooses.

But just as it is a myth that other nations lack the necessary creativity to succeed in postindustrial services, equally it is a myth that they cannot innovate in manufacturing. The ability of the Japanese in particular to pioneer new areas of advanced manufacturing should not be underestimated. As the British management commentator Robert Heller has pointed out, anyone who looks closely at Japanese products immediately sees that they display a high degree of creativity in product design.

The idea that the Japanese lack the ability to make independent innovations in manufacturing is also strongly rejected by the Clinton administration adviser Ira Magaziner, who is a noted authority on Japanese manufacturing. Commenting on one American manufacturer's characterization of Japan as a nation of copyists, Magaziner has said:

This was a common refrain in the early 1980s. Many U.S. business-
men, policy officials, and media analysts saw our entrepreneurial
small companies as untouchable by the Japanese. There were many
pseudopsychologists of Japan with themes about why Japan's collec-
tivist culture did not allow for the creativity and freedom necessary
for invention and entrepreneurship. These arguments have proven
baseless as Japanese companies have shown themselves quite capable
of pioneering new technologies and products.

The proof of this is already abundantly apparent in the marketplace. The
world's electronics stores in particular are now full of products that were
developed largely or totally in Japan. These notably include the Walkman,
the Handycam, the liquid-crystal display, the digital camera, the home
videotape recorder, the compact disk player, the laptop computer, and the
cellular phone. In recent years, indeed, Japan has taken over from California
as the locale where the latest crazes in consumer gadgets appear first. One
notable recent example is car navigation equipment—as of 2002, two-thirds
of all car navigation devices installed anywhere in the world were on
Japanese roads. In recent years, too, Japan has pioneered radio-controlled
watches that tune in constantly to a broadcast signal that keeps them constantly within milliseconds of the correct time. Meanwhile in cellphones,
Japan was first to popularize both Internet and picture-taking functions.

In truth, as the MIT Commission on Industrial Productivity pointed
out some years ago, the argument about superior American creativity in
advanced manufacturing is an ironic one given the historical record. For
America is not the first flagging industrial power that has imagined that
the allegedly superior creativity of its people can arrest its relative decline.
In the early part of the twentieth century, the United Kingdom and other
European nations consoled themselves with similar arguments in the face
of rising American manufacturing might. Up to World War II, Europe
regarded itself as the fountainhead of world creativity, and it talked about
American manufacturers' efforts to commercialize European inventions
in the same condescending tones that Americans now reserve for
Japanese efforts to commercialize American inventions.

Amusingly, that ultimate authority on the human psyche, Sigmund Freud, seems to have concurred with the Europeans' assessment of Americans as copyists. In an interview in 1930, Freud said: "Americans are clever generalizers. They are rarely creative thinkers." Of course, Freud was wrong, and after World War II this became obvious as Americans, leveraging their new advantage in abundant funding, took the lead in many prestigious areas of science, technology, and medicine that had previously been dominated by the Europeans.

Creativity, like beauty, is in the eye of the beholder. While few today would accuse Americans of lacking creativity, the idea that there is something *uniquely* creative about American culture is not a bankable proposition. Rather, it is a dangerous illusion.

So much for the myth of superior American manufacturing creativity. Having disposed of this last excuse for procrastination, we emphasize that drastic action is now urgently necessary. Let's now proceed to a look at what realistic policy options are open to American leaders in their efforts decisively to reverse the deindustrialization trend of the last three decades.

CHAPTER 9

hat should American policymakers do to reverse the postindustrial trend? Any effective strategy would have to be drastic. But in its basic principles, it would be quite simple:

- Boost the nation's savings.
- Channel a larger proportion of those savings into industrial investment, particularly productivity-enhancing production engineering.
- Ensure that manufacturers earn a reasonable return on their investments.
- Upgrade workers' skills.
- Stem the leakage of world-beating production technologies abroad.

Setting aside for a moment the task of raising the savings rate, many practical measures are available to facilitate most of the rest of this agenda. Tax incentives, for instance, can be readily devised to ensure that as much as possible of the nation's savings is channeled into manufacturing. The quality of management in manufacturing industries can be bolstered by ensuring that the nation's educational system places a stronger emphasis on technical subjects. Such a focus would help attract more of the nation's best brains into engineering, and particularly production engineering.

Concomitant measures would be needed to lessen the counterattractions of careers in finance and other postindustrial services whose compensation levels are now disproportionately high. The securities industry's size, for instance, could be drastically curtailed by imposing a transaction tax of, say, 0.5 percent on stock trades.

To deliver an adequate return on manufacturing investment, the United States would have to make sure—really sure—that its exporters competed in world trade on terms at least as favorable as those enjoyed by their foreign rivals. As a first step, the United States would have to dramatically beef up its notably half-hearted trade diplomacy. It might also be necessary to relax antitrust rules to ensure that the nation's manufacturers could agree on product standards and avoid wasteful duplication of effort by cooperating in research and development.

All this would undoubtedly boost the profitability of manufacturing industries. But higher profits are not enough. If U.S. competitiveness is to be boosted, profits must be plowed back into raising worker productivity, rather than siphoned off in large compensation packages for a wealthy elite. Among other things, executive stock options would have to be reengineered to force managers to focus on boosting their corporations' *long-term* prospects. Managers might be required as a general principle to be vested for a minimum of, say, seven years before they could cash in their stock-option gains. Moreover, they would forfeit their options completely in any vesting period in which they laid off American workers. This would powerfully focus management's attention on providing workers with *secure* jobs—a task that requires managers to think long-term in investing both in new production facilities and in research and development. In a regimen in which managers were punished personally for laying off workers, companies would be much more concerned with bolstering the quality of jobs at home; they would have a strong incentive, for instance, not to transfer their most advanced technologies and their most capital-intensive manufacturing processes overseas. The new corporate orientation toward the long term could be further bolstered by financial regulation giving long-term investors more say in corporate affairs, while frustrating the destabilizing activities of short term–minded takeover artists and stock market speculators.

So far so good. But we are left with the fundamental problem that the U.S. savings rate is far too low. How can the American people be induced to save more? Many remedies have been tried over the years, but almost invariably they have only seemed to make the problem worse. This is not to suggest that effective methods to raise a nation's savings rate do not exist. The whole history of the East Asian economic miracle demonstrates otherwise. Even in Singapore, one of the freest societies in the East, the savings rate was successfully boosted by a system of forced savings instituted by Lee Kuan Yew shortly after the city-state won independence.

The problem, of course, is that the United States is not Singapore. Any attempt to impose a Singapore-style savings program on Americans would undoubtedly spark a political firestorm.

Nonetheless, the task of reviving U.S. manufacturing prowess is of vital historic importance and clearly demands exceptional measures. By a process of elimination, only one policy option remains to be considered—an option that has so far been regarded as second only to nuclear war in unthinkability. That option is tariffs. Even the mere mention of the word generates a frisson of fear and loathing among today's generation of American policy makers. That is understandable. After all, many of them experienced at firsthand the unforgettable One World optimism of the Flower-Power era, and like most decent people, they would like to believe that the world is ready for the close economic and political integration that global free trade implies. But after nearly fourteen years studying East-West relations from a vantage point in Tokyo, this writer has no illusions about the practical difficulties that face Western leaders who want to "teach the world to sing in perfect harmony." Certainly, in the absence of major breakthroughs in trade diplomacy in the very near future, the tariff option must be included in any serious consideration of how U.S. manufacturing prowess can be revived. Otherwise, American manufacturers will be condemned to a perpetually unequal struggle in trying to compete with foreign manufacturers that enjoy the enormous advantage of a protected home market.

Let's be clear. As Patrick Buchanan has extensively documented in *The Great Betrayal,* the poor image that tariffs suffer in the current American economic debate is largely undeserved. Their image problem stems almost entirely from the allegedly major part they played in causing the Great Depression. In reality, however, they played a minor role in that disaster and were much less significant certainly than the general mismanagement of domestic demand in the United States and elsewhere in those years. In any case, to judge tariffs by referring to Depression-era experience with them is hardly more appropriate than to judge luxury liners by the unfortunate fate of the *Titanic.*

For any sane consideration of tariffs, the appropriate reference point is not the Hoover years but rather the Eisenhower years. Eisenhower's time, after all, was one of unprecedented prosperity, not only for the United States but for most of the rest of the world. Accompanied by supporting policies, such as careful demand management and fair regulation of financial markets, tariffs clearly played a major role in providing the economic stability needed for manufacturing industries to thrive.

The great advantage of tariffs is that they powerfully counter the effect of other nations' industrial policies in undermining the profitability of American manufacturing industries. Competing with one another behind a modest but adequate wall of tariffs, American companies would be provided with a generally appropriate level of profitability. They would reinvest those profits in the confident knowledge that, if they managed their businesses wisely, they would earn a fair return in the future. Tariffs could go a long way toward end-running the savings shortages and poor returns on investment that have discouraged so many American manufacturers from creating the world-beating production technologies that the American worker needs to stay at the leading edge in world productivity.

Of course, tariffs, like most economic tools, generate minuses as well as pluses. Certainly, compared to a world of perfect free trade, they result in a less than optimum distribution of global industrial capacity. But for an economy as large as that of the United States (or for a large trading bloc, such as the European Union), the disadvantages involved in maintaining some firewalls against the vagaries of globalization are quite minor. In any case, absolute economic efficiency is by no means the only consideration here. It hardly ever is in real life. Remember that if economic efficiency were the only concern, most of our economic arrangements would be very different. Families would live in commune-style accommodation, for instance, rather than in self-contained one-family housing units. Just as people do not consider simply crude economic efficiency and are prepared to pay a bit extra for their own private bathrooms, kitchens, laundry facilities, and so on, it is reasonable for a major economy to waive the dictates of crude economic efficiency in ensuring that it is self-reliant in at least the most important of its fundamental manufacturing needs. Essentially, the point here is that good fences make good neighbors.

The need to build firewalls against the worst excesses of globalization may not enter into economists' equations, but it is a real enough consideration nonetheless for anyone who has a wider concern for the human condition. Globalization might work if all the world's people shared substantially the same cultural values. In reality, however, as anyone who has actually lived for an extended period in, for instance, East Asia can testify, we are still an awfully long way from such a prospect. Those who think otherwise have been misled by the much publicized Westernization that has become apparent in many non-Western nations around the world in recent decades. But this Westernization is typically highly superficial. Certainly the fact that people eat McDonald's hamburgers and drink Coca-Cola is no guarantee that they share an American attitude toward economics or politics. Absent carefully thought-through safeguards, therefore, any attempt to mesh diverse cultures together is likely to end in tears.

Of course, any talk of a pulling back from globalization is likely to appall the American financial elite. And here we come to the nub of the problem: so long as the current economic fashion for laissez-faire holds sway in elite circles, any serious attempt to map out a detailed program to revive American manufacturing would be a waste of words.

The fundamental question is not how to craft a workable program, therefore, but rather how to slay the prevailing zeitgeist.

Encouragingly, the zeitgeist has already been coming under increasing attack from many quarters around the world in recent years. In the United States, the charge against the excesses of laissez-faire has been led by such notable thinkers as James Fallows, Lester Thurow, William Wolman, Clyde Prestowitz, Chalmers Johnson, Bennett Harrison, Patrick Buchanan, George Soros, John Judis, Robert Kuttner, and Barry Bluestone. Even in the United Kingdom, that ultimate font of postindustrial chop logic, laissez-faire is coming under increasing vigorous attack from such authors as Will Hutton and Paul Ormerod. That said, it has to be admitted that on both sides of the Atlantic, the dogmatists still reign supreme. In fact, they have survived a well-deserved measure of opprobrium in the immediate aftermath of the Reagan-Thatcher era to come back in arguably even more potent form in the late 1990s.

In any effort to beat back the dogmatists and vested interests, the media can and should play a pivotal role. After all, the media shape the intellectual climate in which politicians must compete for votes. The editors of the world's leading newspapers should be leading from the front in questioning the obvious contradictions in the prevailing dogma.

So far, however, they have generally shrunk from the task, no doubt in part because they are intimidated by the economics profession's pretensions to scientific certainty. But in truth, they have no reason to be intimidated. Although academic economists delight in cloaking their work in abstruse mathematics, the truth is that real-world policymaking rarely demands anything much more abstruse than simple arithmetic. The advanced mathematical tools used by the "experts" are useful merely in analyzing highly theoretical models that assume away the imperfection and complexity of the real world. By contrast, analyzing the real world generally requires little more than common sense. As John Kenneth Galbraith has pointed out, economists have yet to come up with any worthwhile practical insights that cannot be clearly and completely explained in plain English. Far from hiding important truths, the economics profession's cloak of mathematical abstruseness merely camouflages the worthlessness of its insights in guiding practical policymaking.

Another reason the media shrink from challenging the zeitgeist is that laissez-faire's claims to be the one true faith have been consistently validated by the way the Nobel Prize for economics has been conferred over the years. Most of the prize's recipients have been dyed-in-the-wool advocates of laissez-faire. This naturally has given the impression that there is a general consensus among the world's intellectual leaders that laissez-faire is the only valid form of economics. The truth could hardly be more different. In reality, as *Business Week*'s economics editor, Michael Mandel, has pointed out, the world of academic economics is a seething mass of controversy in which there is virtually no consensus on anything anymore. Thus, the laissez-faire zealots who have won the Nobel Prize represent just one faction in a dysfunctional and demoralized profession, and their thinking is fiercely contested by others in the profession.

The great irony is that the laissez-faire bias in the awarding of the prize seems to reflect nothing more significant than the views of the Stockholm-based Sveriges Riksbank. Known in English as the Bank of Sweden, it administers the Nobel Prize in economics. The pattern it follows in conferring the prize faithfully reflects the tendency of the Stockholm financial elite to seek laissez-faire solutions to Sweden's economic problems in recent years.

One thing is certain: the world needs no lessons in economics from present-day Stockholm. In fact, Sweden's recent history has been an object lesson in how not to run an economy. Since the 1970s, Swedish economic policy making has been increasingly shaped by laissez-faire thinking, and the result has been a consistently disappointing economic performance. Between 1970 and 1997, Sweden's per capita income in current dollars rose a mere sixfold—the poorest performance of any advanced economy with the exception of the United States and Canada. Its recent history contrasts starkly with the early years after World War II, when Sweden ran one of the most avowedly interventionist economies in the Western world. The formula included a powerful labor movement, a government-dominated savings system, high taxes, price controls, and a close partnership between big business and government. The result was one of the strongest and richest postwar economies: Sweden boosted its real output by two-thirds in just the first fifteen years after World War II.

Disastrous though the Swedish economy's encounter with laissez-faire economic dogma may have proved, the Bank of Sweden's baleful orthodoxy has profoundly influenced the world's universities, particularly those of the United States, which vie fiercely to win as many Nobel Prizes as possible. The result is that college administrators increasingly select for advancement those economics scholars whose views are most likely to please the Bank of Sweden and its right-leaning nominating committees.

That the Bank of Sweden's unfortunate influence on American economic thought has been almost completely overlooked in media discussions speaks volumes about the seriousness—or rather, lack of seriousness—with which the editors of the great American media organizations take their responsibility to cover economics. The task for the media is clear: they must move firmly to hold the economics profession as accountable as they would other key players in public life. Although American reporters delight in setting traps for politicians and disgracing them over essentially irrelevant aspects of their private lives, they have rarely done any reality-checking on the economics profession's very public—and generally counterproductive—role in shaping the nation's destiny.

A first step on the road to more reliable and searching media coverage of economics would be for top editors to take direct responsibility for that coverage rather than delegating it to their business sections. They should hire an entirely new cadre of top economic writers who are free from the institutional biases of the business sections. Chosen from the cream of the intellectual crop, such writers would be well versed in the principles of standard economics—and well versed also in deflating those ivory-tower theorists who present standard economics as a set of sacred truths.

By contrast, the current practice of delegating economic coverage to business reporters is a recipe for bias and misinformation. As became abundantly apparent in the egregious misreporting of the final stages of the Internet stock bubble of the late 1990s, business reporters are too close to their Wall Street sources, and they almost automatically identify with the Wall Street view, which happens to be an especially deadly formulation of the prevailing dogma. When reporters from the *New York Times*, *The Washington Post*, and other key media organizations call Wall Street analysts to put the latest economic developments "in context," the result is often pure spin.

Business reporters generally share the stock analysts' knee-jerk tendency to identify exclusively with the interests of capital and are therefore implicitly or explicitly hostile to the much more economically significant interests of labor. Wall Street may be forgiven for focusing tightly on maximizing its own narrow interests, but the press is supposed to be bound by higher ideals. It is obligated to see the larger picture—and in particular to recognize the obvious truth that a nation cannot be rich if its workers are poor. This truth gets short shrift on Wall Street, which cares not at all if American workers lose their edge in the productivity league tables as America's most valuable production technologies are transferred abroad. The only criterion that matters to Wall Street is whether such transfers will pay off in boosting a corporation's short-term profits. But it is the press's job to keep an eye on the longer term and to stand up for the interests of the community as a whole.

The press's reliance on Wall Street for economic insights also introduces into its reportage an irrational bias against regulation. In any discussion of the need for regulatory action to correct the undesirable economic tendencies innate to extreme laissez-faire, Wall Street has a huge vested interest to protect. Not to put too fine a point on it, but the more relaxed the regulatory backdrop in finance, the easier it is for financial professionals to feather their own nests at the expense of the nation's savers. Wall Street analysts thus naturally tend to be unsympathetic toward regulation in all its forms.

But again, it is the press's job to see things in a wider focus, and in particular to look out for the national interest.

The truth is that, for all the glib talk of globalism in recent years, the
peoples of the world still find group strength in their national identities.
We pay our taxes to the nation, for instance, and it is, for the most part,
from the nation that we draw our social security and other benefits.
Moreover, when it comes to helping the sick and the old, it is entirely
natural for us to think that charity begins at home. Even in this era of
globalism, the nation assuredly still counts.

The irony of the global view of economics that underpins laissez-faire is
its assumption that other nations are prepared to abandon all national concerns and behave as true globalists in managing their economies. It should
be obvious that this is a utopian reading of human nature. In fact, in most
parts of the world people are still very concerned about their own nation's
relative position in the world economy. This is true even of the United
States, where globalism has gone much further than almost anywhere else.
There is probably hardly a single American who does not yearn for a return
to the halcyon years of the Eisenhower and Kennedy presidencies, when
American manufacturers paid the highest wages in the world yet nonetheless almost effortlessly dominated world markets. Such concern for one's
nation's economic standing in the world is quite natural and, within reason,
a good thing: it is really just community spirit writ large.

In the issue is one of balance. On the one hand, one's nation should
strive to cooperate to make this planet a better place; on the other hand, it
should stand up for its own citizens' interests when these are at stake.
Striking the correct balance is a matter of common sense, not dogma. It is
time our media led the search for a better way to balance these interests.

NOTES

xiv. almost alone among Tokyo-based observers: See in particular "Why the Japanese banks are shaky" by Eamonn Fingleton (*Euromoney*, September 1987), which was probably the first clear warning in print of the coming mayhem in Japanese finance. The article included this statement: "Two essential ingredients for financial disaster are present: the [Tokyo] real estate industry has clearly been pumped up to giddy heights of folly and the banks have a much greater exposure to risky real estate lending than appears from the crude statistics." As the article recorded, this gloomy view ran completely counter to the mood at the time among Western analysts, who were almost universally bullish about both the Japanese banks and the Tokyo real estate market. (These analysts, moreover, were encouraging thousands of American and European investment managers to pay exorbitant prices for the massive new issues of shares corporate Japan was then making.) The hyping of Japanese investments at that time was notably enshrined in the "Tiffany" credit ratings accorded the Japanese banks by the two main American credit rating agencies. Moody's, for instance, had triple-A ratings on no less than eight of fourteen major Japanese banks in the summer of 1987. Tokyo real estate prices duly slumped soon after the article appeared and a subsequent rally in 1991 stopped well short of exceeding the record prices set in the summer of 1987. That said, it was not until 1992 that the generality of Western analysts and reporters came to see the extent of the problems the mid-1980s real estate boom had created for the banks. As for Tokyo stock prices, see "Making hay" by Eamonn Fingleton (*Euromoney*, February 1989), which predicted "a prolonged bear market." The big bear market in stocks duly arrived in January 1990 and continued until October 1998.

16. Third World imports: William Wolman and Anne Colamosca, *The Judas Economy: The Triumph of Capital and the Betrayal of Work* (Reading: Addison-Wesley Publishing Company, 1997), p. 97.

17. export strength: It should be noted that U.S. exports grew rapidly in the 1990s. But there is less to this performance than appears at first sight— much less. As corporate America's soaring purchases of foreign high-tech parts and materials indicate, typically little of the added value in American exports these days is made in the United States. As the American economy has globalized, American manufacturers have become little more than mere assemblers of high-tech components made elsewhere. In essence in such activities American exporters are merely piggybacking on the manufacturing prowess of Japan and other major manufacturing economies.

21. shoes: Larry Kahaner, *Competitive Intelligence* (New York: Simon & Schuster, 1996), p. 177.

24. hidden army: See, for instance, the annual publication *OECD in Figures*, where unemployment figures for the various member nations are stated on a standardized apples-to-apples basis. Although ill-informed commentators have consistently suggested that the unemployment figures released monthly by the Japanese government are based on a misleading definition that understates the true scale of joblessness, in reality these differ hardly at all from those published later by the OECD (and calculated according to the OECD's definition of unemployment).

24. more universal: To suggest that manufactured goods are more universal in appeal than postindustrial products does not of course imply that no adjustments are needed to sell manufactured goods in foreign markets. Significant adjustments are often necessary to comply with differing tastes and regulations around the world. In the case of Japan's car exports, for

instance, cars destined for the United States must meet different regulatory standards from those of the European Union or of the Japanese home market. But the key point is that making such adjustments generally adds only fractionally to unit costs. Moreover a foreign workforce can manufacture the appropriate products—different car exhaust systems, for instance, for different markets—without the slightest need to understand the general culture of the ultimate customers. By contrast, the adjustments required in the case of exports of postindustrial goods are often not only extensive and costly but may be so cultural-specific that they must be performed largely or totally on the spot in the foreign markets concerned.

26. glass: See John Naisbitt, *Megatrends 2000* (London : Pan Books, 1990), p.7.

32. David Ricardo: As quoted by Doug Henwood, *Wall Street* (Verso: New York, 1997), p. 113.

35. NCR: Robert B. Reich, *The Work of Nations: Preparing Ourselves for 21st-Century Capitalism* (New York: Vintage Books, 1992), p. 119.

47. Another American company: Information in this paragraph is derived from James Wallace and Jim Erickson, *Hard Drive* (Chichester: John Wiley & Sons, 1993).

50. license plate numbers: See *Hard Drive*, p. 264.

66. $600 million: Steven Levy and Katie Hafner, *Newsweek*, June 2, 1997.

69. diminishing returns: See Thomas K. Landauer, *The Trouble with Computers* (Cambridge: The MIT Press, 1996), pp. 1-45.

71. millennium problem: Paul A. Strassmann, *The Squandered Computer* (New Canaan: The Information Economics Press, 1997), p. 284.

72. Jeff Madrick: As quoted by Richard Harwood in the *Washington Post*, May 11, 1998.

80. "mindless freefall": Robert Kuttner, *Everything for Sale* (New York: Knopf, 1996), p. 164.

82. Malkiel: Henwood, *Wall Street*, p. 105.

83. no less than 200: As cited by Prem C. Jain and Hemang Desai, *Journal of Finance*, September 1995.

84. "destroying": Interview with George Soros on ABC Television, *Nightline*, November 5, 1997.

84. "invisible foot": This and other comments attributed to Warren Buffett are taken from *Letters to Shareholders 1987-1995* (Omaha: Berkshire Hathaway, no date).

85. at least $50 billion: This figure is an estimate based on information in a speech in 1996 by John C. Bogle of the Vanguard mutual fund group and is calculated on the assumption that the majority of America's institutionally managed holdings of stocks could be passively managed by low-cost index funds.

89. John Tagliabue: *International Herald Tribune*, July 20, 1998.

93. Steven D. Kaye: *U.S. News & World Report*, July 7, 1997.

103. tends to be irrelevant: The Internet's notorious capacity to serve up "garbage at light speed" was pointedly underlined for this present writer after *Blindside*, his book on the hidden strengths of the Japanese economic system, was published in 1995. Suddenly, Internet search engines began prominently displaying a racist website in New Jersey in search listings for his name. Although he had never heard of the site's operators and utterly abhorred the racist tone of their criticisms of Japanese economic policies, this site typically came up as the number one item for searches under his name—and often appeared in different guises as many as three more times in the first ten listings for his name (the site came up under various headings, most notably "East of the Rising Sun" and simply "Links"). Meanwhile, the search engines overlooked various sites containing major articles he had written and important commendations his book had garnered (from, among others, *Business Week*, which named *Blindside* one of the ten best business books of 1995). To someone who did not know him (and did not know how deeply he abhorred the site's references to the Japanese as "Japs" and its use of Satanic graphics), the conclusion seemed unavoidable—that he was the moving spirit behind the site and, by promoting such vicious hatred, had ruled himself out of the reckoning as a decent and serious commentator on U.S.-Japan relations. His embarrass-

ment was compounded by the fact that the site's use of his name seemed to give credence to earlier allegations emanating from the Japanese economic system's Washington lobby that he was a "Japan-basher"—a label the lobby routinely confers on any writer who writes realistically about Japan's mercantilist trade policies.

Why did the site come up so prominently for his name? As explained by the site's operators, the reason was that the site carried several references to articles he had written for prominent journals such as *Foreign Affairs* and *The Atlantic*. In each case, these references included his name, thus, for search engines programmed to list items in order of the frequency with which keywords are used the site automatically showed up prominently.

Perhaps even more disturbing was the sequel. While he engaged in protracted negotiations with the site's operators to stop associating their vile rubbish with his name, he also notified various search engine companies that he had nothing to do with the offending site. Amazingly, the search engine companies refused to drop the site from listings for his name. In answer to his complaint, David Seuss, chief executive of Boston-based search engine, Northern Light, wrote: "Northern Light's index is generated completely by computers based on the text on the site and the results list are generated on the fly in a completely automated fashion. We simply cannot intervene manually in this process. And philosophically, I don't think Northern Light wants to become the arbiter of what is and what is not appropriate in terms of views to express."

98. Barry Howard Minkin: Barry Howard Minkin, *Future in Sight* (New York: Macmillan, 1995), pp. 54-56.

102. Steve Ward: Cited by Michael L. Dertouzos, *What Will Be* (HarperEdge: New York, 1997), p. 90.

104. subject to spin: The spin in newspaper-clipping databases exists at two levels—not only are primary sources often biased, but a database's selection and ranking of primary sources in response to search requests can be biased. It is not unknown for clippings databases to be programmed to serve a hidden political agenda. Just how politically biased such databases sometimes are can be gauged from the experience a few years ago of one anti-globalist author. Although his books had been generally favorably reviewed by publications of the standing of the *New York Times*, the *Financial Times* and *Le Monde*, they had been predictably panned in a few right-wing publications. In particular, his work had been blatantly misrepresented in a commentary

by the editor of *The Economist* in 1998. As of 2000, this commentary was still being featured very prominently in searches for the author's name at the Factiva database, while favorable commentaries were featured less prominently. Yet many of the favorable commentaries would, by any normal search standards be considered more relevant, given not only that they were more recent but that they were longer and contained many more occurrences of his name. To cap it all, Factiva featured as its Number One item a highly biased review from the *Wall Street Journal*. This review had been so erroneous that—in a rare development—the *Journal* consented to publish a subsequent letter correcting the record. The Factiva ranking system, however, considered this letter so lacking in "relevance" that it would have been entirely missed by most searchers. Pressed by the author to explain how it ranked an article's relevance, Factiva at first refused to respond to his messages. When he threatened to bring a complaint to top management, the company's director of product management finally surfaced but only to refuse to give any details of the ranking system. Nor did Factiva make any noticeable changes in the way it ranked the articles in question. Adding spice to this encounter was the matter of Factiva's ownership: the company had been founded by Dow Jones, the publisher of the *Wall Street Journal*, and was still half-owned by Dow Jones as of 2000.

106. squeezing a profit: Mark Landler, *International Herald Tribune*, January 12, 1998.

106. Nathan Morton: As quoted by Saul Hansell in *International Herald Tribune*, December 2, 1997.

107. innkeepers: Robert Samuelson, *International Herald Tribune*, July 10, 1998.

108. Millipore: As cited by Mary Cronin in *Fortune*, May 9, 1997.

109. cyberquackery: See David Stipp, *Fortune*, January 12, 1998.

112. export superpower: Newt Gingrich, *To Renew America* (New York: HarperCollins, 1995), p. 165.

115. quite small exporters: Valid figures for the overall size of the American entertainment industry's exports do not exist. Such exports are virtually impossible to measure because they take many forms. Typically, when the American entertainment industry sells CDs and video cassettes abroad,

these are manufactured in the markets concerned. Thus, they cannot be considered "exports" for the United States as most of the revenues stay abroad and are expended on wages and overheads in foreign subsidiaries. Of course, this does not stop spokesmen and lobbyists for the American entertainment industry conflating overseas sales with exports and thus giving the impression that the industry is a much greater contributor to the U.S. balance of payments than it really is. Thus, although looking at the audited accounts of major American entertainment companies provides only a partial guide, it is the only method that provides properly audited insights into the true scale of American entertainment exports.

121. Hollywood's leadership: See Paul Fahri and Megan Rosenfeld in the *International Herald Tribune*, October 26, 1998.

123. Samuel P. Huntington: Samuel P. Huntington, *The Clash of Civilizations and the Remaking of World Order* (New York: Touchstone, 1997), p. 63.

134. GCA: Peter N. Dunn in *Microlithography World*, Summer, 1994.

152. $2 billion a year: Martha M. Hamilton, *Washington Post*, March 29, 1996.

161. Harmut Mehdorn: As quoted in *Mainichi Daily News*, May 9, 1997.

167. Brazil: John Naisbitt, *Megatrends*, (New York: Warner Books, 1982), p. 58.

176. "sunset": Robert Kuttner, *Everything For Sale* (New York: Knopf, 1996), p. 222.

176. cut their unit labor costs: The source of the figures quoted in this sentence is the Japanese steel company, NKK.

184. "nobody here": As recounted in *Made in Japan* by Akio Morita with Edwin M. Reingold and Mitsuko Shimomura (New York: Signet, 1988), pp. 305-306.

211. this correlation: This and other comments attributed to Andreas Schafer and David G. Victor are taken from their article, "Global Mobility: Past and Future" in the October 1997 issue of *Scientific American*.

displaced almost overnight: Few who are familiar with the strength of Japan's balance of payments doubt that Japanese exporters would be fully competitive at much higher yen exchange rates than those that prevailed in the first years of the new century. This reflects not only superior productivity in the goods in which they compete globally but the fact that by dint of enjoying crucial monopolies or near-monopolies in a host of high-tech components and materials, they enjoy pricing leadership in Western markets.

Moreover, judging by how violently exchange rates have changed in the past, a dramatic rise in the yen's dollar value is far from a negligible possibility. After all, Japan's current account surplus as of 2002 ran more than three and a half times its level of $35 billion in 1984—and just as soaring surpluses led to a doubling of the yen between 1985 and 1987, the conditions as of 2003 seemed to call for a similarly large revaluation of the yen. One thing is certain: a doubling of the yen's value from its level in 2003 would immediately give Japan the world's largest gross national product.

That said, the Japanese economic system is clearly capable of tolerating an artificially undervalued yen for many years to come. This is because most of Japan's overseas trade is now conducted as internal transactions within Japan's now highly globalized manufacturing and trading corporations. Thus the exact exchange rate used by, for instance, Sony in exporting from its Japanese subsidiaries to its American ones is little more than an internal bookkeeping consideration and merely determines where profits are deemed to arise for tax purposes. Equally because Japanese corporations typically own the foreign coal mines, farms, and iron ore deposits that produce most of Japan's imports, the exchange rate at which such imports enter Japan is largely moot as far as Japan's top policymakers are concerned.

225. contrary evidence: The extent to which the *Economist* in particular is prepared to go to mislead its readers where matters of dogma are concerned is hard to exaggerate. This point was nicely illustrated in the magazine's belated review (in February 1998) of *Blindside*, this writer's 1995 book in which he offered a broad challenge to the *Economist*'s dogma-driven account of the Japanese economy. In virtually every sentence, the review contrived to misrepresent the book. It implied, for instance, that the book's conclusion that Japan would overtake the United States as the world's biggest economy represented an extrapolation from the dollar's momentary fall to below ¥80

in April 1995. In fact this fall took place a month after *Blindside* was published and more than seven months after it was completed. Moreover the book contained a specific caution *(Blindside* p. 353) that at ¥98 as of the book's completion date in September 1994, the dollar had fallen too far too fast and would soon stage a "significant rally." That rally, which few other Tokyo-based observers anticipated in 1994, duly began in the early summer of 1995 and continued until 1998. The *Economist* also implied that *Blindside* denied rumors that Japanese banks were in serious financial trouble. In reality the only rumor the book denied was a quite unfounded one that had been circulated by the *Economist* concerning the banks' involvement in one minor Tokyo real estate transaction. That this writer cannot be accused of being unaware of the Japanese banks' real estate problems is obvious from the fact that he was probably the first Tokyo-based observer to predict those problems—in a seven-page article headed "Why the Japanese banks are shaky" in *Euromoney* in September 1987.

234. large budget surpluses: Take 1995. The American press reported at the time that the Japanese government was supposedly running a huge budget deficit that year. In reality the outturn was not a deficit but a surplus—which according to the OECD amounted to 3.5 percent of GDP. See the 1998 edition of *OECD in Figures* pp. 46-47 (under the heading "Net Government Saving % of GDP").

235. supergloomy foreign stock analysts: It is notable that not one of the many prominent foreign analysts who worked in Tokyo in the late 1980s and then went on to become major proponents of the "basket case" story publicly predicted the coming financial disaster. Quite the reverse: right up to the beginning of the crash in 1990, most of them were conspicuously enthusiastic bulls of Japanese shares—not least banking and real estate shares—and their advice cost tens of billions of dollars (as countless fund managers in America and Europe made huge investment decisions based on their absurd advice). By contrast, this present writer, almost alone among Tokyo-based commentators gave forthright warnings of the multiple financial disasters ahead. See, for instance, "Why the Japanese banks are shaky" by Eamonn Fingleton, *Euromoney*, September 1987. For his prediction of the stock market crash, see "Making hay" by Eamonn Fingleton, *Euromoney*, February 1989.

236. officialdom has played: Even Japanese bankers conspicuously denigrate their institutions' performance in public. They do so in the knowledge that they do

little or no damage to their business. After all, Japan is now such a huge net exporter of capital that the Japanese banks' overseas subsidiaries can fund themselves almost entirely from the ever burgeoning offshore deposits of the Japanese economic system. Meanwhile, at home, Japanese bankers don't have to worry about their image among the general public either. The reason is that the Japanese savings market is so highly cartelized that Japanese savers have no choice but to accept interest rates as low as 0.5 percent or less!

239. *Blindside* has been vindicated: *Blindside* has been vindicated also on virtually all its other major themes. Specifically, it argued that Japan would survive its financial and economic strains of the 1990s without making any significant moves to Westernize its economic institutions. In so doing, the book rebutted almost every major theme of the American press's coverage of Japan in the first half of the 1990s. Some of the more important of these themes were:

- Japan's export industries were supposedly being hollowed out by South Korea and other developing countries.

- Japan's current account surpluses were on the brink of diminishing or even disappearing (this view was associated particularly with *The Economist*'s editor-in-chief, Bill Emmott—see in particular pages 238-240 of his 1989 book, *The Sun Also Sets*).

- The lifetime employment system was breaking down.

- Japan's unemployment rate was set to spiral disastrously out of control.

- Japan's super-high savings rate was supposedly headed dramatically lower.

- Japan's cartels and keiretsus (which are groupings of affiliated companies that favor one another in sourcing of inputs and services) were breaking down.

- The Liberal Democratic Party's long reign as the dominant organization of Japanese politics supposedly ended forever in 1993.

The truth is that, with one partial exception, these themes have now all proved to have been utter illusions. The partial exception concerns unemployment. Japan's unemployment rate did indeed rise in the 1990s, as the press commentators predicted. But even here, the press has been proved largely wrong because the unemployment rate never remotely approached the disastrous levels confidently predicted in the first half of the 1990s. As calculated on a fully internationally comparable OECD basis, Japan's unemployment rate was a mere 5.0 percent as of 2001. Admittedly, this was a fraction higher than in the United States but it was lower than in most other developed nations, including Canada, the United Kingdom, France, Germany, and Italy.

It should be noted that press reports in the 1990s that Japan's system of permanent long-term employment had broken down were, like similar reports dating back to the 1960s, proved wrong by subsequent events. The permanent employment system is based on regulatory requirements which are enforced in varying degrees of strictness depending on the size of the employer, its profitability and the sex and age of workers (the rights of female and older workers to permanent jobs have always been impaired so there is nothing new in the layoffs of such workers). Until Japan deregulates its employment market, permanent employment will continue to form the core of the Japanese labor system.

249. $3 billion: This is a conservative estimate based on figures supplied by the Electronic Industries Association of Japan.

260. boosted its real output: See Sweden entry, *Encyclopaedia Britannica*, 1970.

BIBLIOGRAPHY

Anchordoguy, Marie. *Computers Inc.: Japan's Challenge to IBM.* Cambridge: Harvard University Press, 1989.

Fraser Andresky, Jill. *White Collar Sweatshop.* New York: Norton, 2001.

Brinkley, Joel. *Defining Vision: The Battle for the Future of Television.* New York: Harcourt Brace, 1997.

Buchanan, Patrick. *The Great Betrayal.* Boston: Little, Brown, 1998.

Cassidy, John. *Dot.con.* New York. Harper Collins, 2002.

Choate, Pat. *Agents of Influence.* New York: Touchstone Books, 1991.

Cohen, Stephen S. and John Zysman. *Manufacturing Matters: The Myth of the Post-Industrial Economy.* New York: Basic Books, 1987.

Cusumano, Michael A. and Richard Selby. *Microsoft Secrets.* London: HarperCollins, 1995.

Dertouzos, Michael L., Richard K. Lester, and Robert M. Solow. *Made in America: Regaining Productive Edge.* The MIT Press: Cambridge, 1989.

Eckes, Alfred, Jr. and Thomas W. Zeiler. *Globalization and the American Century.* Cambridge University Press: Cambridge, 2003.

Fallows, James. *Looking at the Sun: The Rise of the New East Asian Economic and Political System.* New York: Pantheon, 1994.

Fialka, John J. *War by Other Means: Economic Espionage in America.* New York: W.W. Norton, 1997.

Fransman, Martin. *Japan's Computer and Communications Industry: The Evolution of Industrial Giants and Global Competitiveness.* Oxford University Press: Oxford, 1995.

Galbraith, John Kenneth. *A History of Economics: The Past as the Present.* London: Penguin Books, 1989.

Goldsmith, Sir James. *The Trap.* New York: Carroll & Graf, 1994.

Gray, John. *False Dawn: The Delusions of Global Capitalism.* London: Granta, 1998.

Hall, Ivan P. *Bamboozled!: How America Loses the Intellectual Game With Japan and Its Implications for Our Future in Asia.* Armonk: M.E. Sharpe, 2002.

Hawkins, William. *Importing Revolution.* Washington: AIC, 1994.

Heller, Robert. *The Fate of IBM.* London: Little, Brown, 1994.

Huntington, Samuel P. *The Clash of Civilizations and the Remaking of World Order.* New York: Touchstone, 1997.

Hutton, Will. *The State We're In.* London: Vintage, 1996.

Ingrassia, Paul and Joseph B. White. *Comeback: The Fall and Rise of the American Automobile Industry.* New York: Touchstone, 1995.

Jasinowski, Jerry and Robert Hamrin. *Making it in America.* New York: Fireside, 1996.

Kahaner, Larry. *Competitive Intelligence.* New York: Simon & Schuster, 1996.Kuttner, Robert. *Everything for Sale: The Virtues and Limits of Markets.* New York: Knopf, 1996.

Landauer, Thomas K. *The Trouble with Computers: Usefulness, Usability, and Productivity.* The MIT Press: Cambridge, 1996.

McRae, Hamish. *The World in 2020: Power, Culture and Prosperity—A Vision of the Future.* London: HarperCollins, 1995.

McVeigh, Brian. *The Nature of the Japanese State: Rationality and Rituality.* London: Routledge, 1998.

Magaziner, Ira C. and Mark Patinkin. *The Silent War: Inside the Global Business Battles Shaping America's Future.* New York: Random House, 1989.

Mander, Jerry and Edward Goldsmith (ed.). *The Case Against the Global Economy—And for a Turn to the Local.* San Francisco: Sierra Club Books, 1996.

Minkin, Barry Howard. *Future in Sight: Important Trends, Implications and Predictions for the New Millenium.* New York: Macmillan, 1995.

Morita, Akio, with Edwin M. Reingold and Mitsuko Shimomura. *Made in Japan.* New York: Signet, 1988.

Motavalli, John. *Bamboozled at the Revolution: How Big Media Lost Billions in the Battle for the Internet.* Viking Press: New York, 2002.

Naisbitt, John and Patricia Aburdene. *Megatrends 2000.* London : Pan Books, 1990.

Nakamura, Shuji and Gerhard Fasol. *The Blue Laser Diode: GaN Based Light Emitters and Lasers,* Berlin: Springer-Verlag, 1997.

Negroponte, Nicholas. *Being Digital.* London: Coronet Books, 1995.

Pool, Robert. *Beyond Engineering: How Society Shapes Technology.* New York: Oxford Unversity Press, 1997.

Reich, Robert B. *The Work of Nations: Preparing Ourselves for 21st-Century Capitalism.* New York: Vintage Books, 1992.

Schenk, David. *Data Smog: Surviving the Information Glut.* San Francisco: HarperEdge, 1997.

Soros, George (with Byron Wien and Krisztina Koenen). *Soros on Soros: Staying Ahead of the Curve.* New York: John Wiley, 1995.

Stoll, Clifford. *Silicon Snake Oil: Second Thoughts on the Information Highway.* New York: Doubleday, 1995.

Strassmann, Paul A. *The Squandered Computer: Evaluating the Business Alignment of Information Technologies.* New Canaan: The Information Economics Press, 1997.

Thurow, Lester C. *The Future of Capitalism: How Today's Economic Forces Shape Tomorrow's World.* New York: William Morrow, 1996.

Tolchin, Martin and Susan J. Tolchin. *Selling Our Security.* New York: Alfred A. Knopf, 1992.

Von Weizsäcker, Ernst, Amory B. Lovins, and L. Hunter Lovins. *Factor Four: Doubllng Wealth—Halving Resource Use.* London: Earthscan, 1997.

Wallace, James and Jim Erickson. *Hard Drive: Bill Gates and the Making of the Microsoft Empire.* Chichester: John Wiley & Sons, 1993.

Wolff, Michael. *Burn Rate : How I Survived the Gold Rush Years on the Internet.* New York, Simon & Schuster, 1998.

Wolman, William and Anne Colamosca. *The Judas Economy: The Triumph of Capital and the Betrayal of Work.* Reading: Addison-Wesley Publishing Company, 1997.

Wright, Richard W. and Gunter A. Pauli. *The Second Wave.* London: Waterlow, 1987.

ACKNOWLEDGMENTS

For help in researching the book, I am indebted to Dirk Heinecke, Michael Henne, Clare Bebbington, Masamichi Shiraishi, Aston Bridgman, Donald Forsythe, Takashi Ogawa, Tsunehisa Yamashita, Daniel Lintz, Firdous Khergamvala, Ashok Syal, Sreenivasan Mohanagopal, Sekhar Chatterjee, Klaus Turck, David Lammers, Yoshiro Sasaki, Takashi Asamura, H. Yamana, Annanya Sarin, Roger Schreffler, and Sam Jameson. I benefited from discussions with various intellectual allies including Ivan Hall, Brian McVeigh, Thomas Flannigan, William J. Holstein, Ivan Schlager, Chalmers Johnson, Margaret Baxter, and Catherine Lemaitre. More generally, I am grateful to James Fallows, whose generous espousal of my work set me on the path to full-time authorship. The original concept of the book was shaped with the help of Joe Spieler of the Spieler Agency. At Houghton Mifflin, publisher of the 1999 version of the book, I am particularly indebted to the firm's then editors, Steve Fraser and Christina Coffin.

The introduction to this edition reflects discussions I have had with Pat Choate, John F. Nash, Jr., Robert Lighthizer, Kevin Kearns, Alan Tonelson, and Bill Hawkins. In updating the argument for this edition, I feel privileged to have worked with Carl Bromley and Michelle Rosenfield of Nation Books.

—Eamonn Fingleton
Minami Aoyama 4-chome, Tokyo
E-mail: efingleton@hotmail.com
Website: www.unsustainable.org

July 30, 2003

INDEX